Money is a Mind Thing

Reinold Widemann

Money is a Mind Thing

Translated by Aafke Kelly

Aspekt Publishers

Money is a Mind Thing

© 2016 Aspekt Publishers
© 2016 Reinold Widemann

Amersfoortsestraat 27, 3769 AD Soesterberg, Nederland
info@uitgeverijaspekt.nl - http://www.uitgeverijaspekt.nl

Cover design: Maarten Bakker
Interior: Maarten Bakker
Cover illustration: Aafke Kelly, 'Lady sings the blues', 2005 oil on paper, private collection

ISBN: 9789463380416
NUR: 740

All rights reserved. No part of this book may be reproduced, stored in a retrieval system, or transmitted in any form or by any means, electronic, electrostatic, magnetic tape, mechanical, photocopying, recording or otherwise, without the written permission of the publisher: Uitgeverij Aspekt, Amersfoortseweg 27, 3769 AD Soesterberg, Nederland.

Preface		7

1 **FOR WHAT IT IS WORTH** 9
   On the return of reading and the right measure

2 **WHAT DOES IT COST?** 21
   On forms and sorts of value

3 **A SEARCH FOR THE START OF THE RAINBOW** 44
   On the sources of value

4 **THE MEANS-END CHAIN** 84
   On the indirect nature and the teleological series of money

5 **A CYCLE OF THE MATERIAL AND THE IMMATERIAL** 102
   On monetary transformation, representation and symbolic money

6 **THE CALCULATING ANIMAL** 129
   On considering pros and cons and on the cult of rationality

7 **(IN)FERTILE MONEY** 153
   On natural and unnatural growth and the prohibition of interest

8 **WHAT ANY FOOL WILL PAY FOR IT** 196
   On the value of money

9 **THE GOLDEN MISUNDERSTANDING** 228
   On gold shadow and gold substance

10 THE CENTRAL BANK AS HORN OF PLENTY   249
   On the belief in monetary omnipotence and the end of scarcity

11 MONEY ART AND ARTIFICIAL MONEY   269
   On the representation of money and value

Preface

This book has been written out of three motives: *interest, shame* and *mission*.

Interest in a subject is of course the first need to start such a time devouring enterprise and to be able to complete it as well. My interest in the phenomenon of money started in college and led to my profession as a lecturer on *Monetary Economics* and to being an author of some books for students of economics. But when looking back I feel some shame. It's not that I didn't' t take my job seriously. I always prepared my lectures conscientiously and managed to be well-informed on the up to date monetary instruments and politics. On the whole my students appreciated my stories that I liked telling them. Unfortunately the results of the students in exams on money- and banking business, interest theory and money creation weren't always up to score. But that is just daily educational practice: doing colleges, studying, correcting and selecting. Nothing to be ashamed about.

Shame came later, long after my retreat from my job as a teacher, when I started studying a much broader field of money and value. To start with, the idea of 'value' hardly gets any attention in education. In Economics a higher Gross National Product (GNP) is invariably supposed to create more welfare and thus more value. But which value? Distinguishing various sorts of values is not an issue for most economists. Let alone that a higher GNP often leads to loss of value in many aspects, such as nature and culture. The connection between money and all kinds of value didn't get any attention from me and my colleagues. For us money was a medium of exchange, a measuring unit and a means of saving, and as such a broad field to teach about, but almost any economist still starts his story with the 'myth of the barter'. This myth was mainly created by *Adam Smith*, but in the meantime refuted by anthropologists like *David Graeber* and defined as fiction. Uncritically having retold this story invented by economists, makes me ashamed retrospectively. Another thing to be ashamed about is the fact that we never considered the relation between money and culture in our lectures on monetary economics. We told a mainly technical story, but never a word about the historical, cultural, philosophical, even religious dimensions of money. Nothing on fertility or infertility of money, on what money represents, on the Christian prohibition of interest or on the belief that money can buy anything. Nothing on the use of money in ancient times nor on the abstract level of thinking needed for our modern symbolic money, not to mention the postmodern money derivates. The latter might be a bridge too far for regular education, but because of the luxury of having more time now, I can at least start filling the gaps of my former educational profession now. It resulted in this book.

And now my third motive for this writing: mission, a feeling a teacher never completely lacks. A person like that wants to share his newly learnt views with the world. However, world is a bit exaggerated, a few well filled colleges would be nice. It started in this way: modestly with small groups of people as an audience for my first ideas on this subject. I owe them a lot.

Reinold Widemann

1 FOR WHAT IT IS WORTH
On the return of reading and the right measure

At a nice day I walked into town wearing no coat. After half an hour the sky became overcast - rain! I ran into a bookshop further on in the street. Just in time as it was pouring now. Leafing through books, always enjoyable, but in fact I didn't need any as I had a big unread pile at home. I started with the books lying on the table, avoiding the bookcases with vertically placed books which always made my neck hurt. I picked up some books, looked at the jacket blurb and put them back. I might come across something I definitely had to read, at the same time realizing I lacked time to do so. No problem, in a few weeks my schedule would be less busy, so why not buy something now. Walking through the shop I caught sight of a book titled *Money is a mind thing*. I wouldn't count on it I thought, money is a thing in my purse or in the bank, but certainly not a thing in my mind. I picked it up and started reading the back flap. It said that money is just an idea, an illusion in fact. I started leafing through the book and came across the assumption that the money value of an object has got nothing to do with the object itself. Nonsense, I thought, this author claiming that this object in my hand, the book, and its price haven't got anything to do with each other. It will have cost money to produce it, won't it? Paper had been used, it had to be printed, bound, packed up, transported and the author, the editor and the bookshop had to make a profit from it too. All of it together will set the price of the book. Holding it in my hand, I evaluated it, leafed through it, read the index and a random page to see whether it was well written. Not bad I thought, but rather expensive too.

I opened the book once more and read: " *If you decide to buy this book you expect the profit you'll get from this item to be higher than what you paid for it."* What a strange thing to say, as I never make my round through a bookshop calculating which profit each book will give me. Okay, I always look at the price, usually too high. Nice book, I often think, but much too expensive. Nevertheless the sentence intrigued me and I thought: does this book suit me, will it be worthwhile? Will I learn something from it? Will I enjoy it? Will it be worth the money I paid for it? Looking back, I realize that unconsciously I put the very sentence above into practice: I calculated to which degree the pleasure or the benefit the book would give me, was going to make up for the price and the time spent on it. So I wanted to know what it would be **worth** to **me.**

Those two words - **worth** and **me** - are quite important, I learnt later on from the text, as they are the essence of any decision to buy something: your personal *subjective value* of a book or what you'll gain from it. What other people think of it is of no importance, nor how much they want you to read the same book as they did, nor whatever positive reviews the book had. "You must read this book", they say, but you are free to decide for yourself which book you want to read.

In the end I decided to buy the book. Obviously I had calculated that it would be worth the money. My decision to buy it was the proof that I expected it would get me more than I had paid for it. But I didn't think like that at all when I purchased the book - suppose you were considering each purchase as a product that would or would not yield a return. That is exactly what you are doing when you constantly compare the yield with the cost. Exhausting. But as a matter of fact, that is just what you are doing unconsciously. For instance when you buy some vegetables it is not only because you must eat, but also because you learnt that eating vegetables is healthier than eating nothing but chips with ketchup. This learning process all children have to get through, is in fact the same as learning to make a well calculated choice like " this will do me good and that is unhealthy". (Though many adults seem to have little knowledge of which food is healthy or unhealthy.) So at the very moment of buying this book I had absolutely no idea that I was calculating whether the yield would balance the cost. And after having read about it later on I still thought of it as peculiar - because would it be possible to measure a book's value in terms of money at all? I don't mean the cost itself, for that is clear: the cost was quite simply the price I had paid for it. Maybe including the time it had cost to select it, well, as it was my day off, I wondered if I could count that as well. And including the time needed to read it, quite a lot of hours, but didn't I do that out of my free will and for the greater part out of fun? Did 'fun' have a price too? Maybe a price in terms of missed opportunities as I could have spent my time more useful elsewhere? These things were mentioned in the book too and the author even considered them rather essential: the problem of the *opportunity cost* or *alternative cost,* as he liked to call them. He introduced the concept in chapter 3.

All right, determining the cost of the purchase of the book seemed rather easy just yet, but determining the profit wasn't immediately clear at all. I thought of concepts like intellectual *enrichment* and of the book as a means of *contribution* to my intellectual *capital.* Those three words: *enrichment, contribution, capital* - suggest something that can be calculated, like a mental profit translated into financial figures. But how? And thinking it over, I suddenly remembered more similar words and sayings, used to express implicit calculation. For instance:

'I'm not going to *invest* more time in that woman, as it *costs* too much energy and doesn't *bring in* anything. I rather *spend* my time on something else.'
'I don't give a *penny* for his opinion.'
'That's put *paid* to.' 'I took no *account* of it.'
'He has a lot on his *slate.*'

In the old times the ancient slate used to be an important financial instrument, I read in chapter 5 later on. The author claimed that you couldn't get round it for a good understanding of what money really is and where it is situated. He connected it to other sorts of money like the big Rai-stones used for centuries at the Micronesian group of islands Yap. An interesting story, I thought, but be patient, it will be dealt with later on.

Later on I just thought of two old similar sayings also connected to cost and yield.

'If you are born poor you will remain poor all your life.' ('A penny is never going to be a dime.' Dutch saying)

'He was born with a silver spoon.'

Those monetary metaphors are understood right away by all of us. But they threaten to pigeon-hole someone by a moralistic monetary label. Nevertheless, comparing each other with social-moralistic standards based on income and fortune is a favourite party game, that cannot be eradicated. The more money, the more prestige, the better a person, it often seems. The book I had bought dwelled upon things like that as well.

But first I want to return to the price of the book. If it had been twice as expensive I would probably have left it on the table. The author presumed the same as he directly addressed his reader asking:

'And? Would you have bought the book as well if it had been twice as expensive? Well?'

At that moment he started treating me as a friend, a little too familiar perhaps.

'Much too expensive!' you might have called out. But in this case you could take the risk as you had already calculated that the yield would be higher than the cost. But looking at it in this strict financial way is not likely to happen. Suppose someone asking you after having read the book: 'And? Did you like the book?' and you answering: 'Certainly, as I enjoyed it for eighty Euros and it cost not even half of that.' People would take a good look at you and wonder how things are with you. He is not sane they might think, he calculates his pleasure in terms of money. For how on earth will you be able to express the pleasure of reading a book in terms of money. Won't it be nonsense to say that for instance *Dead souls* by *Nikolaj Gogol* gave you the pleasure of reading worth €120? And as the book may have cost € 30 the profit or return will be € 90?'

I never looked at it in this way. It would be as if I earned some money while reading.

'By the way', the author continued, 'did you read that book? The book by *Gogol*? In fact this book is about the same, about how you can make money out of something that you don't associate with a calculable product at first sight. In this case a product from which almost anyone would get the creeps when realizing what it meant, namely buying dead serfs: *dead souls*.

But I get off my subject. We were at the supposed 'yield' reading a book might give you. Just like me most people will react that this is impossible, that you can't express reading in terms of money. Ninety Euros profit by reading *Gogol's* book is rubbish, it is impossible to quantify the profit of reading in terms of hard cash. But dwelling on the subject a bit longer I concluded that reading may be profitable indeed. Just think of the success rate of a course. By doing a course you may get a better job and earn more than when you hadn't done the course, anyone knows that. And by reading some other books at the same time you will increase your general education. The lot of reading you have to do for it will give you profit in the end. But how much that will be, is difficult to be calculated. You can compare salary scales and consider which certificates you need to get higher on the career ladder, but then many a job doesn't have a clear ladder at all. Think of a self-employed person, reading an extra (text)book will cost too much time in relation to the expected profit and will therefore not contribute to sound management. This way reading the most magnificent book can have a negative impact on your financial situation, no matter how much you enjoyed reading it.'

At this I asked myself what such a magnificent book might be worth when the time spent on reading affects your income negatively. Did that force you to leave that beautiful novel because it would take up so much time that it was at the expense of your job? If it carries you off to such a degree that you can't concentrate on other things anymore? Does that mean that you would have done better not to buy it? As *on balance* it results in economic loss? '*On balance*' - another term from the financial quarter. But according to the author a term that may put you on the wrong track. For if you want to *count* everything that is of importance to your life *on balance,* it shouldn't be limited to financial affairs. Your health, happiness, fun, freedom and so on are of equal importance, aren't they, he said. And when you greatly enjoy reading a novel, why worry about a little loss of income. Calculation had to stop somewhere to stay healthy, he wrote. I couldn't agree more, but where exactly did it have to stop? Where is the borderline between calculating watchfully and losing oneself in diversion without a brain calculator?

Moderation
In a way Aristotle was already occupied with searching for that borderline, the book told. We don't know if he had numbers on his mind when thinking about it. In *Nicomachean Ethics* he declared that moderation is the art of life. Be moderate in anything you do or want, he lectured. His *phronesis* has become famous. According to him it is the most important human virtue, the insight that makes you choose the 'good' action and the 'golden mean' between reason and emotion. Aristotle thought it nature's imperative to be moderate, to find 'the golden mean', a kind of ethical imperative. It is tempting to connect some numbers to '*moderation*' and '*golden mean*', for instance between 0 and 4. When we take someone's measure, we almost immediately think of a report mark. A term like 'moderation' makes the modern person think of something 'mediocre' like barely a two.

'But I'm sure that this wasn't what Aristotle meant', the author said, 'for if he had to give a mark at all, the way of life he propagated would rather have been graded a three or a four by him. Let's go on about the right way of life therefore, and let's presume that we know where to place the borderline and where to stop calculating and leave things as they are. You picked a sunny outdoor café, a nice place to contemplate on your life. Oh dear, when the waiter arrives with your cup of coffee, he asks at the same time if you mind paying for it right away. *Paying the bill?* You realize with a start that even at this nice place you can't get round it, picking an outdoor café is just a commercially calculable product too. You have to be careful not to let this thought completely spoil your pleasure. Drinking expensive coffee at this place and wondering if all of this is worth the money. Of course it is, it's a nice place and the coffee is excellent, a biscuit included even, but the price of the coffee and maybe a tip for the waiter have to be deducted from the gross value of your outing at once. So, a matter of yield and cost again. Quite annoying to think of it in this way, isn't it? Take care not to become a prune-face!'

That's all well and good, but would Aristotle have scrutinized any of his actions like this in order to find the golden mean? I doubt it. The author of the book seemed to have been reading the reader's mind as he continued:

'Aristotle's 'golden mean' must not be thought of as a narrow borderline but as a path, a path of life. As a matter of fact the whole breadth of that path and not only the white line, because constantly driving on this line causes accidents. This example of picking an outdoor café shows that it is very difficult, if not impossible, to live without any calculating associations. For even your lightheartedly picking an outdoor café, quite soon appears to be labeled with a price tag.'

Unfortunately, I couldn't say anything against that.

'There are many products on the market which give you the fleeting illusion of escaping the daily treadmill, he continued, ' and for all of them you have to pay. Moreover many of them must be consumed moderately in order not to get addicted to them.'

Not my problem, I thought, I'm not addicted to anything. However, defining the term addiction the way the author did, broadly, almost anyone would be addicted to something now and again.

'Many products have just this effect', he said. 'The effect of becoming so mad about them that you get oblivious of anything else. Starting to neglect things. Not keeping things in proportion. The result can be quite destructive when it involves drugs, tobacco or alcohol addictions. "Smoking is lethal", is written on cigarette packets nowadays, and "No alcohol when younger than 18" on signs in supermarkets. The same goes for many other addictions: gambling addiction, shopping addiction, internet addiction, working addiction. Workaholics are often pitiable rats in the treadmill of their burning ambition. Addiction to work can seriously harm your health which may result in a burnout. Each kind of addiction may open the gate to ruin. Various health problems may arise by anything that you are obsessed with too much. Too much eating, smoking, drinking, watching TV, reading - yes, even reading. So even when you have become the lucky owner of this book, you have to take care not be caught up in it to such a degree that you neglect everything else.'

For two reasons I considered the author's final remark a bit conceited: firstly that I should have become a 'lucky' owner by his book and secondly that I could be obsessed with it to such a degree… well, never mind.

By the way, I think that oblivion may be quite a valuable state of mind now and again. Wasn't that what the author meant when he suggested to pick an outdoor café as a means of recreation and diversion? Having nothing on your mind for a while, being released from your day-to-day worries, can make a valuable contribution to your life. As the author already said, 'there are many products on the market which give you the fleeting illusion of escaping the daily treadmill'. Products to intoxicate you into oblivion, call them products of relaxation: holiday trips, movies, CD's, concerts, religion, liquor, amusement parks, zoos, museums, and according to the author: books as well. But as long as we follow Aristotle's advice and oblivion isn't too deep, there will be nothing to worry about. Moderation in all things. If not, you will come to a sticky end, he said. There was a well-known example in the book, namely the Greek legend of king Midas, who met with disaster because of his hunger for gold, and who could only be saved by penance for his sins:

MIDAS
Once upon a time the king of Phrygia had earned the gratitude from the god of wine Bacchus (or Dionysus), because he had saved the drunk satyr Salinas. 'As a reward I allow you one wish', the god spoke, 'tell me what you desire and your wish will be fullfilled'.

As if the king had been waiting for such a favour, he immediately expressed his wish: 'Change everything I touch into gold'.

Bacchus reluctantly complied with this request, for he knew the greedy king's choice to be a silly one. Nevertheless he gave his consent.

Greatly pleased Midas went on his way. He couldn't lose a moment to put the gift to the test - and look, the twig he snapped off the oak immediately changed into shining gold! He picked a stone from the ground: The stone turned into gold! The same happened to a piece of earth that he touched with his hand. The spikes he broke off the stalks did Demeter's gift change into gold in his hand; the apple he picked turned into seductive gold, as if originating from the hand of the Hesperidins.

Midas was beside himself with happiness, when he entered his palace. Whoever would be able to measure up to his richness from now on? His fingers hardly touched the doorposts when they got a gold shine. Yes, even the water brought to him to wash himself changed into liquid gold as soon as he dipped his hands into it.

Overflowing with joy king Midas ordered his servants to prepare his meal. The table sagged below the abundance of delicious food suited to this festive occasion. Midas picked up the bread, a gift of Demeter, goddess of corn - the divine gift changed into gold. He started tasting a delicious meat dish - his teeth bit the hard metal. He poured noble wine into his glass: Bacchus, to whom he owed this fateful power, turned this drink into gold too. Dismayed Midas looked at this ill-fated wonder of change; too late did the poor rich man realize how foolish his wish had been. Cursing the wicked gift the god had given him was no use. Nothing could satisfy his hunger, and a raging thirst dried out his throat.

In despair Midas raised his hands to heaven. 'Have mercy upon me, Bacchus, holy god', he begged, 'forgive me, take pity on me and free me from this shining misery!...'

After Midas' repent the God Bacchus judged him mildly. Midas had to go up the river along the empire of Lydia. At the source of the river he had to put his hand into the water and thereupon bathe in the foaming stream. Midas does as told, is released from his unholy spell, which is passed on to the river, which carries gold in its waves ever since. Midas retreats into the forest where he worships Pan, the god with the goat legs, whom Midas regularly visits in the shady mountain caves. Pan is a virtuoso on the reed pipe and he plays pastoral songs for the nymphs. But Pan foolishly wants to surpass Apollo's divine string music and he challenges the god to a competition. Pan on the reed pipe against Apollo on the ivory lyre. Pan with his shrill tones clearly is the inferior one, so he loses the competition. His friend Midas contests the outcome, being the only one thinking that Pan is the winner. It extremely annoys Apollo. He grabs Midas' ears and says: '*Silly ears like that don't deserve to be human any longer.*' Thereupon Midas' ears became pointed and grown with shaggy ash-grey hair. From then on Midas had to live with two donkey's ears.

But those donkey's ears in the second part of the story obviously weren't the point in the book, the point was Midas' immoderateness in the first part, which caused everything around him to become worthless. Anything he touched, changed into gold, as a result of which he had nothing to eat.

'That overabundant never-ending stream of gold represents the ultimate kind of worthlessness', the author said. 'In this legend Aristotle saw a kind of paradox: 'petrifaction' by 'immoderateness', joined together into the gold transformation of all food being a literal realization of insatiable wishes. Marx spoke of an immoderate *"urge for gathering wealth - the fortune hunter sacrifices his desires of the flesh to the gold fetish"*, he said. The legend shows the paradoxical effect of too much accumulation of wealth, the immoderate hoarding brings trade, that should be streaming, to a stop, so money 'fossilizes' into gold and becomes worthless. Worthlessness as a result of excessive accumulation of wealth.'

He added a remark that concerns myself personally: 'The legend also questions the value of gold as an inedible material that will be of no use in times of need. A lot of people however use gold as a refuge in times of depression, as an allegedly safe investment, as they have the notion that gold will always keep its value. The legend of Midas learns that this might be criticized.' As I had a small piece of gold at home myself as a buffer, I wondered what could be said against it. A chapter a bit further on in the book on "The golden misunderstanding" dealt with it, but I wasn't sure whether I entirely agreed with the author.

DIMINISHING VALUE PERCEPTION
But first he carried on about the legend of Midas, connecting it to the 'laws' of an economist vaguely familiar to me from the classes on economics at school:

'In the story of Midas you may recognize the famous *Gossen's first law*, the *law of diminishing marginal utility*. This law implies that the more units of the same product you consume the less satisfaction it will give you. This 'satisfaction' was called 'utility' by Gossen.'

Oh dear, that story, I thought, how long ago did I hear that one?

'Continuously consuming the same product will soon lead to satisfaction and each next slice of pizza will therefore be less delicious than the one before. And when you keep on eating it you will soon be satiated and it will make you sick. The marginal utility of your last slice of pizza will even have become negative by then. What tasted so well at first, turns your stomach now. The utility we get from each next slice of pizza, Gossen called the *marginal utility* of this slice of pizza. This principle applies to almost any product and even to money. An extra income of some € 100 has got more 'utility' for a poor woman than for a rich lady, peanuts to her, as anyone knows.'

I knew that of course, and in this respect I had nothing to complain about, though an extra €100 is quite a lot to me, such an additional amount still contributes to my personal utility.

'*Hermann Heinrich Gossen (1810-1859)*[1] was a German economist, who formulated the two laws in a book, completely forgotten for years, but which made him famous posthumously. The first law is written above. *Gossen's second law* states that the total utility you can get from your available money can sometimes be enlarged by varying your expenditures. For instance, when you prefer cycling to driving, it is obvious that you use your car less often. But when you think that cycling takes too much time or that it gives you too much saddle-sore, you will go by car. Or by public transport. In this way you rearrange the spending of your money until you think: I can't do better, because the last spent euros on each commodity will get me the same amount of satisfaction.'

As a matter of fact rather obvious points, Gossen's two laws, reading them again now. For isn't that what we do automatically? Spending our money as we think the best? Mmmm, no we don't always do so. For how many purchases don't we regret afterwards? How many wrong decisions don't we make in our lives? The author observed the same as he almost sternly addressed his reader:

'It means that you didn't understand Gossen's laws or at least you didn't observe them rightly.'

In order to be able to act on Gossen's laws, at least you must know what is useful or important to you, I thought, and what it is worth to you. It is quite an achievement to estimate everything at its true value. It won't surprise you that *Money is a mind thing* didn't ignore this and even devoted a full chapter to the subject, titled:

What does it cost?, introduced by the author at the end of the first chapter like this:

'Estimating the value of a product isn't simple. For a start it both is about the value of something itself and the value of it compared to other activities and objects. The value of something itself can be called its *absolute value* and the value compared to other things its *relative value*. The difference between both notions is important and will be dealt with extensively in the next chapter. But right now we can give away that we don't believe in the existence of absolute values very much. We believe that any value is relative in the end, which means related to something else, as it will be immeasurable and intangible otherwise. We shall try to prove this in chapter 2.

Notes:

1. Hermann Heinrich Gossen, *Entwicklung der Gesetze des menschlichen Verkehrs: und der daraus fliessenden Regeln für menschliches handels,* Braunschweig 1854, 1889, 1927

2 WHAT DOES IT COST?
On forms and sorts of value

'After having thoroughly considered and calculated everything, whether or not consciously, you end up at the cash register. Any idea what to do next?' started the second chapter.

Yes, paying of course, I thought, what a silly question.

'Paying, yes, yes indeed, but at that moment you are translating,' the author claimed, 'because paying is translating.'

Paying is translating? Why is paying translating?

'At the moment of purchase and sale, both of you - the buyer as well as the bookseller - are translating the book into an amount of money, which makes it possible to transfer the ownership of the book at a monetary value.'

Oh, that's what he means, I thought, easy, but it was a bit more complicated nevertheless:

'That price is *"the money form of the commodity"*, as Marx called it and this money form is *"a form that is separated from the natural form of the commodity, so it's only an imaginary form"*.[1] That may sound a bit complicated...'

You might say so, I thought.

'... but corresponding to the ideas of this book: *Money is a mind thing.* There are various ideas in your mind and one of the most important of them is exactly this *value-form separated from the natural form of the commodity.* In this case the real form of the commodity is a book and the value-form is the price in the shape of an amount of money.'

Making things difficult, I thought. The book as a natural form and the price as its value-form?

'That amount of money in your mind is a way of thinking. There are even philosophers who suggest that thinking originates from handling money!'

What? It's going too far, I thought. First money and after that thinking? That can't be true, can it? People were on earth before money, weren't they? And those first people must have been able to think, I suppose.

'Nietzsche and Marx suggested this for instance. In their opinion money is related to thinking. They "*both compare money to thinking, not because they have a high regard for money but because they have a low regard for thinking*", according to *Jos Defoort*.[2]

Good heavens, isn't this the world upside down? But the author didn't comment on it. He continued his story by another example of value in our mind and I wondered if that preceded thinking as well.

'But this money, this monetary value-form isn't the only form of imaginary value in connection to a commodity, of course,' he said.

I noticed that those words made me a bit rebellious. Were they of any importance? Of essential importance? Or just fussing?

'Thus the imaginary value of the contents of a book will only be exposed when it takes place in your mind while reading it,' he continued.

Well of course, I thought, you must read it to get hold of the contents, but why does the author make this so complicated? But then he carried on by comparing language with money:

'And you read with the help of language which is just like money "*only an imaginary form, separated from its tangible real form*". For instance, when you read: 'A car enters the street', the real form of the car and the street is represented by only two words: 'car' and 'street'. Enough to evoke the image of a real car and a real street, like '50 Euro' on a banknote is enough to call up a real value of this amount.

'A real value? I thought, does a banknote have a real value? Isn't it just a printed piece of paper? What's real about that? But I was going too fast, for the author explained: 'Of course, this phrase "real value" doesn't mean that bank-paper has a real value in itself, but that you can buy things of that value, you are right, but what about the intrinsic value of the material. So this print '50 Euro' is nothing but a symbolic reference to a potential quantity of goods and services of that value. The potential character of value, that means the value realized by exchanging the banknote for goods or services, also called nominal value. So the nominal value of the banknote becomes real or real economic value at the moment you use it to buy something. More about it in chapter 7.'

I was reassured and I intended to be less hasty with my judgment.

'In fact a small wonder:' the book continued, 'only three characters to evoke the image of a complete car, and two figures and four characters as a symbol for a generally accepted image of value. Characters are the basic symbols to design both language and money. On bank paper quite a range of supplementary symbols are added; besides figures there are signs like the dollar sign and the portrayals of kings, presidents, buildings or landscapes. A bank note looks more like a painting than a story therefore, but in fact it is a story just like the contents of a book: in this case a story on value.'

Alphabet and money

'So characters are symbols to produce words and sentences to deliver a story, but they aren't the story itself,' the author continued.

No, of course they aren't, but he hadn't finished yet:

'They are the materials, comparable to music notes which change into music only by compositions, arrangements or improvisations. Similarly, modern money mainly consists of symbolic signs that give a value message, signs on coins and banknotes and in computers. The French philosopher *Jean - Joseph Goux* compared the development of money to that of the alphabet[3]: *"Money and script have a parallel development",* he said, and: *" The alphabet is the economic moment of script, money is the alphabetical moment of economics. The same principle is behind a character and money: the plural reduced to the singular. One unique element becomes criterion or expression of a multitude. Money is the universal counterpart of products, the means to convert a various and heterogeneous quantity of services and commodities into the same value. The sound of the voice (and later the character representing that sound) is the universal counterpart of anything in the world that can have meaning. A limited series of signs (phonetic and later graphic) can represent, describe, translate an infinite variety of meanings".'*

Not an easy text, I thought, and I had to read it again to grasp its meaning.

'We will go into this symbolic money in chapter 5, but before that we will more than once come across the *imaginary value-form,* which is just what money is,' the author promised. 'But first we will dwell upon the 'money form' of the book, the price you had to pay for it. The chances are that you couldn't negotiate on that with your bookseller.'

No, I didn't even try, for that isn't possible in bookshops, is it?

' "The selling price has been fixed by the publisher", he will say. The bookseller poses as the powerless market party, who has no influence on the price of his products. He plays the part of the humble price follower who can't be blamed and makes the publisher as the price fixer responsible for the price of the book.'

Yes, but who in fact is the real price follower, I thought, the bookseller or I myself as a customer who obediently pays the price that is put on it?

' "The market rules, the market dictates," he might even add when you pay for the book,' the author said.

No, my bookseller doesn't make such poor remarks.

'But hearing such a remark you might frown and think: "There is something wrong here, because the market doesn't rule at all in this case. What I learnt at school about supply and demand doesn't hold for the book market anyway".'

No, that's correct, I thought, for when there is more or less demand for a certain book, it will not influence the price. Only later on when it becomes clear that too many of them have been printed, they will be remaindered for a knock-down price. Anyway, negotiating about the price of the book with my bookseller was no option then, I supposed, for I didn't even try, book prices are fixed in The Netherlands, it's take it or leave it.

'But what does the price of the book tell you about the value of the book?', the author asked. 'In the previous chapter we showed that to you as a buyer its value had to be higher than its price, if not, you wouldn't buy it. The subjective value attached to the book is very personal and different for each of us. Which means that there will be a lot of people who won't buy the book because they don't attach any value to it or because they think it too expensive. A person that doesn't attach any value to a product, is not even prepared to take it for ten euro cents. And if he does appreciate the book, but thinks it too expensive, his value judgment is at any case below the price. This kind of considerations seem to indicate that the price of a product hasn't got much to do with its real value. This goes for the subjective value seen from the buyer's point of view. The seller will probably attach no or hardly any value to his book supply, as it's primarily merchandise for him to make a living from. And to him the value of a book will rather be determined by the price mainly fixed on the basis of objective production cost. Seen from the supply side, we will have to bear in mind those objective production cost, and one of the most important are the various sorts of cost of labour.

Absolute value and fair price
In the past on base of these cost of labour men tried to fix the absolute value of products, a value that had to be translated into a fair price. Next, this value was looked upon as a quality of the product itself. "In the past" as early as in Greek ancient times for instance, when Aristotle enunciated that things had a natural, fair price. This price represented an inherent value and existed independently of any transaction, he thought, which means independently of supply and demand. The concept 'inherent value' is analogous to the concepts 'intrinsic value' and 'substantial value', all of them referring to the value that something has of its own. These and other concepts of value will be dealt with in chapter 8, when we talk about value of money more specifically. But at this moment we should dive into the value-lake a bit deeper in order to dig out which colourful schools of 'value-organisms' are swimming around in it.

Let's start with Aristotle's fair price or fair, absolute value, a value also called the 'natural price' of a product. The 'fairness' he meant, belonged to the domain of the gods.

Which of course doesn't mean that the gods directly interfered in the price-fixing of products, for their power didn't reach that far. The valuation of products had therefore to be left to earthly mortals, who presented themselves as divine ambassadors, people who were in close contact with higher things and understood what the gods wanted. And they were under the impression that the fair price of a product was the result of the sacrifices that it takes, that is of the work that it takes. The terms 'sacrifices' and work that it 'takes' sound negative, as if you can't take pleasure in working. And this is exactly the way it must be interpreted: as a burden on our shoulders, something that costs effort, a hard time, trouble, even a trial that makes you sweat. If we don't look at work like this, it's hard to understand why labour is a cost factor, cost to be made before you can speak of any yield at all.

The ancient Greek did not yet know the curse *'in the sweat of your face you shall eat bread',* by which God punished Adam and Eve after the Fall, but in Greek mythology the evil of unpleasant work came out of Pandora's box.'

Pandora, I thought, wasn't she the woman made from water and earth?

'In Greek mythology, Pandora is the name of the first woman made from water and earth by Hephaestus', the author confirmed. 'The beautiful lady whom the gods in turn endowed with good gifts - Pandora bearer of all gifts - but to whom the supreme god Zeus gave a box filled with disasters and plagues, a box she had to keep closed. But of course she didn't manage to do so because of her female curiosity.'

The story slowly came back to my mind.

'Zeus sent her to mankind to punish them and bring evil upon them.'

I had forgotten all about it. As a punishment?

'She had to do this because Prometheus had stolen fire from heaven to help mankind.'

Ah yes, the fire that made Zeus so angry.

'And for this theft Prometheus was severely punished by Zeus. He ordered him to be dragged into the lonely wilderness of the Caucasus and had him chained with unbreakable chains to a rock above a deep abyss. He had to hang there standing on his feet for many centuries, without food and without ever being able to bend his knees or to sleep. Moreover, every day an eagle came to eat his liver, which kept growing again. Not until hero Heracles, looking for the apples of the Hesperidins, passed, and felt sorry for him, did his ordeal end. Heracles shot the eagle and rescued the prisoner from his torture.'

Nice story, but what about this box of Pandora?

'The other punishment Zeus had thought up, was in Pandora's box,' the author guessed my impatience. 'When she opened the box out of curiosity, all misery and misfortune escaped to be spread around the world as quickly as lightning. When she hastily closed the box, it was too late already. It was even worse, for the only good thing left in the box was Hope. In this way the first woman brought sorrow to mankind.'

Women, I thought, Eve and Pandora…

'What also escaped from the box, was the toil that mankind wasn't familiar with till then, for work had been pleasant so far. In this way the aspect of hardship was added to labour, which made a lot of work change from a pleasant activity into a nuisance. But together with this change of the character of work, from 'joy' into 'suffering', the present perception of value and valuation was born!!', the author called out to me with double exclamation marks, but in spite of the two exclamation marks I didn't fully understand what he meant. Was he saying that enjoying your work is no means to create value? He seemed to suggest it anyway:

'From the moment work required effort, when we started disliking it, suffering from it, being exhausted by it and longing for rest and liberation from its burden, the concept of 'value' lost its gratuitous innocence, you might even say, because from now on value was no longer for free, but had to be sacrificed in the form of labour-sacrifices. Only the sun rose for free, but for all other things you had to work.'

Yes of course, but you don't have to do it reluctantly. Aren't there enough people who like going to their jobs each day, I answered the book aloud as if the author was personally present.

'Of course this doesn't mean that everybody hates his job,' the author agreed with me, 'but there isn't any work on earth which doesn't need some effort.'

Well, I thought, when differentiating like this you can make out with anything.

'The point is that human labour was no longer only pleasant from that time onwards. So human labour being a source of satisfaction before and a means to educate oneself, changed by Pandora's box and Eve's apple from a positive factor of profit into a negative cost factor. But it also caused labour to become the main source of value creation, for without trouble no value, as later on stated both by *Adam Smith* and *Georg Simmel* and many others with them, including *Jean-Joseph Goux* mentioned above. Human labour changed into *'toil and trouble'* as Smith[4] called it and *'Mühe und Plage'* as phrased by Simmel[5]. And also Jean-Joseph Goux frankly claimed that *"only suffering (pain) has value as an objective universal measure"*.[6] We will go into this idea of value in chapter 3.'

When I read those words for the first time, I couldn't agree with them. Why couldn't there be any value without the intervention of men and their labour? I thought. And why had labour to be considered as a sacrifice, as something that made people suffer? Both I thought of as nonsense. Firstly these philosophers claiming that a creation of value couldn't exist without human trouble and secondly when enjoying your work it couldn't result into anything valuable.

Concerning the first point: isn't there nature blossoming and flourishing by itself, aren't there fruits growing on bushes without the presence of human beings, the oxygen we breathe is not produced by human labour and rain gives us water. And when we like watching birds flying in the air, it will give us a positive feeling, a valuable feeling. All of it free and for nothing, and this shouldn't be of any value? Preposterous idea, I thought, completely ridiculous. But when I got on in the book, it turned out that I interpreted the idea of value differently from what the esteemed philosophers meant above. As for the second point, once again: work can sometimes simply be pleasant, can't it? Something that gives you joy and costs not much trouble? Yes, but not much trouble is still trouble of course, I thought, so…well, who lives a life completely without trouble? Looked upon it this way these thinkers might be right after all, living without trouble isn't possible - there would be no need for us to sleep otherwise. Even when you enjoy doing something, you will use energy. Yes, even doing nothing takes energy I knew from my own experience.

'In chapter 3 we go more deeply into labour as a source of value and we will look at other possible sources of value. So we are going to search for the start of the rainbow, where, as everybody knows, the pot with gold is', the author promised and I was really curious about that pot with gold. But he hadn't finished his explanation of the fair price yet:

'The labour-sacrifice, the trouble of labour was translated into working hours and cost of labour, which was the main ingredient of the 'fair price'. This fair price was looked upon as a quality of the product itself, absolute and intrinsic.'

The price of the product as a quality of the thing itself? Did they really think so? So those people saw the price as a kind of physical quality of the product? Did I understand it correctly? Just like weight, size, colour, sort of material? Hardly imaginable, I thought.

'The idea of value as an expression of divine justice could also be found in the Middle Ages, when the Catholic Church controlled nearly the entire economic life. And in that time the intrinsic value of goods was derived from the labour it had cost. *Thomas of Aquino* called a price fair when it corresponds to the sacrifices made for it and the Dominican monk *Albertus Magnus* considered exchange virtuous when the exchanged goods had needed the same amount of work and other cost.

As mentioned before, fixing this fair price was often done by the dignitaries and clergymen who understood what the gods wanted, but when calculating the cost of labour for these products they were forced to look for something to hold on to and for this they probably consulted men with practical knowledge. But after having calculated the cost, the price that came out of it was absolute and fixed, just like the ancient Greek used to do. This price was independent of the price or quality of other goods and could not rise or fall by changes in supply and demand. So even a sharp fall of the supply of, say, corn caused by crop failure, in principal couldn't lead to higher corn or bread prices. It goes without saying that in a situation like that a fixed corn price couldn't be maintained in practice, at least not in short-term. Corn prices did vary along with the amount of crop, but in the long-term they were rather stable. This made Adam Smith being in favour of corn as a more stable basis of value than money when rent had to be paid: "*Corn rents are more stable than money rents*", he concluded. He meant the real value of corn in the long run, but admitted that the corn price in short-term could vary because of variable crops. However, as corn and other products had been produced by labour, it would be best to base value on labour, for *"labour is the real measure of exchangeable value, and the first price paid for all things".* Once more this observation repeats in other words what was concluded above on calculating the fair natural price: labour cost were its basis and this basis of value didn't change much over the years.

But according to *Jos Defoort* 'the modernists' answered this by *"on the contrary, goods don't have a natural price. The value of goods and their usefulness depends on the place where they are. Exactly by moving them, their value can be increased spectacularly. Thus, cloth manufacturers from Bruges were prepared to pay a substantial sum for alum which is all over the place in Italian Tolfa. Salt, openly lying in the saltpans of Languedoc ready to be shipped by anybody who wants to do so, is a great asset to Dutch fishermen and farmers who need it for preserving fish, meat and cheese. So it's the businessman who increases the value of things by removing them from places where they are of no use for anybody and selling them where they are of the greatest use."* [2]

This quotation makes clear that in reality the price of goods is dependent on more factors than just labour cost. To the conclusion that the price of goods is highest *'where they are of the greatest use',* 'the modernists', as he calls them, add the subjective theory of values. More on it in the next chapter.

Exchange or use

The concept *'price'* is synonymous to the concept *'exchange value',* already used by Aristotle as distinguished from *'utility value'.* When fixing a fair price the exchange value for the product was fixed as well. As we saw before, such a fair exchange value was derived from the cost made for the product. Price calculation used to be looked upon from the side of supply and not from the side of demand. In principle a product's demand played no part in it. And for most goods the demand mainly arises from the utility value, from the usefulness it has for the user. We have to go into the concept 'utility' later on, for there are a few snags involved. Let's concentrate on the difference between exchange value and utility value first.

In principle any tangible good has got a double use: the one being a characteristic of the thing itself, the other not being characteristic of the thing. Aristotle presents the following example: *"For instance the double use of a pair of shoes: wearing them as shoes and the exchange. Both ways of use are the use of shoes, for also someone who exchanges the shoes with someone who needs the shoes for money or food, uses the shoes as shoes, but not the proper use, for shoes have not been made for exchange."* The example shows the essential tie between *owning* and *using*. A possession was produced as a consumer good for the owner. By exchanging a pair of shoes for money or food, the shoes change from consumer goods into objects of exchange: they move from *proper use* into *improper use*. The shoes get a value in commercial trade then, a market value or a price, as already mentioned above. According to Marx this process may be described as '*alienation*' of the shoes which is the legal term for '*sale*'. The other person to whom the object is handed over is the stranger; the exchanged object is an alien object. The exchange is improper use, it causes the shoes to be alienated from the proper purpose to be worn. Within this framework Marx speaks of *'the metamorphosis of commodities'* and also of *'a social metabolism'*.[1] In case of the exchange in kind, the metamorphosis of commodities is firstly the change from **utility value** into **exchange value** and then again from **exchange value** into **utility value**: "*When in the process of exchange, commodities are handed over from one person to whom they are utility values to a person to whom they aren't utility values, you can speak of social metabolism. The product of one sort of useful labour replaces the product of another sort of useful labour. When the commodity has arrived at the place where it is used as utility value, it will leave the field of exchange of goods and will enter the field of consumption.*"

The most important difference between the utility value of a commodity and its exchange value is a difference between the qualitative and the quantitative character of the commodity: "*As utility values, goods are primarily different in quality, as exchange values they can only differ in quantity and they haven't got the least bit of utility value.*" So the exchange value, the price, is nothing but a quantitative ratio, "*the proportion in which utility values of the one kind are exchanged for utility values of the other kind.*" And when money appears as a means of exchange, '*the metamorphosis of commodities*', that is the change from quality into quantity, will be broken into two pieces. At first the commodity is exchanged for money: being the first metamorphosis of the commodity, which is the **sale**. Marx called this a leap: "*The leap of the value of goods from the body of goods into the body of gold* [=money]" and he considers this a "*death-defying leap of the commodity.*" But immediately after he observes that the sale is of course at the same time a **purchase** by the counterparty: exchanging his money for goods. The money received by the seller is thereupon used however for the conversion into another product: "*The first metamorphosis of a commodity, its conversion from the commodity-form into money, always is the second metamorphosis of another good as well: its reconversion from a money-form into a good.*"

Good heavens, I thought, what a fuss on a simple transaction between buyer and seller. Was this a difficult matter in those days? Why did the author of this book dwell on it like this? But he kept going on with it:

'Marx illustrates this with the example of a linen weaver, who buys a bible from the sale of his linen: *linen - money - bible*. The last metamorphosis (money - bible) however, is once more the first metamorphosis of another good, in this case from bible into money (= sale of the bible). Next the bible seller uses the profit for a metamorphosis into … gin: *bible - money - gin*. Rereading this explanation, it sounds rather time-consuming and self-evident for modern money users like us: money as an undifferentiated means of exchange between purchase and sale.'

Well, at least he admits that Marx's explanation is rather time-consuming, I thought. My question remained: why? Why did the author bring it up?

'Marx used his elaborate explanation of this '*metamorphosis of goods*' to show that the value form keeps changing during our economic actions', the author guessed my question. 'This form changes from concretely material (linen) into abstractly spiritual (money) and then again into concretely material (bible), in a continuous movement. And during this process the material value form moreover changes from exchange value into utility value as soon as the product arrives at the end user. Simultaneously different images of value circulate in your mind, like the projection of a series of slides of the one tangible thing through abstract money into the other tangible thing. You could consider it a kind of cycle of the material and the immaterial. In chapter 5 we will have a closer look at this cycle.'

These words reminded me of: " For dust you are and to dust you will return". But I guessed that it wasn't meant like this by the author. I wondered what he was going to say on it in chapter 5.

'Let's once again return to the exchange value, that is the price of this book you bought and you are reading right now', the author resumed his story from the beginning. 'From the preceding reasoning you will probably have understood by now that this exchange value hardly informs you on the utility value. The utility value is purely personal and the only thing you can say, is that for you as a reader this utility value is evidently higher than the exchange value, or you shouldn't have bought it.'

Yes, that must be the case, I thought, but isn't this the same conclusion as in the first chapter of his book? Only in other words? My purchase of the book showing that the subjective value of the book as seen by me was higher than the price, so the profit I expected from the book being higher than the cost? And that's why I was going to get a positive return from reading this book?

'If we put the almost anachronistic words 'exchange value' and 'utility value' next to the nowadays generally used terms 'cost' and 'profit', we can say that their meaning is practically identical,' the author agreed. 'When you pay for the book in the shop, it costs its exchange value in the form of a more or less objectively fixed amount of money and when later reading it, or using it, it gets a personal subjective utility value, expected by you to be higher than the exchange value. (Let's hope that this expectation hasn't been disappointed so far.)'

Well, I can't say yet, I thought, as I just started.

'Okay, we spoke about the price of the book. It didn't require a priest or other clergyman. The part of the value and price fixing priests has been taken over by the publisher now, who isn't free to fix any price however. He has to reckon with all kinds of market conditions and he knows quite well that he has to have a look at what is charged for other books. In short he must not only have eyes for the absolute price of his book, but also for the relative price, meaning the price compared to prices of other books and other media and market sectors and a lot more in fact, for when looked upon it in a broad way, everything competes with everything.'

Yes, I can think of a few things myself, I thought, the man may be right in principle, but books competing with bicycles for instance seemed a bit farfetched.

'But it's a hopeless task of course', the author agreed with me, 'for in this case you might compare apples and oranges, but not apples and for instance going to the cinema. Apples and oranges are part of the same market sector of fruit, and books can be placed in the market sector of printed media, but it's still too broad, for the sale of this book doesn't depend much on the price of let's say a cookery book. But when a publisher fixes his selling prices, he has to examine which price suits the market. The only thing in common with the way the absolute price of a product used to be fixed might be that nowadays a once fixed price doesn't change for a while and therefore appears to be an absolute price. But this apparently absolute book price is, as said before, dependent on a lot more market conditions than labour cost alone. Besides hardly anybody will say nowadays that the fixed price of a product is the same as the absolute value. Absolute value? they will ask, what do you mean by absolute value? And probably you won't be able to answer that question.

Here are another three points on absolute, fair prices.

Firstly: does 'fair' mean 'fixed' by definition? Let's look at agriculture and its variable crops. It's clear that the surpluses and shortages the one time cause lower, the other time higher prices of agricultural products, as Adam Smith said too. As early as Egyptian antiquity men tried to subdue these price fluctuations by building granaries, which were filled with surpluses in the 'seven fat years' and from which the shortages could be filled in the 'seven meager years'.

This makes clear that 'fair' isn't necessarily 'fixed'; the supply does play a part in this, even when actually it wasn't allowed according to the almost divine doctrine of the absolute, fair price.

Secondly: isn't an absolute, fair price, always relative as well? My answer is: it must be! For when product A for instance has a fixed price of €10 and product B a fixed price of €20, the relative price of A will be half of B's price, or $Pa = {}^1/_2\ Pb$. It's a matter of price comparison. The concept 'relative value' doesn't have any moral or ethical dimension in this case, it's simply arithmetical work. In the next section we will delve deeper into this relative measure and graduation brainwork.

Thirdly: how many prices are fixed nowadays? Books belong to the few articles having the same price in most shops and not changing for a certain period. Which can hardly be said of food, the supermarkets try hard to be a few pennies cheaper than the competitor. And when it's about vegetables and fruit, prices are different in each outlet and especially at each season. Besides all goods and services are liable to inflation, resulting in sometimes creeping, sometimes running price increases.

But was inflation unknown in ancient times, when these so-called fair, intrinsic, absolute prices were attached to products?' the author wondered straight away. ' Did they never have to deal with inflation, or a general decrease of the value of money?'

Indeed, I had the same thought right then, for I sometimes heard that the supply of gold and silver moved in a herky-jerky fashion, resulting in big price fluctuations. When the supply of these precious metals is large their value decreases, and as a result you have to pay more gold or silver for goods and services, which causes an increase in price. And indeed sometimes out of the blue overwhelming imports of gold and silver occurred, for instance after 1530 when the Spaniards were plundering the Inca's gold and silver for decades. Close to the Bolivian city Potosi is the *Cerro Rico* or the Rich Mountain, where silver ore was discovered in 1544. Potosi is the highest situated city in the world (4090 meters). The silver of the Rich Mountain is exhausted for the most part now, but there are still miners present. Since 1987 the city is on the UNESCO world heritage list for its rich history and the colonial architecture.

But silver mines can be found almost anywhere in the world, I knew. In the 16th century the most well-known European coins were made of silver from the mines in Joachimsthal in Bohemia.

The big silver coins from that period got the name 'Taler' translated into 'daalder' in Dutch. Originally 'tolar' in Czech and 'dollar' in American. But there were more silver mines in Europe, for instance in the Harz, in Sankt Adreasberg's *Grube Samson*, also on the UNESCO world heritage list. Opening all these mines often caused an extra rush of precious metals which decreased their value and didn't this result in an increase of retail prices?

'Surely, the phenomenon of the constantly decreasing value of money was known then,' the author answered, 'caused by the mess made by kings, the unbalanced extraction and import of precious stones, or deficits in the supply of goods by wars or crop failure for instance. And of course this didn't fail to influence the level of the fixed 'absolute' prices. But in the case of a general increase in price of both goods and services an absolute price in principle only changes in nominal terms, so not in real terms, meaning that this price may still be the right reproduction of the labour cost. And when the price of all products increase by the same percentage (which is hardly ever the case of course), the mutual price relation of the goods and services stays the same. These mutual price relations represent the relative prices. We have to dwell on this. We will go into the influence of inflation on the value of money in our minds, in chapter 8.'

I have to keep this in mind, I thought: the difference between absolute and relative prices, which will return in chapter 8 of the book. The idea of absolute prices were familiar to me by now, I thought, so let's continue with the relative prices, the author started to mention above.

Relative value

'So, relative prices. As mentioned before it's about price *relations*, about how many units of one product are equal to a certain number of units of another product. In the example above 1 unit of product B was worth as much as 2 units of product A, represented as the price relation $P_a = \frac{1}{2} P_b$. In other words: the exchange value of product A is half of the exchange value of product B. In the example prices are expressed in Euros. But in fact it's of no importance in which unit of measure the exchange value of prices is measured, whether Euros, cowry shells, cows, fish, axes, corn, beads, rice or salt. All these products used to have the function of means of exchange, of money therefore. When goods like this have the function of money, they are called commodity money. But whether it concerns commodity money or our modern set of money like coins, banknotes and transferable money, all goods and services can be presented by any kind of money.

Representing, relating to each other by random means of exchange can be done with various units of measure. In the days when commodity money was used, measuring the exchange value of that commodity money used to be a problem once in a while, for how to fix the exchange value of an amount of salt to a cow? For this they tried to find standards of comparison for which lengths, weights or measures of volume were chosen. Thus in some parts of Asia and Africa corn was measured by a corn measure like a hectoliter or a bushel (1 hectoliter = 4 bushels) and was equated with a same amount of for instance money cowry, which got the same value in this way. For fish a long measure was used: fish had to be paid for with a row of cowry shells as long as the fish itself. In connection it's worth mentioning that the official name for a cowry shell is *Monetaria moneta* and moneta is money in Italian.'

So that is the source of the word 'money'? The shell? But the author didn't give it more consideration.

'What strikes us in these examples, is that for this kind of value comparison a form of representation was chosen with much symmetry with the traded goods themselves - the length of a fish beside a row of shells, a bushel of corn against the same volume of shells. According to Simmel this *"Neigung zur Symmetrie is allen unausgebildeten Kulturen eigen"*. This inclination to symmetry is also shown in the pictures on some of the first coins. Hence on the first bronze coins of peoples that used fish as a means of exchange, pictures of fish can be found referring to the original means of exchange. For the same reason pictures of bullocks or axes can sometimes be found. According to Simmel a certain intellectual education is needed to be able to think more abstractly in symbols and this progressing abstraction can be seen in the development of money. In chapter 5 more about this symbolic money. But let's go on about expressing the world into measurement proportions.

Nowadays we are able to think in (measurement) proportions without the underlying material having anything to do with one another. With ease we compare a bundle of carrots with a car by attaching a cash price to both of them. As a result these carrots are related in a certain value proportion to the car, whereas they haven't got anything to do with one another.'

Has there ever been anyone who felt the need to compare the value of a car to a bundle of carrots? I didn't anyway. Okay, forget it, but the author immediately put forward Georg Simmel to press home a rather far-fetched example, according to me, and in German at that:

*"Ein Maßverhältnis zwischen zwei Größen nicht mehr durch unmittelbares Aneinanderhalten herzustellen, sondern daraufhin, daß jeder zu je einer anderen Größe ein Verhältnis hat und diese beiden **Verhältnisse** einander gleich oder ungleich sind - das ist einer der größten Fortschritte, die die Menscheit gemacht hat, die Entdeckung einer neuen Welt aus dem Material der alten."*

Magnificent, I thought, I like those baroque German sentences. And in my opinion this sentence was quite special, as it implied that humankind had passed an essential threshold to modern time this way. Or did I misunderstand it? Let's continue reading:

'Relative thinking, thinking in measurement proportions, apart from the quality of concrete material, can be found in different territories', the author explained. 'We use for instance measures of length, surface and volume that are independent of the kind of material - after all it is of no importance whether a room is made of wood, stone or glass'.

Of no importance, I agreed.

'By thinking in this kind of relations, in measurement proportions, the qualitative differences between things are reduced to quantitative proportions'.

I sensed his line of thought:

'And by expressing everything in money we *'monetarise'* the world.'

See? Money! In our minds we are constantly translating the world into money, the author tried to make the reader understand it good and proper. As for me, the message had come across, and I was only as far as chapter 2.

'The monetary human being particularly inquires after *'how much'* and not after *'what',* which shows a well developed sense of abstraction dissolving all qualitative characteristics into quantitative ones', it sounded.

And when those quantities are expressed in money, I thought ahead…

'And by transforming qualities quantitatively into money all human values are reduced to uniform money values', the author completed. 'That's why Marx called money *"that general whore, that general matchmaker of people and peoples."* So money reduces all qualitative differences between people - beauty, creativity, honesty, musicality, strength of mind - into quantitative differences.'

Yes, but that isn't always the case, is it? I thought. Was the author of the opinion that when I bought the book, I was only ruled by a quantitative price comparison with other books and that I hadn't paid any attention to its contents and quality? Or that when buying clothes you only have an eye for the amount of money you have to pay for it in comparison to other articles? Nonsense, I thought, utter nonsense.

'Of course this doesn't mean that modern man exclusively steers by a monetary compass', he immediately put it into perspective, 'but it does mean that in all his acts he carries out a certain calculation, as we already postulated in chapter 1. In chapter 6 the 'calculating animal' a human being is, will be gone over with a fine-tooth comb.

But first let's go on about the subject 'the monetarising of the the world'. The tendency or desire to quantify everything and then express it into money is connected to our wish to get hold of things and events around us. Saying that the value of our effort is one hundred Euros, gives us something more to hold on to than saying 'well done lad!' accompanied by a pat on the back. Just like a gift voucher of thirty Euros gives a numerical idea of the value of your relation with the giver or receiver in a certain situation. Such a voucher translates your wish "sincerest congratulations" into a measurable quantitative variable, measured in money. And whether we like it or not, by this monetary measurableness these 'transactions' are being lifted into the field of economics!'

So giving someone a present is an ecomic transaction? I wondered. Or does this only go for gift vouchers?

'In principle it goes for any kind of gift', was the eye-opening comment of the author, 'for giving something always creates the obligation to do or give something in return. Presents are seldom for free, they are a more or less compelling invitation for something in exchange, the prelude to an exchange transaction. *"There is no such thing as a free lunch",* is said among libertarians and it was also the title of a book by economist *Milton Friedman.*'

He has a point, I agreed, thinking of the invariable envelope with content that was passed on at anniversaries.

'In all cases mentioned above there are measurable, therefore quantitative values, but not until these quantitative values are expressed in money, will we meet with 'hard', economic values. It means that all interpersonal intercourse of any nature whatsoever becomes economic the moment a price is fixed to it. We call economic values 'hard' because they are monetarily calculable.'

I needed a while to fully register this conclusion. So as soon as you give something you paid for, or when you put some money in an envelope or give a similar gift voucher, you are dealing with economics, the author claimed?

'That's how it is', he confirmed my thoughts, 'for when a price is attached to something, it becomes economic by definition and will then be called 'hard' values. But as well as these economic values there are also more 'soft' values, like social, cultural, ethic, esthetic and ecological ones. It's mostly assumed that they can't be measured in the same way and can hardly or not at all be expressed in money. It is to be considered whether there is a substantial difference or a measuring problem. As in the case of ecological values we more and more manage to set a price to it and also the awareness that culture represents a value of money gets across more and more.'

That may be so, I thought, but measuring ethic and esthetic values seems impossible to me. But the author was of another opinion and he tried to explain it by an inversion:

'When you hear that a painting costs a lot of money, you will look at it differently and you will attach more cultural value to it', he said. 'That means that only by coming acquainted with the amount on the price tag you will attribute another esthetic value to it.'

Well I don't, I fooled myself, others may be this suggestible, but my esthetic judgment had never been influenced by how expensive something is. Or had it?

'This example of the painting points in the direction of money being the autonomous source of value. When after having learnt the price of the painting you will see it in a different light, esthetically as well as art-historically and you will attach more value to it, this demonstrates the value-creating functioning of money as it is. By examination of the amount of money something goes on in your mind by which your opinion of the painting started shifting. So in this way money can create value.'

Should that really be the case? I thought again. Should this bother me too? As together with the thought doubt hit home. And when I thought about it a little longer, I had to admit that I was not insensitive either to the psychological influence of a price. I wasn't sure whether you liked something more because it was more expensive or that is was more expensive because it was more beautiful, quite simply causing the higher price. This cheap? - can't be much, you are inclined to think. And the opposite: look what it costs! - must be something special (even when I can't see it).

'Now we have reached the stage that we no longer look at the price of a product as an absolute value, but as a relative variable, it's time for another example', the author continued his reasoning, 'but it's an example that has much in common with the previous one.'

Nice, another example, I thought, I adore examples, can't get enough of them, because without them I am often in a fog.

'As fundamentally any price is relative, any product can comparatively be expressed in another product. Let's take an exchange of goods between two persons without the use of money: Mrs. X exchanges 3 units of product A for 2 units of product B of Mr. Y. The exchange value, or the price of product A, will be two third of the price of product B, shortly $Pa = {}^2/_3 Pb$. Next we fix a cash price to the products A and B. Suppose that product A costs €10. What will be the price of product B? The answer won't be difficult for you, I think, for when $Pa = {}^2/_3 Pb$, product B will cost €15. In this example we started from the idea of a relative price relation of $Pa = {}^2/_3 Pb$. But in a shop those exchange relations are not specified of course, only cash prices are shown there. But when one book is for instance €40 and the other €30, it will be clear that the value relation between those two books is 4:3 or 3:4, dependant on which book is expressed in which book. These ratios represent value relations between products, relative values, or relative prices.'

Well, I thought, it goes without saying that in this way you can relate the value of each product to the value of each other product by means of money, but what's the use?

'The fact that nowadays we mostly realize quite well that any price is essentially relative, also means that prices have lost their absolute character, the character of an absolute and divine judgment of justice. Aristotle and Thomas of Aquino may have said that things have an intrinsic value, independent of any transaction, we know better nowadays. We very well know now that almost all prices also depend on supply and demand. Therefore most prices have become negotiable, and related to this our values are pliable. Our values lost their fixed value by the influence of supply and demand, you might say, they have become consumer products.'

Well, I thought, this is going too far. For, take something like "freedom of speech", to me a value of utter importance, and this man is saying that this value is for sale on the market?

'However, it's often hard to discover how and where these values are sold', the author went on contemplating the matter, 'let alone which prices we pay for them. But the example above of esthetic valuing influenced by prices, shows how easily opinions are adjusted when people learn the price. Much more examples can be thought of. Such as that we have already sacrificed invaluable nature to so-called economic interests and that we easily give up a moral opinion of something or someone when enough money is in it for us. By bribery and corruption even the greatest villains can become a beloved head of state.'

Well, I thought, I could name a few.

'Thus prices are not only relative compared to each other, they also often relate and influence our value judgment of people and things. And this is something that goes on in our minds, this computer filled with monetary moralistic programs.'

Yes, *"money makes the world go round"* sounded in my head, I don't know why, sung by whom? Oh yes, by Liza Minnelli and Joel Grey in the musical 'Cabaret'.

Notes:

1. Karl Marx, *Het Kapitaal*, Amsterdam 2010, Boom, (originally *Das Kapital* Hamburg 1867)
2. Jos Defoort, *Het Grote Geld - keerpunten in de monetaire geschiedenis,* Leuven 2000, Van Halewyck
3. Jean - Joseph Goux, *Elektronisch geld, of de vingers van de onzichtbare hand,* article 1998
4. Adam Smith, *The Wealth of Nations,* New York 2003, Bantam Classic, (originally 1776)
5. Georg Simmel, *Philosophie des Geldes,* Frankfurt am Main 1989, Suhrkamp (*The Philosophy of Money,* London and New York 2004, 2001, Routledge) (originally Leipzig 1900)
6. Jean - Joseph Goux, *Symbolic Economics. After Marx and Freud,* New York 1990, Cornell University Press, (originally Paris 1973)

3   A SEARCH FOR THE START OF THE RAINBOW
On the sources of value

'Do things have a value by themselves?'
This was the question the third chapter opened with. Yes, of course, I reacted spontaneously, that goes without saying.
'And nature?'
No question about that, for we can't do without nature, can we?
'No!!' it sounded almost like a reproof, with two exclamation marks.
'I repeat: no!' Only one exclamation mark now, as if meanwhile he was less sure of himself now, but how wrong I was: 'Things and nature don't have any value by themselves. Reality and value haven't got anything to do with each other.'
How do you know that? I wondered out loud.
'A problematic proposition of course', the author admitted. 'For, to start with, the implicit supposition in a saying like this, is that there is an objective reality. Many philosophers have racked their brains over it. For instance, you may ask whether there really is an objective reality outside ourselves or that it is just an illusion, like Plato thought possible in his *allegory of the cave*.'
It sounded familiar, Plato's cave. Had to do with shadows seen by us as the reality.
'This allegory tells the following story: In a cave without any daylight, there are some prisoners lined up with their backs towards the entrance. They look at the back wall of the cave. They have been chained in a way as not to be able to move their heads or to see themselves or each other. The only thing they can see is the wall. They have been positioned like this their whole lives, they don't know any better. Behind them is a wall and behind it burns a fire. People walk along this wall carrying all kinds of objects on their

heads, like stones and wooden figures of people and animals. By means of the fire the shadows of these objects are projected on the wall the prisoners are looking at and they hear the voices echoed of the people who are carrying the objects. So the only thing the prisoners observe in their lives are shadows and echoes. Because they don't know anything else, they think that those shadows and echoing voices are the reality and when talking to each other their conversation would be about the observing of this reality. But what would happen when a prisoner would be able to free himself of the chains and escape past the fire out of the cave?'

He was going to be blinded if I remember well.

'First the fire would blind him, which will confuse him, so he might be wanting to return to the wall and the shadows, the only things seen as reality by him. But when he doesn't give up and when out of the cave he finds himself in the blazing sunshine, it gets even worse. When his eyes get used to the light, he doesn't understand anything of what he sees. Gradually he gets to know this above-world and he realizes that the only things that used to be seen and heard in the cave were shadows and echoes. If he should return to the cave and tell his fellow prisoners about his experiences in the real world, they wouldn't believe nor understand him, as their language was only referring to the shadows and the echoes.

By this allegory Plato showed that we can never know what is real. Perhaps the objective reality doesn't exist at all and we are therefore living in an illusionary world. Most people will consider this a senseless thought. Of course there is a table when I see one, they will say, I am certainly not imagining it! For convenience's sake, we will take it for granted in this book.'

Quite, we would be lost otherwise, I grumbled. When I hit my head against a door, causing a big lump, or when I cut my finger and it starts bleeding, this is proof of the objective existence of the door as well as the knife as the blood, in my opinion. The idea of the world as a projection of a number of images in my head, doesn't agree with me at all. For when fully considering it - did I exist at all then? Was my own existence only an illusion too in that case? Luckily the author left this cloudy theory alone and for the sake of convenience started from the idea of a tangible, objectively existing reality.

'Okay, we start from the idea that reality exists, but this doesn't mean that this reality has a value of its own. Let's take the example of a blackberry-bush, or a diamond you found in the street. Do you think that these products have a value of their own?'

This introduction made clear what the author's answer was going to be:

'No, these objects don't have a value of their own, for objects nor natural events around us, are aware of any value at all.'

Why needed objects or nature be aware of this? I wondered. For there is no need for a thing to know its value in order to have value, is there? Besides things don't have any knowledge, things don't have brains or a memory, because they are dead. A stone doesn't live, does it? Nor do precious stones. A diamond of great value doesn't know this itself. All of them dead things. Yes, nature is alive, but what does a tree know? I mean what does a tree know consciously? Does a tree have consciousness? I had to take care not to slip down into endless philosophical quicksand.

'When we think that a blackberry-bush has value, it's our own doing and not of the bush or the blackberries', the author continued. 'We express an opinion then, an opinion of value, but it has got nothing to do with the objective reality of the blackberries themselves. Blackberries do have all kinds of physiological qualities, but no esthetic, sociological, psychological or economic ones. When we think that blackberries are beautiful or delicious, or that the sight of a blackberry-bush gives us peace or happiness, or when we attach economic value to those blackberries, it's because of the psychological and economic processes in our minds that lift the blackberries out of their natural value-free context, so from their worthlessness into the domain of values. All of it sheer work of man. And when we include the blackberries into the domain of economics, it's by attaching a price to it. But how do we actually do this, filling the world around us with values, in this case especially with economic value?'

Well, hadn't the author told this before in the previous chapter? Constantly busy calculating in our minds, something like that?

'In the previous chapter we were occupied with it too', he admitted, 'when we extensively dealt with the value of this book compared to its price. We concluded that its price was mainly fixed by the publisher based on cost and market prospects. But that the price wasn't the same as the value you as a buyer attached to it. That value could be higher as well as lower than the price. In the first case it lead to the purchase and in the second to the decision not to buy it. You as a prospective customer had a value-judgment in mind about this product and compared it to its price. The value-judgment in the mind of a prospective customer is a personal, subjective value-judgment, we said in chapter 1. The price of the book however was not fixed on subjective grounds, but on the basis of cost and market prospects and is therefore rather an objective value-judgment. But even when we call the one value-judgment purely subjective and the other objective, in both cases it's about human interpretations of the world around us. This means that even at first sight hard, objective value calculations are subjective judgments after all. Take value calculations based on working hours for instance. They are much less objective than they seem at first sight, because one kind of labour isn't the same as the other and these different kinds of labour will subjectively be judged and therefore also rewarded differently. A certain kind of labour looked upon as quite important in one society and therefore having much social status, can be seen as inferior in another society and therefore be much lower on the wage scale. With a bit of fantasy you might see the actual *number of working hours* as an objective quantity, but not the *kind of labour*. The first is a quantitative, measurable quantity and the second a qualitative, immeasurable factor.'

Quite true, I agreed, for the quality of my own work really is totally immeasurable. I'm rather doubtful about the quality and the value of the things I've done during my life. I don't know whether it has been of some importance what I did or do, but I'm certain that the height of my wages didn't have much to do with it. In my own mind the value of my own work was sometimes high, but often low as well, unfortunately. What am I busy doing? I used to think. A proof indeed that value is something in your mind, I had to agree with the author. My working hours are almost uncountable - x years multiplied by y weeks multiplied by z hours per week, it is still calculable, but as far as the qualitative performances I delivered are concerned, I'm in the dark. It sometimes struck me how some self-contented people considered themselves of great importance. They obviously overestimate their own value. 'He has his nose so high in the air that he can't see the ground' it is called. It must be a pleasant feeling to be able to put yourself on such a high value pedestal, I guess, or do these people on the contrary suffer from inner uncertainty? But let's stop psychologizing, and continue reading the book.

'Value is therefore a human interpretation of the world around us', the book continued, 'an idea: value and values by man attached to nature, objects and events, aren't the qualities of this reality itself, but value-judgments.

Scale of value

We are passing judgments on everything around us, objects, nature and even people. We are continuously placing everything we see in a *structure of value* or *scale of value*. Man is an order producing being and valuing is a way of arranging things in a sequence of importance. We will go into this ordering in a separate chapter hereafter.

The value judgments we give, can be measurable, like a temperature of 21 degrees Celsius, or immeasurable. These value judgment are often emotional values like the warmth felt of the measured temperature. And when two people are objectively in agreement that they both see the same table in a furniture shop, the one may say that it's a beautiful table and the other that he doesn't want the thing in his house, not even for free. Both of them are then placing the table on a personal scale of value, the one by a positive mark, the other by a negative one. By means of this structure of value, reality is given a meaning in relation to man. Our world changes by our continuous value judgments from an objective into a subjective reality.

This duality of 'objective' and 'subjective' is often associated with 'measurable' and 'immeasurable', but from the example of the measured and experienced temperature it's obvious that we don't follow this way of thinking here. In this book we depart from the idea that any criterion is basically subjective, because even the most hard and undisputed measurable quantities are always judged by people in this way. Of course there is a difference in hardness and degree of factuality in various kinds of knowledge and sciences, but this difference is rather gradual than black-and-white. And as far as this book's subject is concerned - money being a mind thing like the value attached to it - we are walking on thin ice in this matter.

Maybe needless, another example: the price of a car. Is it an objective or a subjective quantity of value? At first sight the answer seems clear: objective, because the price is just a measurable quantity of units of currency, fixed on the basis of cost and the estimated proportion of the market. But when having a closer look at how such a price is established, we will discover that the price-making of a car isn't just a matter of objective business economics, but is also subjectively, even emotionally founded. The price range of a certain car has to agree with the customer's social class, that means the reference group he wants to belong to. That's why some cars are deliberately made more expensive as they can't be sold well to the target group otherwise. Products have to be positioned in the market not only as to kind or type, but also as to price, each product has its own market sector.'

Ah well, I thought, which class do I belong to? What is my reference group? In which market sector am I to be placed by market makers? Don't give it a thought, just read on:

'In short, by attaching a certain value to anything, positive or negative, nature, objects and events will get a meaning related to man. Thus the same object may have much value to Mrs. Pope and little or even a negative value to Mrs. King. The latter usually is the case, think of food products, the one person adores boiled sprouts the other gets sick at the very thought. The other way around is possible too, when both ladies attach the same value to two totally different objects. Mrs. King is pleased for instance by a jewel whereas Mrs. Pope takes the same pleasure in an ice-cream and whipped cream. But it's also possible that we are completely indifferent to something, that we couldn't care less, that we aren't interested at all. In this case we are neutral to something.'

Often the case with me I thought, being totally indifferent to something. Soccer for instance, politics, let them blether, I often think, or certain kinds of music I hate - ah no, the latter I'm not indifferent to, but it had rather be placed in the negative part of my scale of value. Get rid of that bloody noise, I think then.

'But how do we make such a scale of value?' the author ignored my grumbling. 'Are we doing that by classifying our needs? On the basis of the quantity of benefit the anticipated satisfaction of these different needs will give us? Or rather based on the quantity of work or trouble it costs to achieve what we want? In other words: we have to consider where the value something gives us precisely comes from: from the **benefit** of what is desired, from the **trouble** it takes to get it, or from both? Or, does value come from a **positive** (benefit) or from a **negative** (trouble) origin? From profit or cost? From pleasure or pain? Or both? To put it differently: do we make our scale of value on the basis of subjective perception of benefit or on objective measurement of achievements? On the basis of *desire* or on *achievement*? Or both? But whether we choose the one or the other, or combine both of them, we always have to be able to rank them well, to be able to *arrange* and *compare* them and know how to *measure* all of this as well. Let's take a closer look at all these points of view and instruments we need to make a scale of value.

Desire and achievement
We have to desire an object, crave for it, to realize that it is something that may have some value for us. But does this mean that value arises from desire? Because satisfying this desire will give us a certain subjective value, a certain **benefit**?'

Yes I think it does, I thought, for when something has some benefit, it will have some value too, won't it? But again this conclusion was too simple:

'Opinions differ on this, just think of what was said about it in the last chapter.'

Did he mention it in the last chapter? I couldn't remember.

'We quoted *Adam Smith* and *Georg Simmel* and also the French philosopher *Jean Joseph Goux*, who said *"Only suffering (pain) has value as an objective, universal measure"*.

Ah well, already forgotten.

'According to the philosophers mentioned above the answer to where value comes from is clear.'

Yes, but in my opinion you can't make it a rule, black-and-white like this, I thought. For why should I do my best for something when I don't see what good it could do? The one thing can't do without the other, can it? So I decided to choose the third option, the option that you only want to incur expenses if you expect a return - just as I had done by the purchase of the book, hadn't I? Hadn't the author already made much of it in the first chapter?

'But of course you may ask why you would make a move for something anyway when you don't expect anything from it from the very start', the author immediately agreed with me.

'Let's try going back in history first to the source of this idea of value, so the idea that you have to make a sacrifice in order to create something of value. And when we go into prehistory, we will discover that making sacrifices and sacrificing are at the basis of the origin of money. According to some people money literally originates from the place of sacrifice. In his book *The Big Money - turning points in monetary history*, Jos Defoort quotes Bernard Laum:[1] *"In his **Holy Money** Bernard Laum claims that money doesn't originate from the market but from the place of sacrifice. The coins would have taken the part of the ox in the course of time. (...) If it is true that coins first appeared at the place of sacrifice, in the centre of the community, visible to everyone, in replacement of the sacrificed oxen, it clears a lot. In that case the coin is something that concerns the whole community, nourishes it, stimulates it and makes it change. (...) In Greek society they penetrated all classes of the population. They appeared at the agora before they were used in international commerce. Owing to their specific Greek origin, coins were primarily meant to be 'divided' among the participants, just like the beef used to be divided. Their part in the exchange process is of secondary importance. (...) Around the altar the priests taught their believers how to weigh and count for the first time."*

The quotation shows that these sacrifices mainly consisted of oxen, cattle which were slaughtered in a sacral manner and then divided 'according to credit and merit'. (Mind: not exchanged but divided!) 'To slaughter' means the same as 'to dedicate to a god', a kind of consecrating and sacrificing. The Latin *sacrifare* points to the same origin: it means to slaughter and to consecrate at the same time.' And the Dutch word 'slachten'/ to slaughter is said to be related to 'slaan'/ to strike coins.'

If that's true, then the striking of coins is in fact a ritual value creating action, I concluded.

'In this light the value of money has been derived from 'the sacrificed oxen'. These sacrifices created value, because they nourished the community and placated the gods. In those days before there were coins, oxen were often used as a unit of account, but not immediately as a mutual means of payment. Sacrificing the oxen was a form of paying, but rather a payment to the gods, whom were expected to do something in return. Coins did change the form of the sacrificial value, but they still represented this value. It meant a step in the direction of the sacrifice becoming spiritualized. Also by this 'coin vehicle of sacrifice' the value of the sacrifice moved to our minds, you might say'.

Money as a sacrifice in our minds? An imaginary sacrifice? So when holding a coin or a banknote, I'm holding a vehicle of sacrifice? Or the sacrifice itself?

'Money isn't only a form of possession but also always a form of debt (more on this in chapter 7). If we pay money, we pay off a debt by this sacrifice. Seen in a broader religious perspective sacrifices can be seen as a means to pay off our sins or moral (primal) debt. This is manifest in linguistic usage. The British sociologist *Geoffrey Ingham* wrote about this:[2]

"In all Indo-European languages words for 'debt' are synonymous with those for 'sin' or 'guilt', illustrating the link between religion, payment and the mediation of the sacred and profane realms by 'money'. For example there is a connection between the German **Geld***, indemnity of sacrifice (Old English* **Geild***), tax (Gothic* **Gild***) and of course the English* **guilt***."*

The elaborations above connect the idea that you have to take pains to achieve something with the theme of making sacrifices. The expression 'spare no trouble or expense' indicates the same and in idiomatic language of business economics concepts like 'cost' and 'sacrifices' are often mixed up.

As we already mentioned, in this connection Adam Smith spoke about *'toil and trouble'*, and because he is often considered to be the founder of the science of economics, here follows the concerning quotation from his book *The wealth of nations:* *"The real price of everything, what everything really costs to the man who wants to acquire it, is the toil and trouble of acquiring it. What everything is really worth to the man who has acquired it, and who wants to dispose of it or exchange it for something else, is the toil and trouble which it can save to himself, and which it can impose on other people. What is bought with money or goods is purchased by labour, as much as what we acquire by the toil of our own body. That money or those goods indeed save us the toil. They contain the value of a certain quantity of labour which we exchange for what is supposed at the time to contain the value of an equal quantity. Labour was the first price, the original purchase-money that was paid for all things. It was not by gold or by silver, but by labour, that all the wealth of the world was originally purchased."* Smith summarizes it brief and to the point as *"Wealth is power of purchasing labour."* If we consider this last thought, so that wealth means the power to buy labour, in fact it says that buying a product is the same as buying a quantity of working hours. *Karl Marx* also concluded this, saying that the value ratio between different things, their relative price, has got nothing to do with the qualities of the things themselves, but are determined by the working hours spent on it.'

The same story again, I grumbled.

' *"A social relation between people appears as relations between material objects"*, he wrote.'[2]

Well, that might be so, but I don't think I enter into relations with the baker when buying a loaf of bread, I thought. And I don't sense any personal relationship between myself and the producer of my garden tools. I am sometimes on bad terms with my garden hose when a kink blocks the reel, which sometimes makes me call out some unpleasant words. Nor do I feel a deep relationship with the author of this book, even when I talk to him once in a while in thought, but we are not acquainted. He may be the labourer - the writer of the book and I myself the reader, but a social relationship? No, I don' talk to the man but to his text. Or is it the same?

'Hence labour was the only source of value according to these philosophers,' he continued. 'Hegel (1770-1831) seemed to claim this too, he posed that the value of things can't be measured or judged by the pleasure they give us. According to him the proportion of value could not be derived from benefit or profit, but only from cost or **sacrifices**. But Hegel did say that sacrifices were made to satisfy our needs. He characterized the 'bürgerliche Gesellschaft' as a '*System der Bedürfnisse*' leading to division of labour, trade and dependence, a century before the Austrian School did: *"In dieser Abhängigkeit und Gegenseitigkeit der Arbeit und der Befriedigung der Bedürfnisse schlägt die subjective Selbstsucht in den Beitrag zur Befriedigung der Bedürfnisse aller Andern um - in die Vermittlung der Besondern durch das Allgemeine als dialektische Bewegung, so daß indem jeder für sich erwirbt, produziert und genießt, er eben damit für den Genuß der Übrigen produziert und erwirbt. Diese Notwendigkeit, die in der allseitigen Verschlingung der Abhängigkeit Aller liegt......"*

Yes of course, I thought, another baroque German quotation, but what does it really say? And what is this Austrian School? Do I read it correctly that according to Hegel value doesn't come from sacrifices but from our needs?

'When reading this quotation precisely, it does **not** say that value **arises** from the sacrifices we make for something, but it only says that value isn't measurable without considering the sacrifices it needed. He only claims that when we want to satisfy our needs, we have to work for it and exchange with one another, because we are dependent on each other for reaching our targets. And this working and exchanging requires sacrifices in the form of costs. Once again, in this quotation Hegel does **not** say that value **arises** from human sacrifice, but that our needs are the motive for our economic actions,' the author repeated again and therefore he agreed with me on this.

'In the same way we have to understand Goux' proposition, that only our suffering is suitable as a universal criterion to define value. Measuring sacrifices in the form of costs is also the only way to *measure* value in his opinion. All that both of them are concerned about is a measurement problem and not the source of value. Value measurement based on the benefit things give us, is impossible, as 'benefit' is an immeasurable concept, it can't be expressed in cardinal units, that is in numbers. At the most we can arrange things according to more or less felt benefit, ordinal therefore. We already spoke about this arranging of our value judgments. How we are able to do so, this arranging, we will deal with in the next chapter.'

This explanation was some help to get a better understanding of Hegel's quotation and Goux' saying, although I continued having some bad feeling about the sketched tension between benefit and sacrifices. I decided not to rack my brains over it for the time being. But this still left the Austrian School.

'The **Austrian School** was an economic movement which explained the value and the realization of prices 'subjectively' out of needs and therefore not out of sacrifices', was the answer to my question. 'This school existed from around 1870 to 1910 and is also known as the **marginal utility school**. We came across this theory of marginal utility in chapter 1 when we dealt with Gossen's laws.'

Ah yes, *Hermann Heinrich Gossen*. That name came back to me all of a sudden.

'This subjective theory of values has early predecessors like Plato and Aristotle: they were also of the opinion that the actual unit of measurement lies in the system of human needs.'

What? A unit of measurement in your system of needs? Value measurement on the basis of enjoyed benefit? It wasn't possible, was it? Only a few lines back the author said that utility is an immeasurable concept, he wrote: ' it can't be expressed in cardinal units, that is in numbers'. And now according to both ancient Greeks the system of needs should be the actual unit of measurement? Something is wrong here, I thought. Let's continue reading:

'This is shown in the following quotation from Aristotle's *Ethics*:[5] *"Everything must (...) be measured by one thing. In reality this is of course need, which holds everything together (...)"*.'

Yes, Aristotle really said it: everything must be measured by our needs. But how? How can needs be measured?

'Money had merely an arbitrary part in this,' the author continued with Aristotle's quotation: *"However, money by agreement has become the substitute of need. Because of this it got the name 'nomisma'; it doesn't derive its validity from nature, but from 'nomos' (the use, the law) (...)"*

Aha! I thought, now the respectable Greek completely changes the matter, as by simply equating money with need, by simply declaring money as the *'substitute of need'*, he pushed *money* as a *means of calculation* between our needs and their value of benefit which can't be measured in numbers. It didn't seem scientifically sound to me, declaring a unit of measure synonymous with what you want to measure.

"*Need, as a certain unit, holding everything together, is shown by this, when two people don't need one another, or one of them doesn't need the other, there won't be an exchange, like when someone needs something that he owns himself (...)*

If we don't need anything at this moment, money is only a security for an exchange in future, when we will really need something, enabling us to acquire it ..."

Yes, okay, but in this quotation Aristotle doesn't speak about money as a means of calculation any more, I thought, nor about the "**calculation** - substitute of need", but about money as the "**exchange** - substitute of need", money as a medium of exchange and in the last line also about money as a deposit, as a medium of hoarding! These are the three traditional functions of money: *medium of exchange, unit of account, store of value* - but I had the feeling that in this case they were more or less regarded as equals and were lumped together. Or did I get it all wrong? I agreed with the author that 'benefit' was an immeasurable unit and that subjective human needs can't be directly measured. The use of money can't change anything about it, I thought, whatever Plato and Aristotle may say.

'However, when holding the previous quotations up to the light more closely, it seems as if the great Greek philosopher had lost his way a bit.'

See? As I said so.

'He simply passes over the cardinal immeasurableness of human needs and benefit by posing that cash prices are their substitute. Which is incorrect, for it would mean that with any purchase the subjective value is the same as the objective value, or the price. In case of the book you are reading now, it would mean that you won't gain any net profit from it, that the return is nil, because the cost you made for it are the same as the benefit the book will give you.'

There you are, I thought, good Lord this dear old respectable Greek.

'Our conclusion above as to the purchase of this book, in principle applies to any commercial transaction: expectations are that any purchase will gain the buyer more than it cost, or he wouldn't buy it. The subjective value of the purchased article will be higher than the price to the buyer. The opposite goes for the seller: the gross value the sale of the article brings in should be higher than the cost, or he won't earn anything. But in his case it's no matter of balancing the subjective values against the objective ones, but balancing one objective value (selling price) against the other one (cost price). This shows that both parties always have to benefit from a voluntary commercial transaction, for if this isn't the case for one of them, he would cancel it. Such a commercial transaction which is paid for with money, essentially is nothing but an exchange transaction. So trade, or exchange is an autonomous source of value.

The exchanging animal
The greater part of human relations can be seen as a kind of exchange, The German sociologist/philosopher *Georg Simmel* wrote in his book *Philosophie des Geldes*: *"..jede Unterhaltung, jede Liebe (…) jedes Spiel, jedes Sichanblicken."* [6] He relates the concept 'exchange' to terms like 'reciprocity', 'relation' and 'interaction' and even to 'action' and 'communication'. The words 'reciprocity' and 'interaction' are most related to 'exchange', for *"Wenn die Menschen in Wechselwirkungen treten, wird gegenseitig gegeben, was besessen wird,"* as expressed by *Christian Papilloud* in an essay on Simmel.[7] As most human acts are to be reduced to a certain kind of exchange, Simmel characterizes man as *"das tauschende Tier"*.

The purpose of all those exchange transactions is the increase of value. By this interaction, this exchange, the total value gets bigger than the sum of the parts. This means that in an exchange the other is given more value than one originally had oneself. How is that possible?'

Yes indeed, how is this possible, I thought. Must have something to do with personal preferences, or something like that, that one person attaches more value to a certain product than the other.

'That has something to do with different individual (subjective) value judgments on the things that are exchanged mutually.'

See?

'When I sacrifice something in order to get something else in return, I will only do so when my profit is bigger than my sacrifice. So, what I sacrifice has got less value to me than it has for the counterparty, or vice versa. In other words: each of us attributes a different value to the things that are going to be exchanged. In the end this is the basis of all trade: You have something that I want and I have something that you want - I want to buy something from you and you from me, namely my money.'

What? My money? Does the seller want to buy my money? Do I read that correctly?

'We agree on a price, and if everything works out all right, we are both pleased with it - the benefit will have risen for both of us after the exchange and the total value will be bigger after the exchange than the sum of the individual values before the exchange.'

Come on, I thought, the man lets it pass too readily, the seller buying the money of the buyer - and the value of 'my sold money' by this exchange transaction getting higher for the seller than it was for me before the exchange, at that! Weird. I mean, ten Euros will be ten Euros after a purchase transaction, won't they?

'The price agreed on in an exchange transaction might be suggesting that both objects of exchange are worth the same, but when this is regarded subjectively, that is from the individual position of each trading partner, this can't be true. The value creation by exchange means that *"jeder dem anderen mehr gibt, als er selbst besessen hat"*.'

Simmel again, those last words? He forgot to mention him this time, the author, but no doubt about it.

'So our new property has got a higher subjective utility value than the old property we gave up, or a higher utility value than exchange value. Owing to this, both parties benefit from an exchange or trade transaction, but

"... there wasn't a bee that not wanted more,
I don't say: than it deserved,
But it didn't dare to show.."

This was written by *Bernard Mandeville* in *'The Fable of the Bees'*.[8] Both parties scrupulously hide the cost price of what they want to exchange (sell) in order to get as much profit as possible, but however unequal the result of the exchange, both of them do well by it.'

Ah, the well-known sales trick, I thought, pretending the object you want to get rid of is really quite expensive, but on this special occasion is to be sold for a knock-down price. Or the other way round, the buyer seizing the opportunity when seeing that the provider hasn't got a clue of the value of the product to be sold and pretending to pay an excellent price for it. This type of sales tricks are particularly stumbled across in markets without fixed prices like jumble sales or antique markets, or where obscure products pass the counter, for which the financial world is notorious.

But meanwhile I still had this money problem, this value of ten Euros before and after the sale.

'Not everyone may immediately grasp that money can be seen as an ordinary product, as a 'thing of exchange' itself, comparable to any random other object of exchange: whether being a garment, food, a tennis racket or an amount of money, all of them things that can be exchanged for one another, the only difference being that money as an indistinct 'thing of exchange' can easily be exchanged for almost any other thing.'

Ah well, I thought, what can I say?

'Just like any other product you can buy or sell money', the author added, by which it didn't become clearer to me at all. Buying and selling money? He just said so, but it sounded like a strange idea to me.

'Someone who buys something and pays for it with money, in fact sells his money at that moment. When you bought this book and paid for it at the cash desk, you were engaged in an exchange transaction: you exchanged your money for the book, or you bought the book and at the same time you sold your money.'

Well.

'And the bookseller sold the book and by this he bought an amount of money from you, you might say.'

Yes, but we should never say it like that, I grumbled.

'A bit unusual maybe to look at it this way, but it may be a way to make clearer that money is just a thing as well, though not a specified thing, but more like an unidentified thing, you might say.'

Yes, you might, but isn't it more like: a thing without content if I read it well - but then it suddenly struck me that this last thought in fact went quite well with the title of the book: "Money is a mind thing". Because your head bristles with all kinds of things which aren't real things yet, undefined things ghosting about as vague images.

'An example!' the author woke me up.

Great, another example, thank goodness, I thought, it may put me firmly on the ground again. Did I already mention that I adore examples?

'Suppose that Mrs. A and Mr. B exchange their respective properties α and β. Both α and β cost € 10 in the shop. Seen from the outside α and β are worth the same. But obviously this doesn't go for Mrs. A and Mr. B, as they wouldn't have any reason to exchange their goods otherwise. Mrs. A happens to attach more value to product β than to her own product α and Mr. B values α more than his own β. It follows that after the exchange the total subjective value of the goods α and β has become greater than before the exchange.'

Did I understand it correctly? Did the author claim that those two products were worth more than €20 after the exchange?

'This doesn't mean, of course, that the shop price of the products α and β have increased after the exchange', he immediately parried, 'for the shop price is the objective value and this won't change by the exchange. Both products will still cost €10 each, even after the exchange. But what did change after the exchange, is the subjective value which increased for Mrs. A as well as for Mr. B. Both gained a subjective profit of value by the exchange transaction.'

Yes, when looking at it in this way, yes of course, I muttered.

'Seen in this perspective it is strange that for example Aristotle or Marx didn't seem to have an eye for this. They judged the exchange and especially trade as a kind of deceit. Also the American statesman, writer and physicist *Benjamin Franklin* (1706 - 1790) obviously took this view when saying: *"War is robbery, trade is deceit"* and Marx fully agreed. The latter posed that by the step from simple exchange of commodities (with money as medium of exchange) to trade (by which money is earned) barter trade has developed into the creation of trading capital. And according to Marx it was impossible to produce the circulation of goods, which presumed equality in his opinion, as the source of surplus-value: *"Turn and twist* as we may, the fact remains unaltered. If equivalents are exchanged, no surplus-value results, and if non-equivalents are exchanged, still no surplus-value. Circulation, or the exchange of commodities, begets no value" Why this blindness? This denial of creation of value arising from exchange or trade?'

Oh well, these people must have had no eye for the subjective creation of value that arose from it, I guessed. For if an international trader for example buys a product in an area where it is relatively abundant and he sells it somewhere else in the world where it is relatively scarce and expensive, he will not only profit by it himself, but he will create value too. These philosophers probably only looked at the price-tags attached to the objects and believed that they would still be there after the exchange transaction, when I correctly understood the author's example above.

'It seems that Marx, Franklin and Aristotle had a blind spot for the subjective value judgments Simmel draw attention to, value judgments which differ for each of us', the author affirmed my assumption which meant that I started to grasp the matter, didn't I?

The marginal utility of money and the distance to the purpose.
'In this book you are reading right now we are talking about money as a conception or an idea in our minds', the author returned to the beginning. 'Money as an *"ideal or imaginary form"* as we quoted Marx in chapter 2, *"a form that is separated from the natural form of the commodity."* Aristotle joins in by the preceding idea that money has become *"the substitute of need"* - which doesn't necessarily mean that this makes our needs measurable, as we substantiated before. After all there are cardinal, so measurable, as well as ordinal, that is only classifiable values, as we said before. But assuming that an imaginary monetary form of substitution did nestle in our minds à la Aristotle, it would by definition be about economic needs, things that are for sale for a measurable amount of money. And if so, this form of substitution doesn't only relate to one thing but to a series of things stored in various brain cells and classified in a cardinal value scale. It bears comparison to a shop-window filled with things along with their prices. This complete shop-window filled with substitutes of need expressed in money is by itself another ideal form,

a concept in our minds. Does this mean that both same laws of Gossen apply to money as well as goods? So the first law of the diminishing marginal utility and the second on maximization the total utility?'

Yes, I guess so, I thought, for it goes without saying that the utility derived from something is related to your need for it. And if money *is the substitute of need*, there can hardly be any other conclusion but Gossen's laws applying to money as well as to the substitute-product.

'The answer is yes', the author agreed with me. Well, I thought, I guess that I'm beginning to understand it.

'You can tell by the utility progression of money when you get more and more of it. To rich people the marginal utility of the last earned Euros is much smaller than to poor people. And if we want to relate money to happiness, which is often done, the proverb will soon pop up "money doesn't make you happy". But as said before, this saying chiefly refers to rich people's last received marginal units of money, for to poor people every extra penny adds to a better life and more happiness. But how does this come about? What is the reason that rich people are not impressed at all by an extra hundred Euros in income, adding nothing to their utility and happiness, as the poorer part of the population is quite pleased with it?'

Well, that goes without saying, I thought, it's just a matter of saturation. But there was more to it, the author said:

'It has got to do with the fact that a person who has to take no trouble at all to get some money, generally won't take great pleasure in it either', he said.

Ah! This trouble again, I thought, Adam Smith's 'toil and trouble'. Well, but a hundred Euros in your hand, free and for nothing, is always useful, isn't it?

'Money is worth much more for those who need to work hard for it than for those whom it simply fell into their laps', he said. 'Value is not only created by desiring something but by the desired object not being there for the taking.'

Repetition again, I sighed. Other words, same story.

'A certain distance has to be narrowed between the desiring subject and the desired object, or trouble has to be taken in order to get it. If something is desired, this desire will incite us to an achievement in order to get the desired object. The trouble we have to take, the effort we have to make, in other words the sacrifice we have to make to narrow the distance between ourselves (subject) and the desired object (object) creates value.'

Narrowing a distance' to create value? He hadn't used those words before, I thought. Why distance? Which distance?

'To start with, this distance can be quite concrete a distance of time or place. For instance, you have to save for quite a while in order to be able to eventually buy that beautiful house, or you have to travel quite a distance in order to be able to visit the Hermitage in St Petersburg or to buy the desired pair of shoes in Milan.'

Well, this 'distance' could just be seen as a cost factor, I thought, as measuring the sacrifices in the form of financial cost, in this way determining the value of something. So just again, it's the same question of a measurement problem, similar to how the author interpreted the concept of value of the philosophers Goux and Hegel, isn't it?

'But narrowing a distance to reach your goal can also be looked at in a more abstract way, in a more psychological sense', the author continued without answering my question. 'It starts with your understanding that there is a distance between you and your goal: I'm here and my goal is there. For this understanding you use your head and language is the tool to put this distance into words. *" Thanks to language our memory expanded enormously and when chatting we can visualize situations which haven't even occurred yet, but which we can plan in anticipation", René Gude* said on this.[9] The use of money rather reinforced this function of language for the memory, for by money as a value - a storage device, we have an extra instrument to narrow distances in time and space between markets. And thanks to modern credit and financing techniques, advanced derivates included, we have been able to make the distances bigger and bigger.

So in order to achieve your aims you have to be able to set yourself apart from the world. You must realize that when you want something from that world, you have to make head for it and the first step will be the narrowing of the mental distance in order to get a clear picture of the object of your aim. Modern man doesn't form an undifferentiated unity with the world, but he realizes that on the one hand he is set apart from it as a subject, but on the other hand he is part of it as an object. So he knows that he is both a person and a 'thing', a subject as well as an object.'

I beg your pardon? A thing? I thought, it's going from bad to worse.

'Take the example of a journey to London you intended to set off for', the author continued imperturbably. 'A journey you have wished to make for some time, and which you expect to be of much value when carried out. Already before you can start narrowing the concrete measurable distance of time and place to London you got the idea to make this trip. This preceding idea goes on in your mind again, among other things implying that you have to make a kind of organization plan and take care of all sorts of things - fixing a date, booking a hotel, tickets, insurances, checking suitcases, and the like. These matters don't take care of themselves, which means that you as the 'I-subject' (so the subjective 'I' at a distance from the world) knows quite well that you have to do something to make yourself transportable as a kind of luggage thing in order to arrive in London and temporarily be part of it.'

There there, what a fuss, I thought, anyone would think that the author is kidding me into a split personality: 'I' as a human being and 'I' as luggage, so as a thing. But I guess this was exactly what he wanted. That I would understand that the things around us don't come to us by themselves, but in order to achieve something you must see yourself as an objective instrument and use it to steer you towards your aim.

'And not until', he continued, 'having listed all the points systematically and having carried them out with due effort, will the journey to London get any value. Solely the need and desire for such a journey won't give you any value at all. The 'benefit' of a journey like that is absolutely nothing if you don't have to do your best to actually carry it out. You have to narrow a psychological as well as a physical distance in order to acquire the value of a journey to London.'

Well, I'm not so sure whether the preparation and the fatigue for a journey to London creates much value. In my experience much of the travel fun was spoilt firstly by the unpleasantness of the journey itself for instance because of the many delays in uncomfortable means of transport, secondly by the tight rooms with sagged or on the contrary hard beds, mosquitoes, failing air-conditioning or noisy neighbours and thirdly the overcrowded bustle of a city like London.

'Of course it's also possible that the sacrifices you have to make for such a journey are greater than the gross fun it gives you. In that case it's the same story as the purchase of this book: your real benefit or profit of the journey is negative. In short: you have to do the usual work to achieve something and to create value, but if that work costs you more trouble than the gross value it gives you, so if the costs are higher than the profit, the real value is negative, and you'd better refrain from it. In that case Adam Smith's 'toil and trouble' and Georg Simmel's 'Mühe und Plage' have been in vain.'

Without a doubt, I thought, for when looking back, I had spoilt quite a lot of time and trouble in my own life.

Comparing, arranging and alternative costs
'A couple of pages ago we spoke about the *value scale* or *value structure*, in which man places all things and events around him. We attach a certain value judgment to everything, from high to low to negative. We do so on the basis of ratio, intuition and emotion. It doesn't mean that everything has got an irrefutably fixed place in this value scale, for we are constantly evaluating and rearranging. We compare our choices with alternative possibilities and when necessary we reconsider our opinions and judgments. What we consider quite important in our youth and place in the top ten of our value perception, may easily drop from this value hit parade, or the other way round, at an advanced age. So our values aren't exactly stable, you might say.'

Well, the man has a point there, I thought, for quite a lot of intellectual and physical matters that I used to look upon as almost sacred, meanwhile ended on the rubbish dump.

'In order to be able to compare and arrange, we must have the skill to get things straight, to arrange them in an order of importance. For this we need the ability to *know* and *value*. 'To know' means thoroughly taking note of things and events by way of collecting the necessary facts, so make sure that you have sufficient knowledge of facts. And as far as the facts are measurable, we must know which criterions are suitable for this. So we must have knowledge of measure units too, of simple measures like length and weight as well as more complicated and often complex measures like economic elasticity or physical voltage units. A problem with all these criterions is the choice of the basic unit. For example, take the peculiar and astonishing history about the ascertaining of what exactly is a metre since 1675. In this year the Italian *Tito Livio Burattini* published the *Misa Universale* in which he fixed the metre at the length of a pendulum moving half a period of 1 second. At that time he didn't know that this pendulum period also depended on the place on earth of the pendulum. (According to the present definition his metre must be 993,9 mm.) Later, in 1795 the metre was defined as 1/10,000,000th part of half the length of a meridian, as measured by Delambre and Méchain; and in 1983 a metre was seen as the distance light covers in 1/299792458 seconds in vacuum. Before that and in between various other metre units passed in review. What this history makes clear however, is that there must always be a reference unit in order to be able to fix a certain measure unit. In this connection Simmel mentions the metaphor of the stick: you can't measure the length of a stick if you don't have a second stick to measure it with. Which in fact takes us back to the value unit as a relative idea: measuring value without a reference unit is impossible.

A well-known way to compare alternatives and to balance them against each other is the one by means of the concept *alternative costs*, also called *opportunity costs*. These are the costs of an (economic) choice, expressed in terms of the best possible alternative, or the best missed chance. The profit of the best possible alternative is compared with the profit of the chosen option then. So It's not profit against costs, but the one kind of profit against the other. You might for instance weigh the profit of this book you are reading right now against the missed profit of another book you could have read at the same time. Or against that nice cycle ride you could have gone for at the same time and which you missed by reading this book now. By doing one thing you have to give up the other thing as you can't do everything at the same time. Choosing is losing, it is said.

Weighing the pros and cons like this is in fact a kind of exchange. If we speak about exchange, we mostly think of two parties, but for a transaction of exchange both of them are not absolutely necessary. In fact everyone of us is constantly weighing pros and cons against each other the whole day long, such as choose this, not that (shown in the example above). Whether or not consciously, we are always busy taking decisions on the basis of plus and minus, profit and loss, yield and cost, and in the case of alternative costs the one realized profit against the other missed profit. *"Unser natürliches Schicksal, das jeden Tag aus seiner Kontinuität von Gewinn und Verlust, Zufließen und Abströmen der Lebensinhalte zusammensetzt, wird im Tausch vergeistigt, indem nun das eine für das andere mit Bewußtsein gesetzt wird",* Simmel wrote.

You don't say, Simmel again, I thought, is it really necessary to drag him in all the time?

'We quote this line by Simmel, because it contains two words we wish to draw extra attention to once more as part of our argument: *vergeistigt* and *Bewußtsein*. Both words refer to our minds, where according to the German philosopher of money the exchange process is being handled and documented. The product we give up in an exchange process, doesn't only disappear from our material possession, but also from our mental bookkeeping you might say and will be replaced by another product. Remaining in terms of bookkeeping for a while: the asset given up in an exchange process is written off materially as well as immaterially, so physically as well as mentally and the new product is booked as an asset. And this transaction is not only handled administratively in some bookkeeping system, but is also registered in our minds. And in fact this mental registration is of more essential importance than the administrative one, because anything taking place in our minds is felt as really existing.'

Agreed, understandable, I thought, but I did need the explanation of what Simmel wrote, though.

'And then there is something else', it sounded when I thought that the matter had been dealt with by now, 'that is that there will always be a certain alienation involved in an exchange transaction. You may remember having seen the *'metamorphosis of goods'* in the preceding chapter?'

Did the author ask me this?

'Marx, you know, the man who spoke in terms of *'a social metabolism'*.

Ah yes, it sounded vaguely familiar to me.

'Well then, this metamorphosis of goods always goes hand in hand with a certain alienation.'

Oh yes, 'alienation' being the legal term for 'sale'. It occurred to me again, and the utility value of a thing changing into exchange value in an exchange transaction, but hadn't he told all this before? What on earth could be added to it?

'The point is that the process of alienation in an exchange transaction is not limited to the exchanged objects but extends as far as our relation with the other person with whom we entered into an exchange or trade transaction.'

Well, I don't believe it at all, I thought, for if I buy a piece of cheese, the cheese monger doesn't become more unfamiliar to me, rather less unfamiliar the more I meet him. But this primitive reaction of mine obviously was proof again that I didn't understand it at all:

'This other person whom is handed over the exchanged object (the buyer) is the stranger.'

Oh, does he mean that I am the stranger to the cheese monger and he not to me?

'With this it isn't important that the salesman sells a 'thing' and the buyer pays with another 'thing' or with money, as money is every bit as good as a 'thing' is, it's just not specified yet, not yet a 'thingified' thing, you might say.

Good grief, come on, I thought, he means of course money as an undifferentiated means of exchange. But why make things so difficult for yourself?

'But then, money too can be looked upon as an object …'

So an undifferentiated object, I finished for him.

' … and the exchanged or sold object becomes an unfamiliar object in the hands of the stranger.'

Because it doesn't belong to me any more, I understood.

'This implies that anything another person owns is unfamiliar to me. On the other hand by a purchase we exchange this alienation for a newly received familiarity. You may remember that in this respect Aristotle spoke about the difference between 'proper' and 'improper' use of a good which he illustrated by the well-known example of the shoes. By exchanging a pair of shoes for money or food, they change from an object for private use (=proper use) to an object of exchange. In this transition the seller alienates from his shoes. But on the other hand the money or food acquired by the exchange has become my *own*, it has metamorphosed from the unfamiliar into the familiar, to say it again in terms of Marx.

The process of alienation in an exchange transaction isn't limited to the exchanged objects, but also concerns our relation to the other. This other person whom has been handed over the exchanged object (the buyer) is the stranger. The exchanged or sold object becomes an unfamiliar object in the hands of this stranger. This implies that everything another person owns, is unfamiliar to me. If this 'possession' is not restricted to material goods, but is extended to immaterial goods like services, spiritual possessions, habits and customs and besides to inbred and acquired characteristics, the other becomes more and more unfamiliar. But the last point is far beyond the scope of this book and therefore we will drop the matter.'

Thank goodness, I thought, for the author sometimes creates the impression of being quite a weirdo.

'But what we can't drop here is the part of money in this continuous process of metamorphosis, in this continuous social metabolism which is the essence of the economic process. The part money has in this comes down to an intensification of this process of transformation as well as making it more spiritualized, because with everything we do money will always be in our minds, as is argued in this book. And in our minds is a switch box where the material is converted into the immaterial and the other way round with the use of money as a lubricant, as oil taking care that the "*cycle of the material and the immaterial*" doesn't get jammed. In chapter 5 we will discuss it at length. But what was I talking about?'

Really, come on, who is the author here, I thought.

'Comparing and arranging, that's what we were talking about. And about the problem of the right unit of measure. To be able to do all this, to sort things out well, you have to be able to *distance* yourself from your surroundings, in other words you have to be able to *objectify*.'

Hey, I thought, it sounds familiar, this distance, the man mentioned it before, didn't he? Let me leaf backward - oh yes, just before, when he spoke about narrowing a concrete or an abstract distance - did he mean the same by it? But he hadn't finished his explanation of collecting knowledge yet:

'Not until having sorted out everything you must know of a certain object, can you start the valuing process. Writing it down like this, it may seem to be about two clearly in time separated phases: first collecting knowledge and then valuing. But it isn't like that, as there is a continuous interaction between both of them. It's true that man as a subject has to start an investigation to get a clear view of the object, but while collecting the facts he isn't able to absolutely rule himself out as a judging being. On the way to his final judgment he is continuously judging the collected parts of information and adjusting his investigation on the basis of it. Hardly ever will he go straight for his goal. Most people are simply not able to do so which is a good thing, as otherwise mankind would fossilize into fundamentalism. The healthy human being has got the ability to permanently adjust his judgments and goals during the interaction between investigation and assimilation.'

Well, I must be pretty healthy then, I thought as I am permanently adjusting my goals too, I hardly ever know exactly what I want and I often want something else all the time. Or wasn't this what the author meant? But of course I didn't get an answer.

' 'Keeping a distance' from things and events in his environment in fact precedes 'narrowing the distance' man has to do to reach his goal in order to create value', he explained. 'Take the example again of your journey to London. Before you can actually start your journey, you must get a clear view of London as a destination. You must know what you want and what you expect of a journey like that. With the help of various sources of information like a travel guide, internet or brochures of your travel agency you start arranging things. This way you get to know the city and on the basis of this first introduction a value judgment is gradually being formed. So you first collect knowledge of the facts and by way of their arrangement in your mind you start valuing them in a certain way. When this process has been winded up, so after having closed the phase of orientation, you will decide whether or not to carry out the journey you planned. If you decide to carry it out, the immaterial distance you first investigated by looking at the journey with a kind of telescope or searchlight shifts into the material narrowing of the distance as soon as you get on the train or in the plane.

Compare it to a hunter who spots a prey from a distance. He probably wouldn't even have seen this animal at close quarters as it would have fled then. The prey at a far distance becomes his target now. By concentrating on this animal as a target he objectifies it and he disposes it of its animal value. The prey becomes a desired object that has changed from a natural into another value for the hunter when he aims his rifle and narrows the distance between himself and the animal by a well aimed shot. This other value can take various forms. If he meant to eat the hunting trophy, it's about the metamorphosis of a natural into an economic value. And finally, when consuming his piece of game, this value will be eaten and get lost by doing so.'

An odd comparison, I thought, and a peculiar conclusion as well. Does he mean that all human beings are hunters? And is he saying that together with reaching our goal its value vanishes into thin air?

Consumptive value annihilation
'This inevitable loss of value after the last consumptive step first applies to *consumable goods* and within this category obviously quite clearly to food like the shot game. It will take a while before the consumptive value of food has completely disappeared, because the consumed nourishment has to be digested as 'fuel' by the body. But also *consumer goods* suffer from obsolescence of value from the moment they have been obtained, on the one hand because they don't last forever technically or economically and on the other hand because we may get tired of them. But this obsolescence of value

doesn't always go by in a straight line at all and the value of an object can even increase during the use of it! Take the book you are reading now as an example once more. This book is a consumer good, but while using (reading) it the subjective value may increase. More than that, the intention of a cultural article like a book often is that you 'profit from it', as they call it, so its value awakening and blossoming during the use of it. Or had we better not speak of 'use' when reading a book, but of the trouble it takes, the work you have to do for it. Then this reading activity is pulled towards sacrifice again: the sacrifice you make to read the book, the time it costs, time during which you could have done something else, once more a matter of alternative costs. The 'toil and trouble' of reading generates value. But however we look at the creation of value that arises from reading a book, in principle this value is cultural by nature and not exactly measurable economically. But as we already stressed in the first chapter, this profit of cultural value may be quite helpful for getting a better position in society.

Technical obsolescence presents itself automatically in time and is perfectly clear: when the television set is broken and can't be repaired, you have to get a new one. *Economic obsolescence* is more difficult to observe. This obsolescence can also be called a kind of *value-reduction*. This inflation is mainly taking place in our minds and is influenced and manipulated by the competition of newer and better products. It isn't necessary that objects are broken before we don't see them as fully valuable any longer. An old television set still in good working order may be outdated for instance by its shape and lack of applications. Advertising is the outstanding instrument to talk us into the idea that we are old-fashioned if we don't replace product A by product B at once or if we don't at least supplement it with C, D, E and F from the assortment. In this way the business world takes care that there is always something left to be desired, but not only this business world is responsible for it. For after all, human desire and needs are unlimited, as also the philosopher *Arthur Schopenhauer* concluded. He said that the will, of which the "*desires are unlimited, the demands bottomless*", is impetuously urging us on in our hunt for permanent satisfaction, which will always be unattainable: "*No satisfaction in the world will do to *satisfy its hunger, to put a final goal to its need."*[10] As soon as a desire has been satisfied, there will be another to take over in a process of continuous desire with disastrous consequences in double respect. Firstly the restless activity of the will guarantees conflicts with other people whose desires are bound to clash with ours. And secondly they guarantee a ceaseless individual discontent, as the pleasure of a satisfied desire pales before the suffering from unsatisfied desires.'

Well, I doubt that, this ceaseless discontent I am said to suffer from according to the philosopher, for I am not all that discontent, I guess. I had to admit that my desires hadn't ended yet as there is always something left to be desired which I didn't have time or money for, but did this imply that I suffered from those unsatisfied desires? I don't think so. But then the author, referring to Schopenhauer, tried to fool me into believing that if I did suffer from it, from this unsatisfied desire, I had to consider it positively:

'Like Schopenhauer keeps stressing, suffering is 'positive' and pleasure is 'negative', that means that the one is experienced as an intense presence, but the other mainly as lacking, absent or removed unease, desire or pain.'

Suffering 'positive' and pleasure 'negative'? I wondered. The problem with it will be the interpretation of the words 'positive' and 'negative'. I usually interpret these terms as something favourable opposed to something unfavourable, but it wasn't meant like that by the philosopher in this connection. He meant it more as a 'presence' opposed to an 'absence', if I understood it rightly. And yes, if you don't suffer from anything, having no pain, you won't feel it, so then the not being present is negative. Compare it to the result of a medical test. 'Positive' means that something has been found which isn't good and 'negative' that there isn't found anything to worry about. This is also a reversal of the concepts 'favourable' and 'unfavourable'. To stress this difference even more, the author quoted Schopenhauer again: [10]

' *"We feel the desire as we feel hunger and thirst; but as soon as it has been satisfied it is like the mouthful of food which has been taken, and which ceases to exist for our feelings the moment it is swallowed. We painfully feel the loss of pleasures and enjoyments as soon as they fail to appear, but when pains cease even after being present for a long time, their absence is not directly felt, but at most they are thought of as intentionally by means of reflection. For only pain and lack can be felt positively, and therefore they proclaim themselves; well-being on the contrary, is merely negative".'*

Again this consumptive loss of value after consuming food, but now put into words by Schopenhauer, and also the 'positive' feeling of loss as soon as we have taken the meal. But all these reversals started to make my head swim. Schopenhauer's quotation affirmed what the author alleged: at the same time as taking the mouthful of food its value gets lost and do we painfully feel this loss of value. This conclusion quite strongly resembled the old saying *'possession of the matter is the end of entertainment'*, I thought - no, it did not only resemble it, it was exactly the same! So consumption is actually nothing else but value annihilation. The pursuit of satisfaction of need creates value by the work you had to do for it, the trouble it took, but as soon as you have achieved your goal, you immediately destroy the value you aimed for. It reminds me of this old piece of wisdom *'the way is more important than the destination'* and of *Peggy Lee* as well singing *'Is That All There Is?'* I had never looked at it like this, that I had been busy destroying value by my consumption. And when I thought it over, I wondered whether this daily consumptive annihilation of value might explain the feeling of senselessness and worthlessness, this nagging feeling that troubles many people now and again. But we have to think of the concept of 'consumption' in the broadest sense of the word, so not only as the consumption of goods and services, but including everything you ever aimed for in life and which you managed to get - not only the car and the house you wanted and you really acquired, but also the family you wanted to start and which you actually got, the job you wanted and really obtained by working hard. All of them imagined as well as acquired goals of more or less consumptive nature. And by obtaining all those goals, the subjectively felt reduction of value hits home relentlessly. So you may have thought that you are discontent because you didn't achieve what you ever aimed for? Because you didn't get any further on the career ladder? Because you couldn't afford that expensive car and because you chose the wrong partner? Wrongly thought! This discontent, this unhappy feeling of being worthless is on the contrary the result of having achieved all the aims you pursued: you have achieved what you wanted and you share your life with the partner you chose yourself, but together with it the imagined value devalued and has been partly annihilated. *'Possession of the matter is the end of entertainment …'* Rather a sad thought, I thought. And actually I believed that I didn't completely agree. It may be true for many things, but not for all of them, I guess. Art for instance. A beautiful painting will be a beautiful painting, won't it? No matter how long it's yours? And you may even start liking and appreciating it more in the course of your life, just like certain music - and just like your partner.

'So if you ask: What happens to the economic value of the desired object if the distance between subject and object is narrowed? Or in other words: if what you desired has been achieved and with it the need has been satisfied, the economic value will have been consumed and will disappear. This is sometimes explained by saying that subject and object have merged - you don't notice any difference any longer between 'I' and the 'object'. A literal example is eating, the *'mouthful of food which has been taken, and which ceases to exist for our feelings the moment it is swallowed'*, as we quoted Schopenhauer a minute ago. After having consumed the meal, the things on your plate have disappeared and with it the distance between 'I' and the 'meal-thing'. The meal has been joined together with your body, its value has been literally consumed and has therefore become economically nil. This consumptive value annihilation goes by definition for all *consumable goods*, but as said before also for *durable goods*, though spread over a longer period.

Another example, but now explained with the help of the concept *'narrowing the distance'*: when you finally have bought the car you have been saving for a long time (= have made a sacrifice by giving up present consumption), you have narrowed the distance between the desired object and yourself as the desiring subject by doing so and the objective 'car-thing' is going to be part of your subjective 'I'. The car has nearly become a continuation of yourself - just like clothes being a part of your personality. Different from the consumed mouthful of food the value of the car hasn't immediately vanished after your consumptive purchase, but it did change its character though. Consumable goods will have come to nought when having been consumed, but durable goods will last a while after consumption. If you wear out your car into scrap heap, you will have totally annihilated the economic value of the vehicle as time goes by. So this economic value of the durable good car will gradually decrease - which is expressed in the concept of business economics' 'depreciation' - but because the car and you have grown more and more together as time went by, the emotional value may have become stronger. And when the thing manages to attain the status of a well kept 'old-timer', beside the emotional value the economic value may increase as well.'

Yes, the thing about emotional value sounded familiar, as once on television I saw someone crying when he had to say good-bye to his *Bugatti*. The man had simply fallen in love with his car. The value of the car in his mind couldn't possibly be measured in money and in front of the camera it was transformed into hot tears. I guess it's a nice example of how painful loss can be, even when it is just material. If we own something we sometimes forget or don't realize how valuable it is. This understanding of the value may suddenly return and show up when we lose it: not until we have lost it do we sometimes really discover its value! The loss of personal properties may feel as an amputation, almost comparable to the loss of artificial aids like crutches or a wheelchair you can't do without.

But what was I doing? I was reading a book, wasn't I? About money that was supposed to be in our minds? But I was carried along by the sound of *Peggy Lee's* song in my mind and my thoughts were floating around the value annihilated and consumed by us. So this value annihilation in connection with our consumption also means that this consumptive satisfaction of needs can never lead to permanent saturation, I concluded. This doesn't only go for food, but for everything. It means that nothing can give you a long-lasting feeling of satisfaction. Temporarily perhaps, but not long-lasting. It doesn't make us much happier either, I considered. And this view was confirmed by the author, who at this very moment, in order to stress this point after Schopenhauer he dragged in the philosopher *Thomas Hobbes*:

' *"The happiness of this life is not the peace of a satisfied mind"*, Hobbes said[11], *"for there is no final end or highest good as meant in the books of ancient ethics."* According to him, happiness was rather a *"continual progress of desire, from one object to another, in which achieving the first was only the way to the second. (…) Constantly succeeding in getting hold of what you want from one moment to another (…), that is what people call Felicity: I mean happiness in this life, for life itself is but motion and can never do without desire, nor fear, no more than without sense"*. According to Hobbes this motion will only be ended by death.'

Well, splendid, I thought, never calming down in this life according to this philosopher. Not a pleasant prospect. So we have to keep toiling till the bitter end?

'Until that time we will be ruled by *"a perpetual, restless desire for power after power, that ceases only in death"*, he added a little extra. 'It isn't a very reassuring thought', the author agreed, 'a thought to be found with many others however, among whom *John Locke*: *" We are seldom at ease and free enough from the solicitation of our natural or adopted desires, but a constant succession of uneasiness take the will in their turns, and before one thing has ended another feeling of uneasiness is ready to put us on work."* [12]

Unease, indeed, only from reading a quotation like that.

'So the individual is mixed up in a restless perpetual, endless pursuit. In Goethe's classic version of the Faust story (1808 and 1832) according to *Robert & Edward Skidelsky*[13] , *Faust* had become *"a symbol of the modern man in endless pursuit, fallible, but in the final analysis worthy of our love. Goethe's Faust may be considered as the literary metaphor of the Felix culpa of the political economy. God sends the devil (Mephistopheles) to humankind (Faust) to awaken her from her slumber. With the help of Mephistopheles Faust does dodgy deals, but in the end his soul goes to heaven because of his 'fierce inner struggle'."*

Yes, all right, wait a minute, I thought, this endless pursuit, this fierce struggle, is just the same as constantly taking trouble for something, an endless 'toil and trouble' and wasn't this creating value in itself? People like Smith and Simmel claimed this, didn't they? Value resulted from our efforts to achieve something, didn't it? We should be happy therefore for always having a new feeling of uneasiness to make us act, which gives us something to do, otherwise we should soon feel worthless.

'Because Faust has been struggling his whole life and never succeeded in gratifying all his desires, he was allowed to go to heaven. His desire kept him going you might say. *"He says to Mephistopheles that if one day there will be nothing left to be desired, he will accept eternal damnation."* [13] With this he showed that he understood quite well that at the very moment that all his desires would have been fulfilled, the acquired value would have been annihilated at once too, and as far as he was concerned life might be over then. But according to Locke he needn't be worried about that, for in view of *"the large amount of needs and desires that harass us in this imperfect State, we are not likely to be freed from uneasiness in this World"* [12] The thereafter has to be a haven of peace or the pursuit of happiness would have no end.'

It might make you religious, if you weren't already, I thought. But the author's last conclusion was rather inconsistent in my opinion. For if the thereafter should really end our industrious pursuit of happiness, it would mean that according to the worldly theory of value-creating labour, value can't be created or doesn't even exist over there, as there would be nothing left to be done. After having read this merry-go round of thoughts I couldn't help thinking that the deity wasn't going to let that happen. Even the Heavenly Vault can't do without permanent maintenance, I imagined, so there may be nice jobs waiting for us over there. He surely wasn't going to let us pine away into idleness in this Upper World and make us feel worthless without daily labour. A haven of peace without continuation of the pursuit of happiness? I doubt it.

And again this referring to pursuit or hunting. Like the apparently never ending hunting of the Indians in their 'Eternal Hunting-grounds', just entering my mind, why else would it be called like that? Weren't those grounds a kind of heaven to them? Something like the Greek and Roman 'Elysian Fields' where the blessed were staying? The hunting itself as a value-creating, happiness-rendering process, with firing the mortal shot as the climax - but as soon as the target has been hit, value collapses like a dead animal.

It made me think of the well-known diagram which shows the connection between the purchase of a desired product or the gain-ing of an achievement and the development of the level of happiness that goes with it. This diagram can have two variants: the first is the *expected level of happiness* after that purchase or achievement, the second the *actually achieved level of happiness*. As for the first: The expectation is mostly that your happiness will be at a permanent higher level after such a purchase or achievement; but the reality in the second diagram shows a line of happiness going steeply upwards, but after that quickly sinking back to the original level of happiness.[14]

'But will this pursuit end after our deaths if we are out of luck by ending up in an eternal hereafter?' the author wondered as well at the same time. Out of luck? Bad luck, indeed, if you have to keep toiling eternally there as well, I thought. But he didn't mean it like that, as he gave it the same twist as I did a minute ago, if I understood it well:

'Imagine a life like this in the hereafter. A haven of peace? And blissfully doing nothing every day? You may ask whether man is capable of this in this Upper world, when he isn't even capable of it in this world. He would probably be bored stiff, though impossible in that situation, or he had to die once again.'

The author of this book surely isn't a happy-go-lucky-fellow, I concluded. I started liking him.

Scarcity
'But let's finally look at this part of consumptive value-annihilation in a larger scope and wonder what would happen if *scarcity* would have disappeared. Economics is the science that deals with the ways in which man tries to conquer scarcity. Scarcity means that our needs are larger than the means we have to satisfy all these needs. The economist assumes that this scarcity will always be there, even when we are rolling in money. Scarcity is therefore a relative notion: the relation between our unlimited needs and the limited means we have at our disposal. Because of this scarcity we will always have to take pains to satisfy our needs, in order to achieve something. Taking pains creates value, as we have emphasized before. But what should happen if mankind would have conquered scarcity once and for all one day? If all our needs would have been fulfilled?'

Well, by now I could guess his answer.

'In that case all the acquired economic value will have been annihilated again!' it sounded rather confidently. 'For by satisfying all our consumptive needs, if we no longer need to work for them, the economic value of goods will be annihilated. If all scarcity has disappeared, everything will be for free, because everything will be there in plenty abundance. Costs needn't be made any longer and all effort will be in vain. Working will be useless and from then on we will be bored, so much even that everything we have acquired during the time of scarcity we would prefer to destroy in order to be able to start all over again. Destructiveness, compulsive destruction, but not destruction that leads to progress, so not *"creative destruction"*.'

Creative destruction, familiar term, wasn't it …

'*Werner Sombart* (1863-1941) invented the term, a German economist and sociologist, but it is likely to have become more famous by *Joseph Schumpeter* (1883-1950), …'

That's the one! I thought.

'… an Austrian economist and political scientist. But by creative destruction he didn't mean destruction for destruction's sake, but a continuous process of technical innovation, in which new techniques displace the old ones. He considered this the most important source of economic growth and thus of value-creation. He wasn't talking about destruction arising from boredom as a result of abundant satisfaction of needs, but about technical progress. Destruction caused by boredom is often more malicious, destructiveness in all known varieties: kicking up a roll, smashing windows, arson, graffiti, bending posts, breaking signs, and quite a range of other breakings-up just for fun, leaving visible marks of degeneration and verging to war hungry. And if these destructive boredom-symptoms of affluence get hold of large groups of people at the same time and become structural, it can end in social disruption. At one side of society are the rich 'victims of prosperity', who by having satisfied most of their needs saw much economic value disappear, and at the other side those who never got that far, because they simply didn't have the means for it. This social divide is actually nothing but the difference between rich and poor. And of course we are talking about the extremes here, as there is a large ordinary middle class with lower and median income in which this problem isn't manifest, but if more people move up towards the well-to-do, consequently the increasing economic satisfaction of needs will involve increasing value-annihilation.

But boredom doesn't only have negative sides, for in itself it can be a source of value creation, because boredom may contribute to creativity. Not fancying anything for a considerable period will help emptying your mind in order to follow new avenues. This is therefore another unexpected source of value creation and again a source that rises from your mind.'

Well, I must have become rather inventive by now, as boredom is a good friend of mine, I thought.

'But we were talking about economic value creation', the author continued his argument. 'And we have concluded that *pursuing* a good life in the form of economic wealth is *creating value* by the trouble it takes us, but that *achieving* it is *annihilating value*. And if we begin to suffer from all the value annihilation that makes itself felt, we may get the desire to burn our boats and start all over again. This can regularly be seen in actual practice. People that were successful and earned a lot, who called it a day and started doing something different. At an individual level nice to read about and rather innocent, but if it happens to large groups of people at the same time and there aren't sufficient alternative ways to fulfill their lives, it may lead to decadent boredom and the need for destruction mentioned above. It may be from relatively innocently setting fire to a banknote to light your cigar for instance to robbing a bank just for fun or joining hunting parties for shooting the last tigers.

Robbing and hunting. The hunt no longer a means to provide our food or to keep the standard, but just for it's own sake, which goes for the drives of the English nobility and for many contemporary hunters. The same with angling. Go and cast a line is for your own amusement, and of course it's nice to hook something now and again, but most anglers don't intend to take the caught fish home and eat it. Here the original means has been a purpose in itself for a long time. The point in an angling match is who catches most fish and not who angles most fish ashore for consumption. The value-creation coming from hunting and fishing in our regions originates from the hunt itself, from the 'toil and trouble' it takes to get a catch, to say it once more like Adam Smith did, but not from the shot or fished catch itself. Means has become purpose here and this is an old philosophical problem: the teleological reversal of object and means, which was also evident in the legend of king Midas. In the next chapter we will have a closer look at this teleological reversal.

Notes:

1. Jos Defoort, *Het grote geld - keerpunten in de monetaire geschiedenis,* Leuven 2000. With references to B*ernhard Laum, Heiliges geld. Eine historische Untersuchung über den Sakralen Ursprung des Geldes*, Tübingen, 1924
2. Quoted from: David Graeber, *Schuld - de eerste 5000 jaar*, p. 70, Amsterdam, Antwerp 2012 (*Debt: The First 5,000 years*, New York 2011)
3. Karl Marx, *Het kapitaal,* Amsterdam 2010. (originally Hamburg 1867) Quoted from: Eduardo Porter, *Alles heeft een prijs*, Houten - Antwerp 2011
4. Georg Wilhelm Friedrich Hegel, *Das System der Bedürfnisse*, Werke, Band 7, Frankurt am Main 1979, S 346 (originally 1819)
5. Quoted from: Dr. W.N.A. Klever, *Archeologie van de Economie - de economische theorie in de Griekse oudheid*, p. 95, Nijmegen 1986
6. Georg Simmel, *Philosophie des* Geldes, Frankfurt am Main 1989 *The philosophy of money*, London and New York, 2004, 2011 (originally Leipzig 1900)
7. Christian Papilloud, *Tausch. Autopsie eines soziologischen Topos,* in: *Georg Simmel's Philosophie des Geldes - Aufsätze und Materialen*, Frankfurt am Main, 2003
8. Bernard Mandeville, *De fabel van de bijen*, Rotterdam 2008 (originally *The Fable of the Bees or Private Vices, Public Benefits*, Oxford 1723)
9. René Gude, *Stand-up filosoof - De antwoorden van René Gude*, Leusden 2013

10. Quoted from: Darrin M. McMahon, *Geluk, een geschiedenis*, Amsterdam 2005 (*Happiness: A History*, New York 2005); quote from: Arthur Schopenhauer, *De wereld als wil en voorstelling*, (originally Frankfurt 1844)
11. Thomas Hobbes, *Leviathan*, Amsterdam 2010 (originally 1651)
12. John Locke, *Essay concerning human understanding*, London 1689
13. Robert & Edward Skidelsky, *Hoeveel is genoeg? - Geld en het verlangen naar een goed leven*, Antwerpen 2012 (*How much is enough? - Money and the good life*, London 2012)
14. Among others in Alain de Botton's *Statusangst*, Amsterdam 2007 (*Status Anxiety*, London 2005)

4   THE MEANS - END CHAIN
On the indirect nature and the teleological series of money

'We humans are always up to something. We intend to buy a new bicycle, to start a study, to make a large journey around the world, to become rich, to redecorate our house, to change jobs, to move, to have a happy life. All those projects are aimed at purposes and those purposes are in the future, because anything is possible in the future, '*the future is the place of possibility*', Simmel said.'

Oh dear, him again, I thought. The chapter only just started and he pops up again, this ancient German philosopher on money.

'But the road to the future is often longer than you may think and never straight. It's a bumpy road with many detours and diversions that you only notice when they are right in front of you. You think to go straight to your purpose, when you have to get out of the way for an obstacle. You see the desired place of arrival looming up, when the spot suddenly disappears from view by an unexpected bend. The journey to the future is a journey with many bends and obstacles. It's an indirect way to an aim, but man can generally manage these indirect ways quite well. The fact is, he is able to look at his ultimate goal from a great distance and to 'calculate' which means and in-between purposes are needed. Thus the means - end chain is created and in this connection Simmel characterizes man as the *indirect being*.

The desired object at the end of the road to the future can hardly ever be reached directly and is even often a disappointment when finally arrived at. Just consider what was said about it in the previous chapter: achieving one's object often means that the value that has been acquired with great difficulty will be annihilated by it.

A problem with all those projects and aims is moreover that a human being can't do everything at the same time. He wants so much but he hasn't got much time. He always has to choose and to choose means to lose, as we have seen before when we were talking about alternative costs. If you do one thing you can't do something else at the same time. Each profit means a missed alternative profit, and each seized opportunity will inevitably be a missed other opportunity. But for this permanent problem of choice money is a way out in many cases. Especially in those cases when an economic choice is involved and therefore the alternative possibilities can be expressed in money, as money gives time for reflection. Money is after all an undifferentiated means of exchange, which means that it can be used for many objects and as long as these objects haven't been realized, money can serve all sorts of purposes. Hence in this connection money can be considered a multifunctional tool. *'Money is the purest form of tool'*, Simmel judges, and in its modern form an instrument of the most sophisticated kind: it's silent, distant, neutral, concealable, invisible, impersonal, 'cool' and multiform, which means that it may be used for multiform objects.

Abstract quality

Money derives all these qualities from its abstract character. Money is an abstraction that translates qualitatively different objects and subjects into purely quantitative variables, as we said before. In contrast with the possession of real goods like a piece of land or a car, or the possession of a certain competence, money doesn't have a character of its own. This impersonal lack of character can be seen as a positive quality of money. In the case of specific properties the tie between *'Sein'* and *'Haben'* is much closer, that is, between someone's personality and the property in question. It's possible to have a certain emotional relation with a certain product and be nearly in love with for instance a car or a work of art, but generally speaking it isn't possible with money - in general it's hard to be in love with an impersonal tool. In this sense money can release you from the sometimes galling bonds between yourself and the specific things you own. You feel more detached with money, less involved than with the personal things you have gathered around you during your life. And a payment with money contrary to a payment with personal things leaves no personal traces. (Which may also apply for the sometimes galling bonds between persons - in connection with this Simmel gives the example of prostitution, an agreement that leaves no traces after payment ...) The monetary settlement of a transaction frees you from further personal obligations which creates a form of freedom. The other side of the coin is that money by itself can never be a means for permanent human relations.

Thus an important value created by the characterless, impersonal money, is the value of free choice. This choice is not nearly as free when money isn't used, for example with an exchange in kind. If Mrs. Taylor wants to exchange 10 apples for instance for 5 pears of Mr. Harris and the latter doesn't accept any other means of exchange for his pears, then those 10 apples are the simple means to the univocal end of 5 pears. As Mrs. Taylor happens to have the apples as means of exchange and she intends to use them to get some pears, the exchange can be established, but if she doesn't have apples in the house and Mr. Harris doesn't accept another product of exchange for his pears, the exchange is off. The aim to be pursued by this exchange is moreover a short-term aim: Mrs. Taylor and Mr. Harris are talking about an exchange of this moment of 10 apples for 5 pears and not about an apple - pears transaction that will only take place in a year, for in a year the apple and pear crop may turn out differently which changes the exchange ratio. If the apple crop is disappointing by apple disease for instance, whereas the pears are on the trees abundant and healthy, the apples will get more expensive and the pears less expensive. The exchange ratio will possibly be the other way round then, 5 apples for 10 pears or if the apple crop is even worse only 3 apples for 10 pears. But not only the supply may turn out differently, for the taste of both trading partners may have changed after a year. Mr. Harris for instance may have got an apple allergy so that he can no longer eat any apples at all or Mrs. Taylor may have started turning up her nose when thinking of the taste of pears.'

The same for me with fish, I thought, merely the smell in the fish market makes me grasp for breath. So if someone offers me a beautiful fish in exchange for let's say a croquette, this exchange transaction surely won't be established.

'And we haven't even mentioned the sort or the quality of the fruit to be exchanged, for it's rather unlikely that both trading partners aren't interested in it, that they are randomly going to exchange apples for pears without having seen them. Besides there are only two parties involved with two products in this game of exchange. The exchange problems that occur with an exchange in kind are calculable, but will become much more complicated when large groups of people are involved, for in that case the one must have precisely what the other wants. In Adam Smith's book *The Wealth of Nations* from 1775 and in almost any subsequent handbook in economics there is always the same kind of invented examples. Invented indeed, because these exchange practices have never actually existed according to anthropologist David Graeber. He calls this the 'myth of barter'[1] and this myth will be discussed in great detail in the book hereafter in connection with money in our minds.

Myth or not, with money as generally accepted means of exchange the sort or quality of the product to be sold is important but not problematic, because the qualities of the product are simply translated into money. And as long as the transaction hasn't been realized, the undifferentiated money can still serve all sorts of purposes.'

But as soon as you have spent it, your freedom of choice has ended for this amount of money, I grumblingly added. There you are, reading this book and meanwhile thinking of that nice outdoor café where you could easily have taken coffee and cakes and whipped cream for two persons for the same amount of money.

'But let's go back first to our plans and choosing aims. Because man has to determine his aim(s) before he calls forth his means. And an aim always lies in the future, …'

The place of the possibility, yes I know, I added somewhat grumpily, but where did this grumpiness come from all at once? Maybe from the thought that instead of reading this book I might have done something that would have been much more fun? The picture of the outdoor café at the waterside had suddenly made me realize how high the alternative costs of reading this book were. 'Choosing is losing', I grumbled loudly to myself.

' … but in order to reach our ends, we have to be capable to do so, that is, the ends must not be unattainable. That's the question of 'capability'. That doesn't mean however that the end will really be achieved, for the future will always be accompanied by uncertainty: everything that can happen, doesn't necessarily happen.'

No, I know all about it, I thought and the thought almost made me feel sorry for myself.

' In order to make something happen that you want to happen, action is needed', the author continued imperturbably. 'And for this action man in principle has got two sources: the **will** and the **intellect**.'

Yes, that's the point, I thought, the will and the intellect, two sources I had the feeling not to be very gifted with. But don't keep bleating on about it, let's just continue reading:

' By the will the end is defined, by the intellect the means are selected. In order to attain an end, sub-purposes are often needed. These in between-purposes are the means for the more distant sub-purposes and the final-purpose. Hence a *means - end chain* comes into being. It follows that making a distinction between 'money as a means' and 'money as an end' isn't that simple. Of a person who's careful with his money and saves up for a rainy day can hardly be said that he considers his money as an end. Saving is simply necessary, for instance for a big purchase in the future or for a good pension. And money makes it possible.'

Money as a saving-tool I added.

'Thus money makes it possible to postpone a choice, the choice to put off a part of our consumption to the future by saving for example. That is one of the values money has created: it creates the possibility to save goods that can not or hardly be stored because they are perishable or unwieldy, save them by way of their substitute, money. Aristotle considered this *hoarding up-function* of money a danger, as we have seen in chapter 1 where we talked about the legend of king Midas. Because by this we can ignore nature's imperative to be moderate and start being engaged in the skill of exceeding moderation: capital accumulation at the expense of the natural balance in nature and society. Aristotle claimed that this morbid growth was the consequence of weakness of perception: man strives for satisfaction of economic needs, a certain wealth, but with gold, even when you have loads of it, you may starve to death, as king Midas' legend showed. In this connection Aristotle spoke of an abnormal reversal: what should be a means to reach an end - realizing a good life - becomes the ultimate end. But as said before such an 'abnormal reversal' of means and end can't be easily diagnosed in practice, for where is the limit? And who prescribes it or who can judge it? The example of the savings makes clear: how much do you have to save to get a sense of financial security in future. How much do you need? When do you feel financially independent or 'safe'? What is a 'good' pension?'

Well, how much do you need? No one can answer these questions, I thought, for anything can always be better, whenever do you have enough? How much is enough?

'End and means, that's what we are talking about. And about the teleological 'abnormal' reversal of end and means Aristotle pointed out to. Money as means or money as end, that's the question. But the answer to that question isn't as simple as it appears to be at first sight. If our goals lie in future, intermediate steps will always be necessary to attain these goals, and the farther away they are the more of them we need. Thus we must know which are the intermediate steps, which sub-purposes must be achieved in order to reach the final goal. But what can be the actual character of such a sub-purpose? Is it a real goal?', the author seemed to put the question directly to me.

Well, I thought, why not, for is there a final goal in life anyway? It made me automatically think of the story of Croesus. That story had been written down by Herodotus in his *Histories*.[2] Croesus was the immensely rich king of Lydia (560 - 546 before Christ), who thought that he was the happiest man on earth, as he lacked nothing. But the wise Solon, Athens' legislator, thought it an illusion and he tried to open Croesus' eyes by pointing out that nobody should be called happy before his death: '*Let no man be called happy before his death. Till then, he is not happy, only lucky.*' Croesus thought it foolish and sent Solon away. It was the beginning of a series of events that finally caused the fall of Croesus and his kingdom and pushed the Greek and Persians into a long war. Cyrus, the king of the Persians, sent Croesus to the stake where he loudly whined 'Oh Solon! Oh Solon!' and from which he was saved only just in time by a downpour and Cyrus' curiosity when he heard Solon's name.

But what took me back to that story? Because only death might be the real final goal? And that the whole road to it is paved with sub-purposes? That each step of mankind can actually be reduced to a mini-sub-purpose in life? What does life amount to, people sometimes ask and the answer often is that it comes down to putting one footstep in front of the other, 'just simply going on'. Each step is therefore a mini-sub-purpose, and a couple of steps are a larger sub-purpose, until you end where Croesus also ended. So returning to the author's last question: yes certainly, each sub-purpose is a real purpose too, except when you consider death as the highest final goal of life and all steps on the way to it as almost trivial. Because in that case all goals are ultimately only sub-purposes. But, forget it, that's going too far, I thought, that overshoots the mark, the author won't have meant it like this.

'On the one hand a sub-purpose is a goal, but at the same time also a means to attain another sub-purpose or the final goal', he continued. 'If for instance the final goal is to graduate, the sub-purposes are passing the examinations. Each examination is a separate goal as well as a sub-purpose, a means on the way to the final goal of graduating.'

Was I still engaged in sub-purposes then? I wondered loudly at that moment. And do I have a final goal at all? I must have, mustn't I? For even when I suggested a moment ago that only death may be the real final goal of human life, it can't be the meaning of life, can it? Stop ruminating about it, just keep on reading.

'And like this a means - end chain is being created, in which each goal may be a sub-purpose and each sub-purpose a means to keep travelling to the next sub-purpose, on the way to the final goal, the final destination where the journey ends and where the ultimate goal will have been attained. But after arriving at that final destination there appears to be another final destination further down, full of promises for a better life, just further down, behind the horizon maybe. Thus the journey will get longer and longer and the intermediate stations are being threaded on the means - end chain, a continually lengthening chain.'

Isn't it sad, I thought, a slow train like that with more an more intermediate stations, but obviously the author disagreed:

'But actually this is a good sign', he said, 'as it proves that mankind is getting smarter. In general it can be said that there is a connection between the length of the means - end chain and the development of society: the higher the development of society, the greater the distance from means to (final) end. And to succeed in getting a good view of this greater distance and bridging it, more and more intellect is needed. Simmel characterizes man as an *indirect being* because of this ability. As mentioned before, he has to set a distant goal (with his free will) and think of the instruments and tools (with his intellect) in order to be able to reach that goal.'

Well, if Simmel says so ...

Indirect production
'In economics the term *indirect production* is being used in this connection, which means that a final product almost always comes into being by the roundabout way of investments in capital goods combined with an increasing specialization, by which the final product can be produced much quicker and in larger amounts. For instance: instead of hand-woven cloths first an automatic loom is constructed that can produce at least a 100 of those cloths against 1 before in the same time. And as we all know this mechanization and automation progress is unrestrainedly causing the roundabout way from raw material to final product getting longer and longer. It isn't necessarily a roundabout way in time; hence not every extra link in the production process leads to longer production times. On the contrary, as it can often go faster with modern techniques. But there will be more and more intermediate steps with specialized service providers and components makers who sometimes hardly know where their specific tiny bars or screws end up. That's the effect of specialization: from raw material to final product more intermediate stations are created in the stages of production, by which human labour becomes more and more indirect, a smaller and smaller impersonal link in the means - end chain. According to Marx it risks that man alienates even more from his labour, because he doesn't know any longer where the result of his labour ends up. In his opinion this alienation began much earlier when people were forced to work in factories, as a result of which they stopped producing for personal

use or people in the immediate vicinity. And producing only for anonymous sale (for the exchange) at a distance, this labour becomes 'abstract' in Marx's opinion. He called this abstract labour alienating, labour only being done to get a salary. So, producing a pair of shoes for the reason that one needs a pair oneself isn't abstract labour, but producing shoes in a factory to earn money is. The cause of this alienation, which he also discerned in exchange, the *'metamorphosis of commodities'*, is placed before the exchange by him, namely at the (capitalist) way of production. Abstract labour alienates the labourer from himself and his surroundings, because he must produce things which he can't control. These things, products leaving the factory, are the property of the employer and not of the employee, and therefore strange to him. While with an exchange transaction the sold commodity originally was still personal property before having been alienated by the sale, wage work for market production is alienating from the very start.

This Marxist idea of alienation with labourers who don't work for themselves, but are in the pay of an employer, fits in with Aristotle's idea of wage work being the least valuated form of labour, hardly different from slave labour. Under the appearances of formally free labour fixed in a wage contract, the employer-employee-relation has got much in common with the master-slave-relation. Thus the abstract, alienating labour Marx talks about is a form of slave labour, in which the employee is not only not the owner of his own production but has also sold himself to the employer. That's a double alienation, you might say: being no owner of one's products and no owner of oneself, in addition to which the utility value of both forms of commodity has been metamorphosed into exchange value, or into market price.'

Well magnificent, excellent, but where does the money come in? I said to the book rather impatiently. Which part does money play in this story? Isn't the book about money in our minds? But as usual I was too hasty:

'And with this exchange value money is involved again, for the simple reason that all market prices are expressed in money nowadays. What does this mean for the exchange of goods, the production and the 'abstract' labour?'

Does he ask me this question? I thought. Well, there will be even more intermediate steps in the production chain, I guessed, the way from primal producer to consumer will be even longer.

'This money enables us to lengthen the roundabout in the production process even more'

See. The correct answer.

'Besides, Simmel saw an analogy between the development of money and the increasing division of labour: both have become more and more functional in the course of time. Not the substance of money is of importance but the function. In modern time labour as well as money are especially seen in terms of relations, functions and interaction, as instrumental and impersonal things for exchange.'

I can be replaced by a dozen others, ran through my head at the last observation. Labour as a salable thing, a marketable instrument. At that moment I thought of myself as a tool that cold be thrown away when it had become out-dated or worn.

'What counts is whát a person produces and not who does', the author intensified my feeling of being a tool. 'And the value of this labour is always expressed in money. In ones work one will always be judged by the quantity of money it has raised and not by the quality of that work itself or the production it has created. And if one day one doesn't bring in enough money: get lost! Money as well as labour are instruments, they are means not goals. And the more functional they are, the more the means-end chain can be stretched.'

Ah well, I'm just a tiny link as well, I sighed. And my functionality was and is rather limited. Maybe because my individuality has always been standing in the way too much? Because I was self-willed and didn't want to be a continuation of a machine? But if I had been a bag of money I would have been multifunctional and game for anything.

'Money as a multifunctional and undifferentiated instrument enables us much better to take some intermediate steps than a simple means of exchange like apples and pears for example. Money enables us to stretch the means-end chain enormously. With money as intermediary we simply jump from one commodity or service to the other, and back again to money and continue to the next product, and so on.

Goods → Money → Goods, that's the exchange in a roundabout way with the help of money in a nutshell. And by the hoarding-up function of money more intermediate stages can be created in the stages of production and the production-process - at least if money itself has not been hoarded to a degree that it paralyses the circulation of money (by putting it under the mattress or in a shoebox for instance). Aristotle had this paralysing form of hoarding-up in mind too when he spoke about the paradoxical combination of 'petrifaction' by 'immoderateness', which has been described so expressively in the legend of king Midas and has been characterized by Marx as an 'immoderate desire for storing up treasures' by which money petrifies into gold and blocks the exchange-process. 'Money is there to be spent', meaning that the hoarded money must keep functioning. How? By putting it in the bank for instance. By doing so the hoarded money gets a different character, namely that of savings. And with these savings investments can be financed. By hoarding up in the pure sense of the word the flow in the money-river gets blocked, like blocked by a beaver dam, but by savings the money-level in this river can rise and the flow can choose monetary roundabout ways, which can lead to extra investments and extra consumptive spending in future.

Monetary roundabout ways mostly run through the financial sector with banks as important intermediate stations. A lot of our payments, savings and investments are channeled through them and transformed according to place, risk and term into various 'bank-products' as they are called in technical terminology. Those are the well-known bank products like payment and savings accounts, deposits and credits. And in all these products a part of our future plans has been stored, undifferentiated but present in a spiritual form if by looking at the sums of money we think of the car that can be bought with it, the holiday or the new garden terrace. The saved money in our accounts evokes an image of the goals we think to attain with it in future. Our money also being used for credit for companies, we mostly don't think about. As long as we get it back with interest when we need it, it doesn't worry us. Not until press reports on imminent bank deficits appear, do we get restless - but as long as our savings are guaranteed by the government or the united banks, we calmly go on dreaming about whatever nice things we can do with those savings in future, while visualizing them.'

Inspired by these last lines I tried to imagine which images my savings evoked. But I'm afraid that it was rather vague and even if a more detailed image would appear, I'm not going to dwell on them in public here.

'Goal-images as it were. Spiritual images promising to become possible materialization in future.'

Did I hear an echo of Plato here? Of the ideas preceding things or something like that? Did the author adhere to the school of philosophical idealism by any chance?

'Money that lies at the basis of these images is in itself an abstraction, but as soon as this abstract value develops itself in our minds into a concrete image of some salable object, the first step to materialization of the goal-image has been made. Money being an undifferentiated means flitting through our minds, has by then turned into the road to a specific goal.

The teleological series of money
When determining a goal through a means - end chain with the help of money as an intermediary tool a *teleological series of money*[3], as Simmel calls it, also arises. This series consists of the following steps *Acquiring* → *Possessing* → *Spending* → *Enjoying*. The arrows suggest that every next phase logically follows the preceding one and that man automatically goes through these steps to the end of Enjoying.'

Well it seems logical, I thought, for you must first earn your money before you can spend it and enjoy this. And the intermediary step of possessing seems to be inevitable to me too, for you must possess it first ... well, of that I wasn't that sure, for you can borrow money too of course.

'At first sight it seems obvious that money is being acquired as a means to enjoy it in the end by way of spending, but not necessarily so all the time. Dependent on the type of person you are, the end can be aimed at any phase of the teleological series. Simmel distinguishes six types in this connection: *the greedy one, the miser, the spender, the ascetic, the cynic,* and *the relativist*. He connects this distinction to the phases of *acquiring money, possessing money, spending money* and *enjoying the purchase*.[4] The greedy one is primarily interested in acquiring money. The miser thinks possessing money the most important. The spender enjoys spending money most, but is hardly interested in the things he spends it on. With the last three types - the ascetic, the cynic and the relativist - the connection between their characters and what they want to do with their money is less straight-lined. The ascetic basically doesn't care about money, for he doesn't care about the things you can buy with money. He denies the value of things and oddly enough this makes him equivalent to the spender, who doesn't really enjoy his spending. That leaves the cynic who thinks that money can buy anything. A type of person who knows the price of everything, but the value of nothing, as he is often characterized. And finally the relativist, whom is said to be blasé, dulled by overconsumption and therefore insensible to what other people can enjoy.

The different typifications of this teleological series seem to implicate a moral judgment on a whether or not 'sound' handling of money, but it's not a simple matter at all. They are just six possible ends for which you need money and it isn't necessarily at all to go through the whole series in order to be considered 'sound'. Each phase in the series may be an end in itself and a psychological judgment on the measure of being (un)sound with each typification is too simple. Just compare the possession of money (phase 2) with any other form of possession, for instance land. Is there a substantial difference? Could you say that someone who is very much attached to his landed property and doesn't want to part with it, is therefore a miser? Or that a philatelist collects stamps out of greed? Because the terms 'saving' and 'collecting' are almost indistinguishable from each other in this connection.

The psychiatrist *Robin Skynner* once said in a dialogue with *John Cleese* that sound people have got a clearer idea of what really satisfies them than unsound people and thus have a better idea of how much money is required for it.[5] Cleese concluded from this that this satisfaction can also lie in the **symbolic value** money gives them.

Hence on first sight greedy or miserly types may for instance attach value to the possession of money as *"a **symbol of their power or status**, so of their position within the hierarchy; for other people, especially for a **certain kind of puritans**, the possession of money gains them **moral plus points**; and for other people who suffered poverty in their youth, it is a **symbolic safeguard against a return to that penniless existence**."* To the last words Skynner added that it wasn't always about financial poverty: *"For many people who lacked love and emotional security, money becomes a substitute, a source of security and satisfaction they totally control. That is the reason why many people never think to have enough; their real need will never be satisfied."* He added that as to this kind of people he never had met someone who was happy, whereupon Cleese wondered if he could conclude *"that the more someone compulsively strives for the possession of money, and the more money is a symbol for something else, of which the person in question is not aware, the lower is his level of mental soundness?"* Which the psychiatrist agreed with.'

Well, I must be rather sound, I thought, as I don't compulsively strive for the possession of money, do I? But on the other hand I did buy a book on money, so is that quite as sound as it seems?

' Anyway the different types in this schedule of the teleological series of money can be recognized less univocally than you might think at first sight. Like this a connection is often made between greed and (extravagant) generosity in order to avoid the appearance of greed. In the book by *Simon Schama* on Dutch culture of the Golden Age, *The Embarrassment of Riches. An Interpretation of Dutch Culture in the Golden Age* is the following passage on this[6]:

"According to the official doctrine of Calvinism as well as that of humanism profit was dirty and pursuit of profit a defiling idolatry. Desire and greed at the worst kind could deprive someone of his conscience and senses and change free minds into slimy slaves. This strong understanding that earning money was condemnable remained, even while the Dutch were gathering a personal and collective fortune. This discrepancy between principle and practice had the peculiar consequence that **in order to avoid the appearance of greed money was spent instead of saved**. It's true, the expenses had to be approved collectively and be considered morally acceptable by clergymen as well as by laymen, but they could vary from unmistakably virtuous gifts for philanthropic causes to less altruistic gestures, like long-term low interest loans for public institutions or to create a comfortable domestic environment in which a patriotic Christian family could be started. In this way Louis de Geer, who no doubt was a devout Calvinist as well as an energetic entrepreneur, could combine a dignified lifestyle with devout expenses. He bought the house with the heads at the Keizersgracht (...) But it was generally known that by way of compensation he levied tithes on himself for the poor and that he offered heartfelt help to the Calvinist refugees from Middle-Europe during The Thirty Years' War."

Another aspect of the connection between greed and generosity is the **power** that can be exercised by it. All those who have sufficient means can also decide how to divide them and place the receiving parties into a guilt-position of gratitude and subordination. To put it differently: the possibility to give money = the power to dominate.

In current time we also know various rich philanthropists, with well-known names like *George Soros, Bill Gates* and *Warren Buffet,* who spend enormous sums on good causes. In the light of the above one may wonder if they are doing this out of a kind of sense of guilt, or to avoid the appearance of greed? These superrich like to show that their only concern is not self-interest and luxury and create the impression to be sincerely interested in the fate of the world. There is no reason to doubt this sincerity, but with their part of good Samaritan we must always keep in mind that it's based on an extremely distorted distribution of income and wealth. It expresses a certain sense of guilt - posh philanthropy as a kind of indulgence. They don't want to be branded as greedy or as misers, who in the teleological series of money got stuck in the phase of collecting or possessing. Nor do they wish to get the image of a spender, but spend their money on good causes and make sacrifices by doing so.

These sacrifices bring us back with a wide bend to chapter 3, where we talked about sacrifice as a source of value. These sacrifices made by rich philanthropists may not be immediately recognized as such by everyone, but nevertheless their donations involve due effort, hence sacrifices. They have to take great pains to make all these gifts arrive at the right place, judged by the large staff they hired to sensibly head down their heaps of money.'

Well, sacrifices like that I'm willing to make too, I thought, for they are luxury problems, aren't they? This kind of problems aren't mine at all, what a lucky thing!

'Our detour along the pains the philanthropists have to take to give away their money in a sensible way, raises the question whether for each (sub)end in the teleological series sacrifices have to be made.'

Making sacrifices to enjoy for instance? I wondered. But along with this thought the concept of alternative cost entered my mind, mentioned by the author a minute ago: that you can never do two things at the same time, that you always have to choose - so either you enjoy a sunny sidewalk café by the waterside or you pay attention to a book on money in your mind for example. But is it impossible to do two things at the same time? I wasn't convinced. Because reading a book by the waterside will be at the expense of enjoying the view … won't it?

'The answer to this question is yes, for whichever phase you concentrate on in this teleological series of money, reaching it will always be accompanied by a certain sacrifice. For collecting money work has to be done; for just possessing it you have to give up consumption; spending can only be done on one thing at a time: a sacrifice therefore by not buying something else - a form of alternative costs - and to enjoy the purchase another choice has to be made as it takes time at the very least.

By the way, it's doubtful whether the last phase in the teleological chain of money, the phase of enjoying, is attainable for man as an ultimate goal. We discussed it at length in the last chapter. We quoted *Thomas Hobbes* among others, who stated that this was impossible, because the phase of "enjoying" suggests that the stage of "happiness" has arrived, a certain "peace of a satisfied mind" and this peace won't be granted to man during his lifetime. According to this idea there will be no end to the human means - end chain until we die.'

Yes, I know, you rubbed it in before, I thought a bit grumpily.

Man and flower
'To end this chapter let's return once more to man as an indirect being in another somewhat more frivolous way, showing the difference between a direct and an indirect being. To indicate this difference Simmel used the example of the 'work' a flower must do to bloom as opposed to human labour. Both kinds of activities differ in the following ways:

The flower doesn't have to trouble itself to bloom, whereas human labour always costs sacrifices.
 To man labour (usually) is a means to attain something. As to the activity of the flower there can't be made a distinction between means and end. So human labour is instrumental.
 The blooming of a flower has been programmed by nature; human labour can be chosen (though not necessarily by the employee himself).
 Man works out of necessity; a flower doesn't bloom out of necessity.

There may be difference in opinion to what extent these differences are really provable, but there is no doubt about man being able to keep a distance between himself and his surroundings and set oneself a target at a distance. That's why Simmel called man the *objective animal*. And an important instrument to bridge that distance is money, which improves the possibility to delay direct satisfaction of needs.

Conclusion: even when Aristotle considered the hoarding-up function of money a danger, money, exactly by this function, enables man more to design his indirect being than (perishable) goods do. Money is the ultimate intellectual tool to enable us to lengthen the means - end chain and develop society more by it. In this respect it's a **value-creating tool** too.

Notes:

1. David Graeber, *Schuld - de eerste 5000 jaar,* Amsterdam, Antwerp 2012 *(Debt: The First 5,000 years,* New York 2011)
2. Herodotus, *Het verslag van mijn onderzoek - Historiën,* Amsterdam 2005 *(Historiès apodeksis, the Histories)*
3. Georg Simmel, *Philosophie des Geldes,* Frankfurt am Main 1989 *(Philosophy of Money)* (originally Leipzig 1900)
4. Derived from Ton Bevers, *Zuinigheid en verkwisting - Georg Simmel over geld en cultuur in onze tijd.* Lezing in het Geldcultuurcafé, Geldmuseum Utrecht, 14 June 2007 (Lecture in the Moneyculture café, Moneymuseum Utrecht ... closed in 2015)
5. Robin Skynner & John Cleese, *Cleese over het leven,* Utrecht/Antwerp 1999 *(Life, and How to Survive it,* London 1996)
6. Simon Schama, *Overvloed en onbehagen - De Nederlandse cultuur in de Gouden Eeuw,* Amsterdam 2006 *(The Embarrassment of Riches. An Interpretation of Dutch Culture in the Golden Age,* London 1997)

5 A CYCLE OF THE MATERIAL AND THE IMMATERIAL
On monetary transformation, representation and symbolic money

' Is money material or immaterial? Object or thought? Substance or function? Concrete or abstract?'

A new chapter, a new question - but after what I had been reading in the previous chapters, the answer the author wanted to hear shouldn't be that difficult.

'It depends on the kind of money, you might say. Because there is material as well as immaterial money, as there are circulating coins as well as virtual bank balances.'

And what about paper money, banknotes? I hastily added. Are they material or immaterial?

'Of course there are also banknotes', the author subdued my impatience. 'In which category are they to be placed? It might be a point under discussion: it's true a banknote is a material piece of paper, a concrete little document you can hold, but is it really a 'thing'? We will exhaustively go into this question in subsequent chapters a few times. And it will become clear then that the 'thing-proportion' of most coins is rather meagre nowadays too.'

A banknote not a thing, I thought. Not a real thing? Well, I sensed what he was driving at.

'It's usually assumed that there has been a development in the history of money from the material to the immaterial (some say from the material to nothing), or from substance to function, from thing through symbol to thought, an historical development that can be schematically represented as:

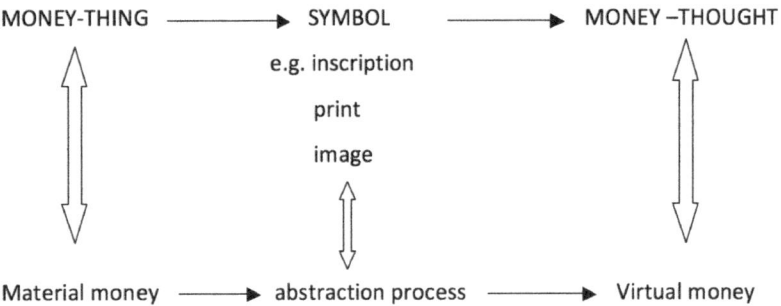

In this diagram 'money-thing' represents the whole accumulation of things (objects, agricultural crop, animals) that once served as a means of exchange or still do. Such a money-thing might also be called currency, the type of currency or currency unit. But this word currency unit possibly causes confusion, because a currency might be anything. Thus anything from cattle, corn, beads, shelves, rice, salt and a lot more including the precious metals gold, silver, whether or not being coined. Even slaves have been used as means of exchange! In Genesis 37:28 is said that merchants (in the beginning of the second millennium before Christ) got patriarch Joseph out of prison and sold him to Ismail merchants for twenty silver pieces (no coins). And Aristotle classified slaves as personal possession and considered the fundamental human inequality a natural thing: "*The one being a ruler and the other being ruled is inevitable as well as useful*".[1] But although in Greek times slaves were treated relatively well, slave trade in the seventeenth century was quite awful. Dutch boats departed for West-Africa with among other things rifles, alcohol and textile and there these commodities were exchanged for slaves that had been supplied by African or Arabian traders. The slaves were transported by the same boats to America, where they were exchanged for sugar, cotton and tobacco. Thereupon these goods went to Middleburg or Amsterdam.'

A striking example of Dutch business sense, I thought, a bit of VOC-mentality in optima forma.

'But did all those material things serving as money precede the thought of money? It's doubtful. Wasn't it rather the other way round? Shouldn't the horizontal arrows in this diagram go the other way round, in fact? Or at least into two directions? In such a way that it becomes clear that on the one hand the material shapes the immaterial, but on the other hand the immaterial shapes the material? Hence not one-way traffic, but two-way traffic, as in the next diagram?

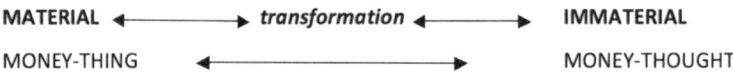

The term *transformation* in this diagram when read from left to right corresponds to the indication **abstraction process** in the previous diagram, but reversed it can be seen as a **concretizing process**. This means that in our minds on the one hand a conversion takes place from the things around us into representations or images of them which are being filed in our brains. But human is also capable of doing the opposite. He can also make concrete things from images and representations that are ghosting about in his mind. That's why the linking arrows point to both directions here because modern man is capable of immaterializing the existing material (=abstracting) as well as materializing the immaterial (=concretizing).'

Yes, modern man might be, but does this also go for ancient man? I wondered. Did our distant ancestors have the same capability as we have of translating their ideas into products? Well yes, in principle they did of course, as quite early they also made instruments which they used for hunting or housekeeping, primitive in our eyes indeed, but even so. Hence inventing something first and then making it, is an essential characteristic of man and probably as old as humanity itself.

'Compare in this connection the creation of the 'product' money to the realization of other products made by man', again he author seemed to be able to read my thoughts. 'They never come out of the blue, but are the result of an intentional product development from design to end product. So once again: idea first and then thing.'

The first spear made from a stick became design before the term existed, I thought.

'And it might have been like this with money too: money having come into being first as an idea in the human mind and only then having been materialized into a tangible form. Many anthropologists support this idea and we have to go into the matter in great detail presently.'

So with regard to the development of money in the diagram above these anthropologists are thinking from right to left, I concluded, so from the immaterial to the material, from idea to material. Well, logical in fact when considering it from the point of view of product development: in that case there was the money-idea first and only then the money-thing. But you must look upon money as an ordinary product then, comparable to any other article that man has ever invented, from peanut butter to an airplane.

'So, money as a human idea that belongs or stems from the human mind, comparable to intellect, morality, religion and esthetic experiences', he added.

Well, well, I thought, quite an allegation it seems to me. In this way the dross of the earth is being put on quite a high spiritual throne.

'But let's continue first with the things that certain communities generally accepted as a means of exchange', the author descended to a more earthly level, 'the things from cattle to gold as mentioned above. In practice not all of these generally desired things were just that suitable as a means of exchange however - the reason why being quite obvious.'

Is it? Why?

'Cattle is perishable, as it dies as time goes by. Agricultural crop is less problematic in this respect, as it can be stored for a longer time (think of the granaries we mentioned before), but then again its supply is very irregular: a bumper crop alternated with crop failure, causing the exchange value of these products to fluctuate a lot. Shells (like cowries) and salt are abundant in certain parts of the world, so when these products got the character of money, it wasn't long before smart numbers started collecting them massively causing a large increase of supply and a fast decrease of value.

The most suitable means of exchange were goods that were desirable as well as durable and represented a great value in relatively small quantities. Moreover it had to be impossible to increase their quantity strongly enough to decrease their value of exchange (= inflation). In this way a certain selection took place from all kinds of commodity money, out of which the precious metals gold and silver emerged as the most suitable means of exchange. These metals met the requirements *durability, stability in value* and *high value in small quantity*. (by the way: this so-called stability in value of gold and silver has been and is being belied rather often in practice. Look at what we said about it in chapter 2 for instance and what will be mentioned in chapter 8.)

By the replacement of the different kinds of commodity money by gold and silver the *commodity standard* disappeared and the *metallic standard* arose. In the whole succession of goods serving as commodity money this last step to metallic money with the help of precious metals hasn't ended yet. Especially gold is still generally considered the ideal basis for a monetary system. We will try to find out and enfeeble the underlying idea of this "golden misunderstanding" in chapter 9 of the same name.'

Well, I wonder how, I thought, because money has to be covered by gold at least for a part. Hasn't it?

'But first we have to take a few steps back into the history of money. Let's ask ourselves how human economic relations took place before the time that those generally accepted and desired means of exchange were being used. Did barter exist? There are differences of opinion on this.

Linear or circular?
Let's critically look at the diagram above once more and question which representation is most correct. Did the history of money develop linearly from thing to thought? From the material to the immaterial? So from concrete material to abstract money? Or was it the other way round? Or did it go forwards and backwards like a mantel clock?'

Well, look, those arrows into both directions in the second diagram are a clear answer to that question, I thought.

'This mantel clock-option is comparable to a circular movement of the history of money, as in both cases history repeats itself again and again. And this historical movement swinging backwards and forwards would mean that periods with material monetary systems are being alternated with periods with immaterial monetary systems. If that would be the case, in present time we might just be at a temporary point of the clock or the circle pointing at a transitional phase from material to immaterial, from material to immaterial money, or in jargon: from a decrease of notes and coins in circulation to an increase of transferable money. But if this development is really a clockwise swinging or circular movement, this virtual monetary phase will end again: after this phase having been fully developed, the money circle might go off like a kind of monetary kitchen timer and the money clock might revert towards material kinds of money. This is quite imaginable when more and more people start considering the present monetary system as a form of monetary hocus-pocus and lose confidence in the whole monetary mysticism. (Is this why in times of crisis the homesick call for the gold standard keeps sounding again and again?)'

Monetary mysticism? Homesick call? Rather suggestive use of words, I thought, but it had become obvious meanwhile that the dear chap didn't fancy gold as a monetary standard at all, I guess. He was going to explain the matter in chapter 8.

'But not until recently did most economists believe that history of money has developed from concrete, from a monetary system with notes and coins in circulation, to more abstract transferable money systems, so in the diagrams from left to right … until in 2011 this belief was relegated to the realm of fiction once again by anthropologist *David Graeber*[2] Once more, because this had been done before, but hadn't been noticed by most economists or hadn't been taken seriously. In the past decennia anthropologists have been searching quite a lot, into the very ends of the world, but they didn't come across Smith's barter trade anywhere. Graeber classified the described system of barter trade by Smith therefore as a myth, the myth of the barter.'

Smith? Adam Smith?

'For he was the very man who propagated the fairytale of the barter further into the world after Aristotle and John Locke among others. He merely deductively assumed that there had been something like barter in former times which had been made much easier by money. So as not to drag ten bags of potatoes each time when you wanted to take over a few chickens.'

So a myth, I repeated loudly, merely made up, incomprehensible.

'But among many professional economists the generally assumed idea that originally economic transactions took place by barter, still exists.'

The myth of the barter, I emphatically said once again, as I liked the sound of it, like the title of a novel. Maybe something for this Spanish author, Isaac Rosa, who wrote a novel about *The invisible hand* too.

'Many economists kept or keep telling this traditional and linear money-story from their teaching chairs. Graeber wrote about this in his book:

"When economists speak of the origins of money, debt is always something of an afterthought. First comes barter, then money; credit only develops later. Even if one consults books on history of money in, say France, India, or China, what one generally gets is a history of coinage, with barely any discussion on credit arrangements. For almost a century anthropologists like me have been pointing out there is something very wrong with this picture. The standard economic-history has little to do with anything we observe when we examine how economic life is actually conducted, in real communities and in marketplaces, almost anywhere one is more likely to discover everyone in debt to everyone else in a dozen different ways, and that most transactions take place without the use of currency."

Thus this standard story on birth and development of money always starts with this myth of the barter. In it man lives in a supposed world without money, in which economic transactions develop by barter trade.'

Yes, but wait a minute, I addressed the author in thought, didn't you give a few examples of it in your book yourself? For instance when you made Mrs. Taylor and Mr. Harris exchange apples for pears? And somewhere else where you put on the stage an imaginative Mrs. A and Mr. B, who exchanged their possessions α and β with each other? And also elsewhere a certain Mrs. X an a Mr. Y, who exchanged their products A and B? And, that reminds me, he also mentioned Marx, who made someone exchange a bible for gin - or, no, the latter was by way of money.

'Imagine a world without money, the myth always starts, what does it mean?'

That people have to turn to barter trade to satisfy their needs, but this was a myth, as you already said before.

'We mentioned several examples of barter in the preceding chapter of course, but we mainly did so to explain the term 'relative value'. In this chapter however it's about painting a picture of the development of money from the time that man didn't pay with money and settled their transactions by way of barter trade.'

Which is a myth, you wrote, so why this difficult carry-on? I thought.

'To pay a meal in a restaurant the owner of the restaurant has to be offered something of equal value. One can of course offer to do the dishes, to wash the car or sing a song, but an economy based on barter trade will have difficulty in assigning the scarce resources in an efficient way. An economy like that requires a double accordance of needs, i.e. the unlikely occurrence that two persons possess a product or a service that the other wants.'

So this is the next made-up exchange-story, what a silly example, because in a world without money there won't be any cars nor restaurants, will there.

'Of course, this is a silly example', the author immediately agreed with me, but nevertheless most handbooks on economics offer something comparable when trying to explain the coming into existence of money. It's meant to indicate that in a society with barter trade problems will soon arise when several products are to be exchanged with each other. Firstly for each product one wants to exchange an exactly right counterparty must be found and secondly the determining of the right exchange-ratio soon will be a complicated matter. And sometimes it's accompanied by a calculation example, like the one below:

Calculating the number of required prices with barter trade.
If in an economy there are only 2 commodities to be exchanged, money won't be required, for there is just 1 exchange price; for instance 2 apples for 3 pears. When a third commodity is added there are already 3 exchange prices: for instance 2 apples for 3 pears and 3 apples for 1 peach, from which follows that 1 peach costs 4.5 pears. What to do if there are 10 commodities people want to exchange with each other? How many prices must we calculate when money doesn't exist? To do so we must find out how many different commodity-combinations these 10 goods can form in pairs. And there are already 45 of them! As a consequence 45 exchange prices are needed as well. The formula for the calculation of this number of prices with exchange in kind is ½ n(n-1). In it n is the number of commodities. From this can be calculated that with 100 commodities there will be 4950 exchange prices and with 1000 commodities no less than 499,500!

An example like this makes clear the convenience of money as a means of exchange and calculation unit. For 1000 commodities only 1000 prices are needed instead of nearly half a million.'

Well, the example is much more complicated, I thought. We are lucky to be able to use our money, but of course it's purely hypothetical, this example. In practice something like that couldn't possibly exist.

'In search for generally accepted means to simplify the exchange, the idea originally came up of the so-called *goods money* (cattle, beads, shells, rice, salt etc.) as dealt with above. Some words in our language still remind of them: the Latin word *pecunia*, originating from *pecus* (= cattle). And our word 'salary' has been derived from the Latin *sal* (= salt).'

True, but, I thought, and again: True, but ... Hadn't the author suggested a minute ago that it hadn't been like this? That the historical development of money hadn't started with barter trade and next the tangible commodity money?

'That's once more in a nutshell the traditional linear history of money, starting with the tangible things of exchange and nowadays ending for this moment with the abstract exchange function by means of electronic money. This assumed linear development from barter to electronic money has filled many people with suspicion in the past. They thought that by the ongoing abstraction of money nothing but a 'shadow' of real money would remain, a kind of apparition. In a separate chapter this 'shadow of money' will be dealt with. There an extremely curious novel will come up containing a description of people's fear when paper money was introduced. This book was published In 1867 and was written by *David Ames Wells* (1828-1898), who filled the position of *Special Commissioner of the Revenue*. It's called *Robinson Crusoe's money* and predicts all kinds of possible misery if the gold standard will be given up and the money press will run wild.[4] More on this later on.

Thus, *David Graeber* and others deny this kind of stories. According to them the historical development of money didn't go from concrete money to abstract money, but the other way round and besides not linear.[2] Originally transactions in local communities were being settled by way of *credit systems* without intervention of money, so with the help of mutual credit based on mutual trust. In his book *Debt* he discusses this at length. A quotation:

Admittedly, the usual impulse is to imagine everything around us is absolutely new. Nowhere is this so true as with money. How many times have we been told that the advent of virtual money, the dematerialization of cash into plastic and dollars into blips of electronic information, has brought us to an unprecedented new financial world? The assumption that we were in such uncharted territory, of course, was one of the things that made it so easy for the likes of Goldman Sachs and AIG to convince people that no one could possibly understand their dazzling new financial instruments. The moment one casts matters on a broad historical scale, though, the first thing one learns is that there's nothing new about virtual money. Actually, this was the original form of money. Credit systems, tabs, even expense accounts, all existed long before cash. These things are as old as civilization itself. True, we also find that history tends to move back and forth between periods dominated by bullion - where it's assumed that gold and silver *are* money - and periods where money is assumed to be an abstraction, a virtual unit of account. But historically, credit money comes first, and what we are witnessing today is the return of assumptions that would have been considered obvious common sense in, say the Middle Ages - or even ancient Mesopotamia.

A similar opinion is found with *Jean-Joseph Goux* in his article *Electronic money, or the fingers of the invisible hand*, we came across in chapter 2.

Representation
Together with the transition from commodity money to coins, money became more abstract. The first users sometimes had difficulty with that. Therefore images on the first coins often referred to the commodity money used before and thus on the oldest coins we find images of for instance cows, fish, axes or corn. This *"Neigung zur Symmetrie (ist) allen unausgebildeten Kulturen eigen (…)"* according to Simmel. The same conclusion has already been mentioned in chapter 2 when we spoke about the idea of 'relative value'. Why do we repeat this statement once more here?'

Yes, I'd like to know that too, I thought.

'As nowadays we too have a long way to go in managing to get rid of the tendency towards symmetry. The more so, as in symbolic pictograms for signposting for instance such a 'symmetric' reference is often to be recognized: on the sign directing to a hotel a picture of a bed can be seen, a restaurant is indicated by a crossed spoon and fork, an industrial zone can be recognized at the contours of a factory with a smoking chimney, for a marked walking trail you follow the signs with the silhouette of a little walker and along a cycling path are signs with abstracted two-wheelers. Having an eye for it once, you will see more and more of these symbols of representation, including the Facebook-thumb-up shooting from a well recognizable little fist. And this longing for symmetry is also apparent from the design of our money, even in the size of the coins and banknotes: the higher the value, the bigger they are.'

Why, yes, I thought. I never consciously noticed this before.

'But, well, what have we done so far in this chapter? Which road did we walk on?'

Walk? Road?

' The first part of the road from thing to thought. Supposing that preceding the generally accepted 'exchange things' functioning as money, there must have been barter, then the following historical money-road has been covered: *barter → commodity-money → coins → paper money → transferable money.* This road shows a development from concrete to more and more abstract thinking. But once again: this way is an assumed way, because according to Graeber and others history of money started at the end of the way, with a kind of transferable traffic in the form of credit. Let's first see therefore whether there are examples to be found of it in practice. We will return to the standard story afterwards.'

It gives me the heebie-jeebies, I thought. First from material to immaterial and then back again from thought to thing; why is the man doing this?

'We can imagine that the reader might be off track a bit', he guessed my slight despair. 'But the arrows in the diagram pointing into two directions, show that history of money doesn't go one way, as we argued before. And that's why the reader might get the impression that the story in this book isn't going linearly one way either.'

No, it absolutely isn't! I called out loudly.

'But that's exactly the intention, as history of money doesn't develop linearly either, but more in a circling and turning way.'

Or like a pendulum clock, then, I added.

'Dependent on the circumstances different monetary systems seem to have taken turns with each other, or even have existed side by side! It has especially got something to do with trust in society: the more balanced the society is, the greater the trust and the more transferable money and credit is being used. But the opposite, in instable situations with threats from all sides economic dealings often relapse into notes and coins and even in barter trade - the latter occurred quite recently in Russia after the disintegration of the Soviet Union during the rouble crisis in the years 1992 till 1998.'

The rouble crisis? I had never heard of it. Or had it completely escaped my notice? Or had it just slipped my memory, I'm forgetting more and more.

'This rouble crisis started with a galloping inflation', the author explained. 'In 1992 the inflation in Russia was 2000 percent or more! When money loses its value this quickly, companies and merchants avoid this currency and start paying each other with commodities or with (uncollectible) bills of exchange, or they let their debts increase. The surprising thing however, was that money didn't even return as main currency in Russia in 1995, even though inflation had decreased considerably by then. In 1998 more than half of all payments was still not done in money in Russia, including wages and taxes. Not until in the same year when a financial crisis had put things right, did the rouble return as most important currency. We quote this example only to show how vulnerable a monetary system can be when the underlying economic situation is instable. This instability is even much greater in war situations and with banking mostly completely on its last legs then, so there is often nothing else we can do but exchange, pay in cash, in complementary IOUs or substitute currency like cigarettes and coffee.

But well, first we were going to look whether there have been or still are any examples to be found in practice to support the proposition of anthropologists like Graeber.'

All right, Just do it, look at this first. But which proposition again?

'The proposition that the granting of credit preceded the coming into existence of money'

Ah yes, first credit then money.

'The most well-known is perhaps the slate.'

Ah yes, I'm familiar with that one, I thought, for if you put something on the slate, you have done something wrong.

'Originally a slate is a stick in which snips were made for counting and remembering what one person owed another.'

Hence a mnemonic device, I understood. A kind of primitive bookkeeping system with which receivables and debts were registered.

'Slates were physical IOUs. They functioned like this: when a deal was made, both parties carved the indebted amount in a hazel or willow twig, which was divided in two thereupon. Each party kept a half and this half was the visible proof of the receivable or debt.'

A beautiful system, but how long ago was this?

'Those slates were already used in prehistory, but for instance also in the days of Henry II, who was king from 1154 till 1189. He ordered part of his subjects' tax arrears to be registered this way. But what did he do with those slates thereupon? He often didn't wait for payment of the indebted amounts, but he sold the sticks at a discount. By doing so he got his money sooner and the slates were put in circulation as IOUs - comparable to our present-day government bonds.'

That's why our government has a lot on her slate, I thought.

'In England slates remained in use quite a long time however and not until 1782 did the Chancellor of the Exchequer abolish them as bookkeeping instruments. But it took until 1834 before the last slate was replaced by a paper document. Thus the slate used to be a means to register debts, a proof of credit, but it wasn't money. And in prehistory this kind of visible, but also often invisible IOUs existed before money.'

Invisible? I thought, in what way invisible?

'As a matter of fact most credits used to be arranged verbally, merely on the basis of trust and 'registered' in memory. More in the way of you-scratch-my-back-and-I-scratch-yours, based on mutual verbal acceptance of debt. But this memory registration fairly often lead to problems, as not everyone could or wanted to remember everything correctly, resulting in disagreement or struggle. This is the reason why there was need for credit mnemonics like slates.

Another classic example of this kind of currencies or credit systems is the **Rai**. The **Rai** had been the currency for centuries on the island of Yap, part of the Micronesian group of islands. These round yap stones had been carved out of limestone and could vary in diameter from a half to even four meters. The stones are still scattered all over the group of islands, along the roads and against houses. Their owners may have changed with payments, but their place seldom did. Because it was difficult to move them, everyone in the village remembered which stone belonged to whom.'

Yes, but those people were obliged to remember it then, I thought, who was the owner of a certain stone, as they didn't write it down, did they?

' In order to avoid trouble about property claims in future, witnesses were present at each exchange transaction.'

Solved. But how reliable were those witnesses? The author didn't go into that question.

'The value of a stone among others depended on size, shape, colour and the age and history of the rai. The stones were always put upright. It was considered an insult to put a rai down or to drop it or to sit on it. And only men were allowed to own a rai.'

That's rather a bit of patriarchal stupidity, I thought, because women are often better than men in managing money. Often, but not always, of course.

'Nowadays the rai have been replaced by the American dollar and a large part of the stones have been sold meanwhile and are no longer on the islands. Worldwide there are probably 6000 to be found. The rai has become a symbol of the federal state and its depiction can be seen on local number plates.

Which takes us back by the roundabout way of this last example to the idea of the 'symbol'.'

It's called a link, I thought.

'And with it we'll return for a moment to the (partly invented) standard history of money which develops from concrete to abstract money.

Symbolic money

We were just talking about the use of symbols which can represent all sorts of things. But now it's about time to concentrate more on the use of symbols. In the diagram in the beginning of the chapter the term *'symbol'* has been mentioned as an instrument to help shaping the abstraction process of money. This development goes hand in hand with the use of symbols in the form of signs and pictures which represent the value of the money, for example numbers indicating the nominal value, exchange symbols, stamps, royal portraits full-face or in profile, gods, horsemen, coats of arms and much more. All these symbols were originally meant to support trust in the currency. They refer to the state power or central bank which guarantees the value of the money and which is presented in the pictures and in the symbolic signs. Only by these signs money gets its value, the French philosopher *Michel Foucault* claims.[4] He thought that money didn't derive its value from the material it was made of at all, but exclusively from its form, for instance from the portrait or the stamp of the sovereign. Money "*completely derives its value from the **function of the symbol** it holds*", he said. The printed symbols on money represent the power or authority that issues it and which guarantees its value. This put him in the camp of the **functionalists** and monetary nominalists, who don't think the intrinsic value of money important. This view puts him diametrically against people like *John Locke*, who thought that the value of money could exclusively be found in the material or intrinsic value of money. Locke therefore can be classified as a **substantialist**. (Contemporary advocates of the return to the gold standard are to be found in this quarter. That's why we will also encounter this substantialistical way of thinking in the chapter on "the golden misunderstanding".)

The relation between substance and sign (symbol) raises the question where the value of a currency may actually be found: in the substance or in the symbol.'

According to Mr. Foucault exclusively in the sign, I understood.

'Gold and silver coins used to circulate with a print or a portrait of a sovereign, who rendered the money a hallmark of value this way. But suppose a coin like that starts wearing out and the portrait disappears completely - will this coin be still money then?'

Well, as long as it has sufficient gold value, why not? I answered, but the author hadn't finished his question yet:

'Or the other way round: the coin disappears and only the portrait remains, for instance on paper. Will this portrait be money then?'

According to the French philosopher it will, I thought. And we don't have any problem using banknotes that are nothing but printed little papers, do we? And transferable money from which even the 'sign' has disappeared? Or is this still rudimentarily present perhaps? Oh well, I think that the author did promise to return to it later, if I remember well.

'When sharing *Foucault's* argumentation the image in itself is sufficient to pass for money', the author agreed.

'Centuries before theologian and philosopher *Thomas of Aquino* (1227-1274) seemed to have had the same view as Foucault. As it happens he alleged that the acceptability of money as a means of exchange follows from an agreement between the government and the community and mutually between the members of that community. The first step with it was that an authority guaranteed the weight and the value of the nuggets of precious metal; so he certainly wasn't an adherent of monetary functionalism, but by this agreement between government and community he on the contrary wanted to guarantee the substantial or intrinsic value of money.

Foucault's view seems rather debatable therefore. If he is right, Aristotle for instance has been wrong when saying in *Politica*: *"For barter human beings agreed to exchange* **a good easily applicable to the purpose of life** *and easy to handle as well, like iron, silver and the like. The amounts were* **first determined by size and weight**, *but later by printing marks on the metal."* Hence Aristotle clearly says that 1st the metals in question are useful in life and 2nd minting coins (printing marks) came in existence after nuggets of metal had been used as money for some time, because *"it would obviate the need for measuring and weighing."*

In his book *The Night of Capital, A. Th. Van Leeuwen* also challenges the 'sign' idea as defended by Foucault: " *The stamp is a sign (…) of the quantity of metal, serving as a means of exchange. Not for a moment the illusion which started fermenting in the theory of economics in the Age of Reason can arise, that money would be mere fiction, because the coin is nothing but a sign of the real material. The phase in which the quantity of metal has been chosen for a coin with inscription and mintage, is indeed the beginning of an evolution developing by way of paper money and ending in transferable money. But exactly in his analysis of the crucial first phase Aristotle shows the essential relation between sign and reality. Completely against appearances, transferable money isn't a fictive machination with numbers either, but it's just a more developed form of currency, for its part stemming from money as a substantial means of exchange."* [5] And finally the use of all kinds of silver objects as money in Mesopotamia in ancient Egypt doesn't support The French philosopher's thesis either.'

Yes, but ... Yes, but, I muttered. It's becoming a bit of a confusion now. What should I believe now? Aristotle and Mr. Van Leeuwen are obvious supporters of **substantialism**, I guess, of the idea that the value of money is derived from the value of the material, the material money is made of. And *Thomas of Aquino* can be placed in that quarter as well, I think, just like *John Locke*. Whereas *Foucault* was diametrically opposed to this and therefore a pure **functionalist**. For him the value of the 'thing' itself didn't play any part in the value of the money. But what was the opinion of the author himself about it? Closer to *Foucault* probably, or the book wouldn't be titled *Money is a mind thing*. And oh yes, also close to *George Simmel* of course, as he was rather fond of the abstract character of money. And indeed, the German philosopher of money appeared on the stage once more:

'*Simmel* called this the "*Entwicklungsgang von der Substanzbedeutung des Geldes zur Funktionsbedeutung*". This traditional way has taken up many centuries in the history of money - at least, when departing from the existence of such a linear historical way, which as being said before is a deductive myth.

But however this way has gone by, linearly or circularly or twistingly, money always represents some kind of value. Our modern money refers to a value outside itself, because it isn't worth anything by itself, or it doesn't have any intrinsic value. The value of the paper of a banknote is practically nothing and a transferable credit is just a number in a computer. So money represents something else. That's why it's a symbol, a 'sign', as it was called by *Michel Foucault*, a sign that, as said before, represents something else: "*For classical thought (...) money is that which permits wealth to be represented. Without such signs, wealth would remain immobile, useless, and as it were silent.*"[4] This sign often has the shape of a number with a portrait on coins and paper money, as we have mentioned before, but is shapeless in virtual money. But whether shapeless or not, even 'invisible' transferable money is a sign that represents a value. But which value?'

Which value? Does the author start repeating himself? I thought. As by now he has devoted two complete chapters to this value, hasn't he? Whatever new information could he possibly add here?

'We did dwell on kinds of value, forms of value and sources of value in chapter 2 and 3, of course, but now the time has come to see from which modern money derives its value', he promised.

Well. I can't wait, I thought.

'Nowadays this value is first and foremost being associated with the purchasing power of money, meaning the goods and services that can be bought with money. As such money represents and substitutes merchandise. This 'merchandise' can be looked at from our income and spending - the well-known cycle of money and goods -, but also from the total value of our possession. In the first case it's about *quantities of flow* and in the second about a *quantity of stock*. A quantity of flow is a quantity measured over a certain period, for instance the returns or the cost per year. A quantity of stock represents a certain value at a certain moment, for instance a stock of goods or a savings balance on 1 January. In both cases it's about an **object representation** of money.

However another idea of representation is possible too, namely not starting from goods and services but from people. This approach emphasizes the concept of *relationships*, that is relations between people. Economics is not so much a system then in which mutual relations of merchandise and its value are being fixed, but more a system of relationships between people who set and estimate values. In this approach there is a **subject representation** of money.

Object representation
First something on object representation. The question, exactly of which money is a symbol, a 'sign', which objects it represents, has been answered differently over the centuries. *John Locke (1632-1704)* for example, mainly saw money as a security, so as a kind of token, a fictitious money-token that can be exchanged at any time for the same amount of merchandise or something of equal value. And as stated above, he also thought that the value of money was determined by its intrinsic quality, that is by the value of the material money is made of. In his time this meant a certain weight of silver.'

So that man was a real **substantialist**, I repeated to myself once again.

'*John Law (1671-1729)*, a Scottish financier and repeatedly convicted criminal, however thought that circulation of paper money was possible, guaranteed by the main source of property, that is landed property. Law tried to get this concept going in France, which failed and he had to make a business enterprise vouch for the guarantee of the money.'

So this Law wasn't a substantialist, I concluded, because he argued in favour of paper money which doesn't have any intrinsic value. But was he a proper functionalist? I had my doubts, as he thought that money had to be covered by a physical security like land. And for a true functionalist this isn't necessary, if I had understood rightly. Or is it? For if they say that money represents something else, this 'else' will represent a certain value, won't it? Let's continue reading.

'Nowadays the guarantee of our money is no longer linked to a specific product like gold or land. At the most you might say that the value of money is 'guaranteed' by the total value of the economy. This value is usually defined as the sum of all goods and services produced and sold in a year. The total value of all these produced goods and services is the national product which is always expressed in an amount of money. And the amount of money we earn with this total production is our national income. As both quantities are measured with the same unit, namely money, they are similar per definition: national product = national income. In financial reports this is usually abbreviated as GDP = Gross Domestic Product. There are also other ways to measure the national income, but they are of no interest for our argument at this moment.

The thing we want to stress once more right now, is the fact that all produced and sold goods and services are always expressed in money, in other words: transformed into money. We have come across this **monetary transformation** several times before, as the transformation of things into money plays the first fiddle in this book. This monetary transformation is going on in our minds. There we transform goods and services into money, or a real sphere into a monetary sphere, to put it in terms of economics. And these two spheres go against each other like streams in a cycle: a cycle of goods against a cycle of money. In other words: a material cycle against an immaterial cycle. In a highly simplified form this cycle looks like this:

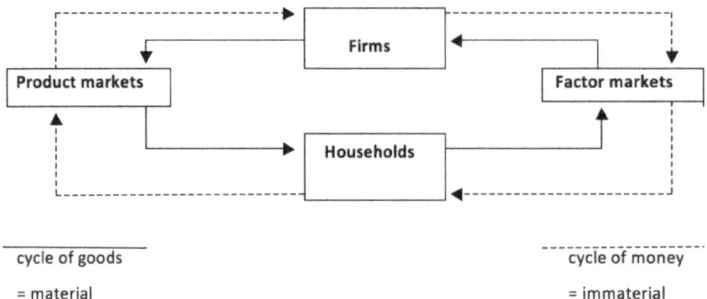

This diagram is highly simplified, because there is a lot missing. No place for instance has been made for the government and foreign countries. So it's a closed national economy without a government. But nevertheless, it's quite obvious that there will always be a stream of money against a stream of goods. In terms of the idea of representation: the stream of money represents the stream of goods. If we question what the relation between the immaterial and the material is like here, we have to bear in mind what both streams basically represent in this diagram. There is no doubt about the cycle of goods: goods = material. ('Goods' are meant to be goods + services here.) And as has been said before, money belongs to the intellectual sphere of the immaterial. With money we transform or translate qualitatively multiform goods and services (things) into a quantitatively uniform criterion of comparison (money). In our minds a diffuse variety of things becomes a subjective scale of value (see chapter 3), which thereupon are being objectified into measurable units by means of money. Thus we objectify subjective relations with money.'

Isn't the author repeating himself now? I wondered. Oh very well, it's not bad, really - ***frappez toujours***, the French call it, and for my kind of memory it's the only way to make it sink in at all.

'We recognize in this cycle of economics once more Marx's idea of metamorphosis, who rather laboriously formulated it in *The Capital* like this: *"First commodities stand opposed to money as units of value, which - in someone else's pocket - get a commercial, hard reality, and thus the owner of some commodity will be opposed to the owner of money. As soon as a commodity transforms into money, money becomes its temporary equivalent, which use-value or content exists in other beings of commodities. (...) Both opposite phases of circulation of the metamorphosis of commodities are a cycle: form of commodity - end of form of commodity - return to form of commodity."*

Well, laborious indeed, or rather forced I would say.

' ...but by this objectifying, money doesn't need a concrete form like cattle, shelves, gold, coins or whatever. Since this value-comparison is going on in our minds. Concrete, physical money is at the most a tool to give this value-comparison a handle by attaching a visible amount of 'money-material' to it. But owing to our present well advanced transferable money system, we realize more and more that money is essentially virtual, i.e. imaginary, an idea. Once more: money must be placed in the ideal or mental sphere: money is mind!'

See: just as I thought his answer would be to the question at the beginning of this chapter.

Subject representation
'Above we dealt with objects that can represent money. Objects like land, gold, merchandise or the total set of goods and services produced in a country per year: the GDP or Gross Domestic Product. But another idea of representation is imaginable too, namely that money represents human relationships or relations. Then, money isn't linked to goods (objects), but to people (subjects). This approach emphasizes the concept *relationship* in the sense of *relations* between people.

A limited part of those relations are employment relations. If we consider money the representation or equivalent of our employment relations and labour performance, we must look at the right side of the cycle diagram. It's the representation of the market for production factors and in this market labour, capital (goods) and natural resources like land and minerals are being sold. Thus the labour market is part of the total market of production factors and in this market human labour is considered a marketable product, a kind of 'thing' to be bought or sold for a certain price.

We may raise many ethical objections against this objectifying of an essentially subjective and varied qualitative phenomenon, but fact is that money reduces this qualitative multiformity into a uniform and quantitative quantity, namely the price of labour, the labour costs. The various kinds of labour reduced to and represented by amounts of money. Hence money represents certain human qualities and transforms them into seemingly objective quantities. The annoying thing about the matter is that a lot of people are inclined to transform this into quite another kind of quality, namely a quality of character. And in such a way that a higher wage and more money is associated with a better character.'

What? I thought, I can't imagine a person being judged from his money like that. From his appearance, yes I'm familiar with, but from his money?

'Wealth often used to be linked, and still is, to the owner having certain character traits. *"and it's only a small step to imagine that 'extremely good behaviour' and many virtues must be at the bottom of the acquisition of (...) yachts, mansions and jewellery"*, Alain de Botton wrote.[6] And: *"The concept of a status symbol, a precious material object giving its owner respect, is based on the widespread and not unlikely idea that the acquisition of the most expensive commodities needs the best character traits."* Reversed, this makes a person who is forced to spend his whole life gathering useful primary necessities of life an obvious member of the less decent social classes. It's a liberal view still existing, especially among Americans: anyone who wants to and does the best he can, will succeed and poverty is one's own fault.'

Oh well, Americans, I thought. Americans, but in Europe we don't share this view, do we? Don't we have better social services than they do over there? But the author didn't go in on this.

'Thus regrettably the subject representation of money may degenerate into a moral evaluation of man based on the height of his financial income and fortune - money as a criterion and symbol for whether or not having succeeded in life and as a quality mark of character. Sometimes this subjective evaluation literally appears in language. We've indicated this in the first chapter. We speak of 'investment in friendship' for example, which suggests an aspect of costs of relationships, and we sometimes say 'that person isn't worth much' and 'every man has his price'. Consciously or unconsciously we are inclined to measure a person with the money-yardstick. In *'Dead souls'* by *Nikolaj Gogol* a nice illustration can be found of a couple of ladies who suddenly discover that the main character Tchitchikow is actually a billionaire: *"… From the very moment rumour spread about his billions they discovered new qualities in him. It's not that they loved his money, no the mere word billionaire was to blame; the mere sound of the word always has this effect on people of all sorts, on villains, good people and the average man."*

In his book *Freud, Marx: Economie et Symbolique*, the French philosopher - economist *Jean-Joseph Goux* put quite a different and rather peculiar Freudian explanation to the subject representation in 1973.[7] Economics, he said, isn't a system in which mutual relations of merchandise and its value are determined, but first and for all a system of relations between people who have made it a habit to set values and appreciate them based on certain developments and growth processes. The monopolizing of gold and money is an example of the historical symbolizing process Goux compares to the gradual development of the object relation between child and father and the monopolizing of the father figure. This development happens in four phases.'[8]

Object relation between child and father? I thought. Subject relation rather, I imagine? A relation between people? But when reading on, I understood that the author definitely meant object relation:

'According to Goux the first phase in the development process of money can be compared to the first object relation of mother and child. It's a simple relation, analogous to a simple exchange relation between two products. The very first self only needs the one in which it recognizes and reflects itself, as with exchange the value of one object is completely expressed into that of the other. So, we are talking about a simple relative valuation, like product X having a certain value relation to product Y. The value of one object is completely expressed into the other. There is only 1 value-equivalent.'

But hold on, I thought, won't you be engaged in the myth of the barter right away if you take your departure from this starting point? Aren't you defining the value relation between child and mother simply as an exchange relation between two products? And how on earth can this be measured? Apples and pears may be possible, but mother and child? My feeling stubbornly resisted this supposed analogy. But then, it was a kind of Freudian explanation, according to the author, which has always been a mystery to me.

'In the second phase history meanwhile has evolved more and then the meaning of the child or the merchandise that is to be exchanged will be expressed into various other forms. With it one form is seen as more valuable as the other. The relation between child and mother has extended to a larger environment with room for others: brothers, sisters, a father, other relatives, visitors. The simple relation model has extended to a multiple, but still limited relation model. Several value relations have been added, more value equivalents - besides into product Y, product X can be expressed into product A, B, C and so on.'

But still a matter of relative value determination like the myth of the barter, I thought. Rather unsatisfactory, I thought.

'In the third phase the relations are being extended more and more. The world around the individual gets larger. Whereas being a matter of complete equivalence and identification in the first object relation (between mother and child; between one object of exchange and the other), we have arrived at a situation of ambivalence now. Although this often is a rather instable situation of potential rivalry, conflict and crisis too. There are so many different relations and value relations that factors like dominance or subordination may play a part. A situation in which differences of opinion may arise or being accentuated and fighting may flare up. In order to put an end to this undesired situation, in this fourth phase these multifarious relations, these relation forms and value criterions are leaped together with the help of one superior valuation and direction indicator and made similar. In Goux's Freudian view this part in the family is granted to the father and in economic transactions to money. This father image suits the western patriarchal masculine culture. This image functions as a general value equivalent - everybody has been made relative compared to the father, whose 'relatives' they are. Thus Goux describes the development of barter into contemporary economy with the gradual monopolizing of money as having taken place along the same symbolic basic principle as the historic development and growth of the bourgeois family, with the gradual monopolizing of the father image.'

Hence it's our common father, I concluded, the monetary father we serve and obey - yes, the latter is correct in a way, but isn't the rest a bit of nonsense? And in matriarchal societies money should be seen as mother, I presume? But the author didn't go into it. Instead he finished this chapter with an almost heavenly final chord, which resounded in my ears for a while:

'If we add a fifth speculative phase to Goux's Freudian story, we almost end up in the clouds where the Holy Ghost resides. Is it possible maybe that our contemporary virtual money which circles the earth quicker than light, represents this Holy Ghost? And may *Peter Sloterdijk* have had this idea in mind when he said: *"The fundamental fact of modernity is not that the earth orbits the sun, but that money orbits the earth."*[9]'

Notes:

1. Quoted from: Dr. W. N. A. Klever, *Archeologie van de economie - de economische theorie in de Griekse oudheid,* Amsterdam 1986
2. David Graeber, *Schuld - de eerste 5000 jaar,* Amsterdam/Antwerp 2012 (*Debt, the First 5,000 years,* New York 2011)
3. David A. Wells, *Het Geld van Robinson Crusoe - populaire uiteenzetting omtrent de oorsprong en het gebruik van geld als ruilmiddel* The Hague 1919 *(Robinson Crusoe's money,* New York 1876*)*
4. Michel Foucault, *De woorden en de dingen,* Baarn 1966 (*The Order of Things,* New York 1966)
5. Arend Th. Van Leeuwen, *De nacht van het kapitaal,* Nijmegen 1985

6. Alain de Botton, *Statusangst,* Amsterdam 2007 *(Status Anxiety,* London 2005*)*
7. Jean Joseph Goux, *Symbolic Economies after Marx and Freud,* New York 1990
8. Source: Etty Mulder, *Freud en Orpheus,* p. 59-62, Utrecht 1987
9. Peter Sloterdijk, *Sferen,* Amsterdam 2009 *(Bubbles,* Cambridge 2011)

6 THE CALCULATING ANIMAL
On considering pros and cons and the cult of rationality

' *"Nowadays people know the price of everything and the value of nothing"*, is *Oscar Wilde's* famous complaint in his novel *The picture of Dorian Gray* from 1891. But is he right?'

Right away another question as a warning shot, I thought, and by now I knew that this author wasn't going to answer it with a heartfelt 'yes'.

'In order to be able to judge this, we must first and foremost know the exact meaning of the terms *price* and *value*,' he went on as expected. 'Because as we must have gathered by now, these concepts have several meanings. And besides it can be questioned whether the content of both words differs as much as is often assumed and whether they even may be the same when looked at them closely. Price is mostly seen as the amount of money to be paid for a thing or service and in chapter 1 we did see that such an objective amount of money never is the same as the subjective value the product gives the buyer. As you know, this subjective value should always be higher than the price, or else he would not have bought the product. But *Oscar Wilde* didn't refer to this meaning of course. His saying was meant to indicate that people don't have enough appreciation for many valuable things or don't even recognize their value when there isn't a price tag attached to them. It's about values as mentioned before, like cultural, social, moral, esthetic and environmental ones. Most certainly people underestimate this kind of values, but the question is whether this is caused or strengthened by money, the uniform means of reduction. For it might be the other way round: exactly the lack of a good monetary calculation may be the reason why the value of many things is being underestimated. It's certainly the case with environmental values for instance: The idea that nature, air and water are free inexhaustible litterbins led to massive environmental pollution. *"Economists call this a 'negative externality': the negative effects not being expressed in the price, and therefore a surplus as the real costs are being overlooked",* wrote *Robert & Edward Skidelsky* in their book *How much is enough?*[1] This 'negative externality' was even there in the days of the great author, when the industrial revolution had left its negative marks, but it hadn't been realized yet that the real costs hadn't been completely expressed in the price. So if *Oscar Wilde* would have lived now, his saying should rather have been that people don't know the price of many values.

Valuing is, let's say, a specific profession, a skill that has to be learned. In business economics this valuing skill is in several varieties at the top of the 10 skills a business economist must have to practice his job properly. Think of balance valuing for instance, profit-and-loss-account, making investment plans or estimating the shareholder value. Especially this last doctrine of the *shareholder value* is quite at the centre in estimating the value of a company, even that dimensionally central to make *Douglas K. Smith* characterize it in his book *On Value and Values* as an ideology of *value fundamentalism.*[2] The fact is that there are other interested parties than just the shareholders, like employees, customers, suppliers and people living in the neighbourhood. In order to consider the values of all those involved, the attention must be focused on their mutual interests, on *stakeholder value.'*

Quite so, I thought, for it's my interest too that for example Unilever or Shell supply me with good products at a fair price and save the environment at the same time. So I have an interest in Unilever or Shell too as well as they have an interest in me and the environment.

'Money only plays an instrumental part in this. It's a tool to help with the quantitative calculation of our valuations, comparable to an abacus, but it isn't the valuation itself. This valuation takes place in our minds as a matter of fact. There value judgment comes into being and this is subjective by definition. Even value judgments that are purely objective at first sight, like calculations of the cost, can on closer consideration be reduced to subjective value judgments, as like mentioned before, any price or value has its origin in our minds. This mind is the great calculator and starts working as soon as it sees the light of day. And who knows, maybe even before.'

You're kidding? Calculating fetuses and babies? The young human being as *infans economicus?* Is this what the author claims? I tried to imagine it, but got stuck in the image of little squeaking robots.

'From a very young age we have to make choices and we are born with a certain taste and preference. But this doesn't mean that this innate taste will be a fixed blueprint for the rest of our lives, as on our way to the end it will be continually readjusted. Making the right choices doesn't go smoothly, it needs consideration and a lifelong learning process.

A first step in this learning process is reduction of things into functions. As long as our mind hasn't got a clue what's the purpose of them, it can't understand them nor associate with them. A thing must be 'consumable' for instance or 'cuddlesome' to make the young mind see the use of it. We link our first values to these functions, like delicious or dirty, soft or prickly. The appearance of things plays a part too. The baby brain thinks for example that a multicoloured rattle or ball functions better than a grey one. Hence, appearance must be considered part of the functions of things as well. We think of something as beautiful or ugly and during our whole lives we judge things on their design too.

Selecting and valuing is a skill we must have mastered in order to make the right choices in life. This doesn't only apply to business economists but to anyone. During our lives we develop a system of *'mental accounting'*, a kind of mental bookkeeping with which we calculate yield and cost from the past, present and future. Also on the basis of this we make our plans and decisions. This mental bookkeeping takes place partly automatically and unconsciously, but this bookkeeping is a mental administrative instrument that has to be refined more and more during our existence in order to be able to make the right choices.'

Mental bookkeeping? Was I doing it too? Yes, you will always think before you decide, but is this bookkeeping? Well, okay, you put the advantages and disadvantages side by side and you might see this as a form of debit credit. This always goes for things you buy, as the author elaborately explained with the purchase of this book. And yes, when I think it over more closely, you might never be able to escape this habit of mental calculation. It would always be 'either' this 'or' that, you had to choose all the time, and to deal with those damned alternative costs the author mentioned before. Those annoying opportunity costs that deprive you of your peace, as afterwards you never know for sure if you have made the right choice. Hadn't I rather …, you may think.

' So from a very young age we continuously have to deal with choices. In the beginning we make do with ordinal value judgments like better/worse, higher/lower, beautiful and ugly, revolting and tasty. We place these judgments on a subjective value scale, dealt with in chapter 3, even when the young brain doesn't realize it. Next this brain must learn to translate these ordinal value series into cardinal units and this translation from words into marks requires the necessary abstraction skills. Part of these skills is among others the ability to think in numerical relations, of which, within the scope of this book, cash prices are the main representation.'

Ah here we are again, I thought, the relative values!

'Through money, the ultimate means of reduction, prices will connect almost anything in the world to one another. And as anything has its price, the young brain learns soon enough: "How expensive bread has become!", he hears without grasping what's it all about, and "Can we afford that car?", "We must go out with the baby, but what does it cost to rent such a cottage?" By this the young brain starts getting prepared a bit for a cost-benefit analysis, a tool without which it will go wrong in later years.'

Once more this initial impetus to the *infans economicus*, I thought, and again the image turned up of a calculating squeaking little robot doing a cost-benefit analysis.

'If the parental voices come to the conclusion that a journey is out of the question because of a broken washing machine, the young brain witnesses a small case study of the calculating principle of exchange: 1 washing machine costs 1 journey. Hence at a very young age the brain gets acquainted with the basic principles of barter and learns something on relative prices. But for the time being it can't join these price discussions, as it doesn't know the language used for them. At the beginning its language is often restricted to incomprehensible gestures and sounds that have to be developed into signs comprehensible to everyone. Among these signs are not only words and images, but also figures, which are essential for thinking in monetary value relations.'

Yes, right, prices he means, I thought, I know by now.

'Anything will become comparable this way - heterogenic qualities change into uniform monetary quantities.'

I had heard him dwelling on it before, so what's the point in doing so once more? Didactics I guess, probably a rudimentary psychological remnant of his old job.

'Thinking like that is a form of thinking in relations of measurement, we have stated in chapter 2. Comparable for instance to lengths and weights, which are uniformly applicable too, regardless of the matter to be measured. Modern man inquires especially after 'how much' and less after 'what', he is mainly interested in quantities and less qualities, as we have stated explicitly a few times before, and by this he shows to have developed a good sense of abstraction.'

See, frapper toujours - go get your favourite German philosopher of money to state that abstraction skill belongs to a civilized world and the circle is round again, I thought.

'For the moment this calculative capacity of abstraction has reached its highest development stage in the monetarisation of the world view. Almost anything is expressed in money nowadays, by which the connected qualitative definitions are resolved into monetary quantitative units. Money is the ultimate means of reduction, as we stated before, following various philosophers.'

Sure enough, once more.

'The question is whether this is bad and whether it deprives society of part of its qualitative value perception. According to *Oscar Wilde* it does obviously, or he wouldn't have made his famous saying in that novel. And also according to a moralist like *Michael J. Sandel*, who almost nostalgically warns us that not everything can be bought with money.[3] But as a neutral answer to that question is impossible, we leave it at that and as calculating animal let's concentrate on our calculating brain.

At the beginning of chapter 3 we posed that nature, the things and events in themselves, don't have any intrinsic value (at any rate no value we have knowledge of) and the reality and value haven't got anything to do with each other, as our idea of value is subjective. All natural phenomenon and things are neutrally equal originally, was and is our opinion, following *George Simmel.*'

I groaned.

'The human brain starts arranging this amorphous unity and imposes value judgments upon it. It starts distinguishing sorts of values and places them in a subjective value scale, as we have said before in chapter 3.'

A rudimental didactic disorder, I thought once again.

'These values are intellectual abstractions of our experiences of reality and the way we handle things. By attaching value the brain first reduces things to functions, as we have said before. This reduction also means that the brain looks at things as tools. Tools to design life and tools to become happy.'

Oh dear, I thought, do I see everything around me as tools?

'Just try inventing an example this doesn't go for', the author challenged me.

I tried but failed.

'Take your bicycle for instance. It has the function of taking you to your job or to enjoy the scenery or do your shopping. All this is functional. Even cycling for pleasure serves the object 'pleasure'.'

Oh well, like that you can go on a while, I thought. But in fact I didn't succeed in finding a totally non-functional thing, or it had to be a piece of art - however this for its part had the function to please, annoy or surprise. So, if he meant it like this …

'It's hard to think of non-functional things, as our brain will probably not be able to see those things at all, to the brain they are just invisible. Even an insignificant thing like a dead twig broken off a tree, the human brain can't make much of it. It might out the corner of its eye unconsciously observe a functional necessity of natural processes or it might consciously see an example of the functional sadness of the cycle of life and death.'

Go on, the functional sadness of life and death, I repeated loudly, but what is the connection with money here?

'And our brains attach a judgment to all these things and each judgment is a value judgment that is going to be placed in a value scale. And because a lot of people have problems with mere qualitative judgments, they grasp hold of quantitative scores. Valuing, evaluating, calculating: with this our brains occupy themselves from birth, and what can be more obvious in our monetary society than translating these calculations as soon as possible into money, the uniform criterion?'

I've no idea, I thought. Mental accounting reduced to monetary mental accounting.

'Even though balanced verbal value judgments are indispensable in good and pleasant communication between human beings, with the help of numbers we arrange the greater part of our (mainly urban) surroundings. And in this world of numbers money has a special position, as besides being a means of exchange and hoarding, money is a means of calculation as well.'

Might be true, but money isn't going to help you in creating good human relationships, is it, or is it? But the author didn't go into that question.

Grading

'Hence the development of a wide verbal value spectrum also lays the foundation of value estimations in figures much resembling calculating report marks. 'Junk' means 'bad', so an 0 (F) or a 1 (D) at most, 'is okay' is 'good', a 3 (B), or 'great' means 'excellent': 4 (A).'

Or a number of stars as in art reviews, I thought. A book or a movie with 3 out of the maximum 5 stars got the report mark 2(C) from the art critic. And 5 stars is a 4 (an A). So real teachers they are these critics.

'Giving marks is just like giving verbal qualifications a way of judging. Actually giving marks is nothing else but translating these verbal value judgments into numerical judgments. I hope we have made this clear by now.'

Yes sort of, I smirked a bit in a forced way.

'It can be misleading because a quantitative judgment like that might suggest something being objectively quantifiable. Which is mostly the case for physical phenomenon, but hardly ever for psychological, social, nor for economical phenomenon. These are in most cases subjective value judgments, embroidered with a figure hoping to get the aura of scientific objectivity. But in spite of the apparent suggestive use and misuse of figures, we can't do without numbers.'

Related to this I suddenly remembered *"How to lie with statistics"*, a famous book by *Darrell Huff* from 1954, which I had never read however. But the title started leading a life of its own, being a warning sign for blind faith in numbers, schedules and diagrams which can easily give a biased view or be manipulated.

'So you have to be careful with the use of figures in territories in which there will be value judgments. There are hardly any fields where these judgments don't play a part. Perhaps in the so-called exact sciences, but for the rest? In the mental bookkeeping in our minds the figures are at least soft and pliable, as our valuations will be subjective and changeable. That means that mental bookkeeping certainly isn't a rational process and that a mind thinking in numbers isn't a guarantee either for the development into a rationally choosing human being. This assumption of a rationally thinking and acting person actually underlies the idea of the *homo economicus*. This 'economic human being' is a rationally working being driven by self-interest, aiming for maximum profit and maximum benefit. This in reality non-existent being is a concoction arising from the cult of rationalism, especially held by economists of the *Chicago School of Economics* with famous names like Milton Friedman and Friedrich von Hayek. These neoclassic economists based their rationality doctrine on two premises: the first is that man is a perfectly reasonable being and the second that he is completely well-informed on anything he buys or wants to buy.'

Well, it seems a lot of nonsense, I thought, because we are drowning in the deluge of shop supply, aren't we. Just look at a random product like jam in the supermarket: the amount of varieties you can buy!

The distorted money brain
'This model of the homo economicus is a rough and highly controversial simplification of human behaviour, because man is by no

means always a rationally calculating being. On the contrary, he is actually quite often an emotionally and illogically acting being, driven by many passions, and even cursed with a *'distorted money brain'* according to psychologist *Jaap van Ginniken*.[4]

This distorted money brain means that our financial observations are asymmetrical. This goes for our perception of profit and loss for example: the fear of loss is much stronger in most people than the hope of a profit of the same size. This greater fear of loss ('loss aversion') arises from the aversion to risk ('risk aversion'), which causes our distorted money brain making illogical choices in many economic and financial decisions, when looked at it statistically. This was researched by *Daniel Kahnemann* and *Amos Tversky* who developed the so-called *prospect theory*.[5] 'Prospect' means anticipation and Kahnemann and Tversky discovered that we practically always misjudge the risks of future uncertain situations. Unlikely chances will mostly be seen as much too high. For instance: there is a slight chance that a new washing machine will be broke within five years and yet we are prepared to take an extra (expensive) insurance for the years after the standard warranty period.'

Well, I suppose so, I thought, but my computer happened to crash after three years and I was very grateful for the extended warranty I had bought. Owing to my personal loss and risk aversion I saved quite a lot of money.

'This prospect theory is based on a few simple assumptions. The first is the relative character of money and profit and loss. We get used to a certain level of income or property and we mainly react to changes in it. The feeling in connection with it can turn out quite contradictory. Say you expect a rise in salary of about £300 a month, but instead you get only £100, it will feel more like a loss of £200 than like a profit of £100. The reason why is that this £300 is a *reference point* you expected. Such a reference point determines whether something will be charged as a profit or a loss in our mental bookkeeping.

The second assumption of the prospect theory is the already mentioned dislike of loss, the *loss aversion*. Loosing a certain amount of money or another valuable thing is more painful than the pleasure of winning something of the same value will give you. A famous experiment in which this is proven, is the bet in tossing a coin. The participants of this bet will get a loss of £100 if the coin falls on 'head'. They are asked next how much profit there has to be on 'tails' to accept the bet.'

Well £100 too, of course, I immediately responded. But I was wrong:

'Research has proven that there are only few people that accept an 'honest' chance of a profit of £100. The fear of loosing this £100 is that big that there are only a few who accept £110 as possible profit and those who go into such a bet for that amount are often gamblers, arbitrageurs or economists. But the average man demands a profit of about £200 on 'head' to be able to psychologically stand the chance of loosing £100 on 'tails'.

This fear of loss can become that great and the confrontation afterwards with it that painful that people take their lives. The German billionaire *Adolf Merckle* threw himself under a train after a loss of 400 million Euros in a bad speculation with Volkswagen-shares. He expected these shares to drop after the economic crisis of 2008, whereas the price actually started increasing highly during a short period. Because of shame and loss of face he decided to commit suicide. More often news may be heard on the increase of the number of suicides after financial disasters - bankers and traders jumping out of the window or from the roof, but also 'ordinary' people who are up to their necks in financial trouble and don't see another solution.'

Yes, but these are exceptional cases, I thought, for who does really jump out of the window for a loss of roughly a hundred pounds? Well you might when you haven't got a red cent. Because according to the first assumption of the prospect theory loss and profit are relative, aren't they. So once more: indeed. It's all a question of psychology.

'Another well-known example of the functioning of our distorted money brain is our price perception. In our culture we read from left to right, so at our daily shopping we first see the whole pound figure in front of the decimal point and only then what's next. Because of this a price of £1.99 rather enters our minds as £1 than as £2 and that's why the greater part of products will be labeled this way.'

Yes, psychological pricing, I know, I thought, but I won't fall for it. I immediately round up everything - plus an amount on top of it, as it costs time to buy something and my time is valuable. And I mostly add a part for travelling expenses, with the result that a bag filled with shopping from the supermarket of roughly £50 sooner will be calculated at £60 by me.

'In psychological pricing the figure 9 often has a key role. Jaap van Ginneken calls it *'the dictatorship of the nine'*.[4] Also apparent in great amounts. A car doesn't cost £30,000 but only £29,990 and this last tenner pushes our distorted price feeling towards £20,000.

Another example is the discount we can get. We sometimes make a long detour to get a few pounds of discount for a small purchase, but won't do this for the same discount for a big purchase. Our feeling tells us that we got (relatively) much advantage in the first case and that in the second case the same small amount of pounds hardly makes any difference.'

Well, relatively this may be true, but to my knowledge I never fall for it. If I read in a advertising brochure that my brand of shampoo is ten percent cheaper in the next village, I most certainly won't step into my car for it. I would only do so when I had to be there anyway.

Elastic purchasing behaviour and Gossen's second law.
'The calculating animal can be looked at in quite a different way, namely through his purchasing behaviour. "Tell me what you buy and I'll tell you who you are", to vary a well-known saying on reading behaviour. By this the calculating animal indicates what he appreciates and what he doesn't and what he is prepared to do for it in the practice of every day life.'

Why of course, I thought, but isn't this the same issue with which the author started his book? I mean the issue of balancing the subjective value against the objective value in the form of a price?

'This approach embroiders on what we started with in this book,' the author admitted, 'but let's try here and now to look at it from a different angle, the angle of the price and income elasticity.'

Oh dear, I thought, it's vaguely familiar to me from my schooldays, but if I remember well it was rather complicated.

'The price elasticity of a product indicates to which extent the sale or the sold quantity of that product reacts to a change of price. If the price of product X increases with 5% for instance and the sale of that product doesn't react to this or hardly at all, then economists will say that the demand for product X is inelastic and therefore we are dealing with a useful and non-luxury first necessity of life. But if with a price increase of 5% the sale declines with 10% for instance, then this product obviously isn't in great demand, and it isn't a first necessity of life. In terms of the value calculation we are dealing with in this chapter, it has to be concluded that in the first case product X is placed relatively high in de scale of value by the consumer, and in the second case much lower. In general we may take for granted that the first products the consumer buys and which he continues buying regardless of the price, must be the most valuable for him.'

Really? I thought, I'm not sure. Because I can think of a number of to me quite valuable things I definitely can't afford.

'This doesn't mean of course that you can buy all you can possibly wish for', the author immediately reacted. 'As most people are tied to a limited budget.'

Just what I meant, I thought.

'Let's have a closer look at that budget. Its size is determined by the income and of course the capital has a part in it. But here we just confine ourselves to the income and question what's the effect of a change in income on our shopping behaviour. And again the conclusion is that the effect is related to the kind of products we want to buy: first necessities of life or luxury goods. If the family income decreases with eight percent for instance and the family continues buying as much potatoes as before, the economist will conclude that potatoes are part of the necessary and therefore useful first necessities of life for these people. Hence the *income elasticity* for potatoes is 0. (In very poor families the consumption of potatoes may even increase at the expense of other more expensive food when the decrease of income gets larger - the economists calls it an 'inferior good' (which doesn't indicate the quality). But mostly the income elasticity is positive, because if you earn more you will generally spend more and in case of a decrease of income spending will drop too. When the income elasticity for a product is quite large, it's mostly a luxury good we give up first at a decrease of income. So when someone immediately gets rid of his car at a decrease of income of eight percent, the car obviously belongs to the dispensable, hence to the luxury goods.'

Immediately getting rid of the car at a decrease of income of 8%? Why not trade it for a smaller one? Rather a black-and-white example, I thought.

'Let's leave it at that with this short explanation of income elasticity. Most people are dealing with a limited income and they have to spend their money as well as possible within this budget restriction. But within this budget restriction the price elasticities of the quantity in demand nevertheless are a good indication of the things that are more or less valuable to consumers. And this idea of value is the central item in our reasoning.'

Why, of course, the idea of money and value always going on in our minds, it almost escaped my mind.

' Such a price elasticity is usually expressed in a number. In the example above we made the price for product X increase with 5%. In the first case the sale hardly decreased, let's say with only 1%. The proportion of 1% quantity decrease to 5% price increase means a price elasticity of -1/5, which is inelastic. An inelastic demand like this suggests a relatively valuable first life necessity. In the second case, when with a similar price increase the quantity demanded decreases by 10%, the proportion is a quantity decrease of 10 % to a price increase of 5% therefore or a price elasticity of the quantity demanded of -2. The economist evaluates the product as being less valuable to people, a luxury product. This might look a bit contradictory, a luxury product being less valuable than a first life necessity, but when seen from human need, it is though. So it's called *first* life necessities for a good reason. Because without things like water, food and basic clothes we will die. Luxury goods aren't first life necessities exactly for this reason, as we can live without these products. Perhaps not as pleasantly, but nevertheless.

In the terminology of utility and marginal utility: first life necessities are generally more useful than luxury goods and the marginal utility of the last spent pounds on first life necessities is mostly higher therefore.

In chapter 3 the concepts 'need' and 'utility' as starting points for value creation have been dealt with extensively. As we also mentioned there, Aristotle saw money as a substitute of needs. With the help of this need-substitute the connection between price, need and utility can be represented nicely. Economists often use a demand curve for this. It's a diagram that shows the connection between various prices and the belonging sold quantities of a certain product during a certain period. This curve usually shows a decreasing line, which means that in case of lower prices more of this product will be sold and less when prices are higher.'

Rather obvious I thought - the more expensive a product is the less it will be sold.

'It seems a matter of fact', the author guessed my thought, ' but what is the cause of it?'

Well, I thought, well, if objects become more expensive, you can buy less, or is this too simple?

'The cause is dual.'

See? Too simple.

'A price change has two effects, namely: a *price effect* and an *income effect*. If a product's price increases, some people are going to look for a cheaper alternative. They want to replace the product that got more expensive by a cheaper substitute. That's why the price effect is also called the *substitute effect* of a price change. This effect usually functions in such a way that the cheaper alternative substitutes the more expensive one, but not always. The fact is that there are people too who on the contrary find it interesting to buy expensive things instead of cheaper ones. Those more expensive products are of better quality for instance according to them or are of higher standing. The reader may be able to think of a few examples of products of high standing.'

Well, it isn't that difficult, I thought. Caviar for example, expensive wines, a three-star restaurant instead of the Chinese takeaway, cabriolets, a luxurious cruise instead of a boat trip along the Rhine ...

'But what exactly happens to the value perception in the consumer's mind at a price change? Does the product get another value to him? Has a product that got more expensive become less valuable to him and is this the reason why this price effect caused a sale decrease of the product?'

It's not just that, I thought, as you will have less to spend by it: the income effect, as the author called it.

'The answer is yes and no.'

Exactly, I thought, it's economics, isn't it?

'Moreover it's the question whether we ask the right questions.'

A bit of a scatterbrain this author, in my opinion.

'Let's start with this yes and no answer to the question of the change of value by the price effect. On the one hand the answer is yes, because the utility of the spent money on that product decreases by the price increase. But on the other hand the answer is no, because the value of the product itself doesn't change by the price increase. And this will mainly answer the question whether we ask the right questions on value.'

Oh dear! What? I don't get it! I called nearly in despair. Explain yourself!

'We not only look at the product itself when we buy it, do we, but we look at the price as well.'

Yes sure, but hadn't he started his book with it? By saying that the subjective value I expected to get from the book had to be higher than its objective cost, that is the price, or I wouldn't have bought it? Is he starting all over again?

'But what are we doing exactly, when we oppose a thing to its cost or its price? What are we looking at? Exactly which value do we judge?'

My goodness gracious me, what a silly question, in that case we consider whether this thing is worth the money of course, I thought.

'We mainly look at the subjective value or the utility of the amount of money we had to pay for the article in question then and less at the value of the article itself. A good example of this is our behaviour during the clearance. In the clearance we buy clothes for example that we find too expensive when they are 'new', but that we want when they have been reduced in price. Has this article of clothing become more valuable by the reduced clearance price? No of course it hasn't, but the subjective utility value of the pounds spent on this clearance article has increased by the decreased price. It's caused by the increase of the proportion *Value clothing article X/Price clothing article X* due to the decreased price. This proportion shows the experienced benefit by the pound. We'll get into it in a minute.'

He has a point there, I thought, as I had to admit that I sometimes buy things in a sale that I normally find much too expensive.

'We wish therefore that our pounds bring in as much benefit as possible. And when we think that those pounds bring us more pleasure elsewhere, we take the money there. And which law can be recognized in this? Which famous law we have already mentioned in the first chapter?'

Do I have to guess? I thought. I'm not fond of riddles. A bit childish.

'Gossen's second law!' the text triumphantly crowed at me.

Of course, what else could it have been, I grumbled.

'Do you remember? It's the law that says that the total benefit you can get from your income can be enlarged by shifting your spending. So we mainly have an eye for the benefit money gives us when spending it and not immediately for the thing we buy with that money.'

What? But aren't they inextricably bound up with each other? I thought. For the benefit of money is a derivative of the things we buy with it, isn't it? Or is it?

'This may sound a bit odd, as you go to a shop to buy something you need or you think you need and hope to derive great pleasure from. That you have to pay for it, oh well, too bad. So you think of the things first and only then of the money - you believe. But do you? If you judge a product and think: gosh, how expensive!, what exactly are you thinking?'

That it isn't worth its money, I thought, but it's a lot of thinking in succession, I thought.

'Then you will think: I won't spend my money on that, as I can use it in a better way. And by 'better' you mean more useful. Meaning that the money needed for this expensive product can give you more benefit elsewhere.'

Rather obvious, I thought, but why does he make it so complicated?

'It may sound rather long-winded, but actually it boils down to the fact that you really only look at how much benefit your money gives you if you spend it. But I have to admit: this benefit depends on the proportion between the benefit of the bought product and the price of it', the author explained, 'like above with the article of clothing X.'

Hence the benefit of the thing itself as well, I concluded. What a whirlpool!

'That means that a price decrease of the product can give a higher benefit by the pound and you may want to buy more of it, because you get the feeling that you spend your money in a better way, that is more useful. Agreed?'

Agreed? Did the author want to know if I agreed? Or that I understood? Yes sir. I understand, I said as a good boy as if the master stood in front of me in person.

'Now that we have got this far as to having reduced the benefit of a purchase of a product to the benefit of the money given by the purchase, we have to go one step further and ask ourselves which benefit exactly we are talking about: the average benefit or the marginal benefit?'

What? Average or marginal benefit? What's the guy talking about?

'So, are we talking about the average benefit of for instance our total monthly spending or just about the benefit of the money of our last bag with shopping or the last thing we just bought?'

What does that matter? I thought somewhat grumpily.

'Because as in each spending it's by definition at the moment of this spending always about our last spent pounds, we are dealing with the marginal benefit of those last pounds. And to be more precise within the framework of Gossen's second law, we had better look at our last spent pound only and ask ourselves how much benefit this pound has given us.'

What a load of nonsense! I cried out loudly. Why not the benefit of the very last penny then!?

'But this is pure theory,' the author tried to calm me down, 'theory used in textbooks with which you can do nice number work. Let's just check our steps here and joke about these sums presented to pupils or undergraduates. In short, a didactic intermezzo therefore, a small calculation example as a kind of entr'acte 'for education and enjoyment':

Intermezzo: Gossen's second law in an imaginative practical example

Mary Cameron got forty pounds as a birthday present to buy a nice object for her windowsill. She decides to spend the money on flowers and plants and wants to put a few pounds in her piggy bank too. She supposes that a bouquet of flowers will cost £3 and a pot of plants £5.

Mary is a lady with a rather rational attitude and therefore she is going to find out exactly which benefit the sale of the flowers will give her. For that purpose she designs the schedule below for her total number of expected 'utility units' or subjective value units. She calls her total benefit TU (Total Utility).

FLOWERS			PLANTS			SAVINGS		
Number of Bouquets	TU		Number of plants	TU		Number of pounds	TU	
0	0		0	0		0	10	
1	54		1	75		1	19	
2	99		2	135		2	26	
3	129		3	175		3	29	
4	138		4	200		4	31	
5	141		5	215		5	32	
6	138		6	220		6	32	

Mary aims at a maximum total benefit by spending her £40.

How many bouquets of flowers and how many pots of plants does she have to buy to succeed? How much does she save in that case? In order to assist you as a calculator we added some extra columns in which some intermediate calculations can be filled in. But which ones? Think of both of Gossen's laws when doing so.

We'd like to keep the reader dangling on this puzzle's right answer, which we will give at the end of the chapter. Try to find out the correct answer for yourself first. The next digressions may be of any use.'

Ugh, I thought, a school sum! I detest doing sums and I have no intention at all to put any energy in doing them. What other readers intend to do is up to them.

'In real life there might be nobody to bother with this kind of calculations.'

Good lord, you don't say! A fellow or girl has better things to do!

'Nobody will worry about the quantity of benefit it will give her when buying a bunch of flowers. She buys the bouquet when she feels like it, period. But this 'feeling like it' obviously is nothing but a value variation, just like what we call a 'nice' flower bouquet or a 'snug' plant for our homes. All of them ordinal value judgments, that is utility judgments.

But our Mary evidently knows exactly that her purchase of the first bouquet gives her a number of cardinal 'utility units' of 54, whatever that may be. And the next bouquet will give her 99 utility units total. Hence an extra or marginal benefit of 45 units ... but I won't give away more for the time being.

Let's go on first with the underlying line of thought in this. For, however silly all this may seem, when we buy something, we implicitly give a value opinion in terms of the benefit the money spent on it will give us. And this benefit is the proportion between the marginal utility of the product and the price. So when you bought this book, you unconsciously had in mind the proportion *"Marginal utility of the book / Price of the book"* with which you determined how much benefit or subjective value this spending was expected to give you. And next you also compared in your mind this marginal money utility with the marginal money utility of another potential spending, a CD for example. As you could only spend that money once, you had to choose and consciously or unconsciously a second calculation went on in your mind of the type *"Marginal utility of a CD / Price of a CD"*. (Is it going to be a bit clearer what you must fill in in the empty columns of the example above?) And if you belong to the group of consumers who read the advertising brochures word by word and who look twice at their money, there will be a third and a fourth calculation of the same type, and after that a fifth and a sixth and perhaps even more. People who are keen on spending each pound as useful as possible, are true followers of Gossen's second law. They will spend entire days on comparing prices and looking for the best special offers. At the start of the sale they will be pushing forward until the doors of the shop open in order to be the first to throw themselves on the reduced articles and enlarge the benefit of the pounds to be spent there. Their marginal money utility as a matter of fact.'

I started to get the feeling to be in a merry-go-round. Wasn't the guy saying the same all over again?

'After having presented Gossen's second law as a comparison of proportions between marginal utility of a series of products and their prices, it's obvious at a glance which three factors may cause an increase of the benefit of a spending of money. Namely either a greater utility of a certain product, or a lower price, or a switch to another product.'

Or all three of them of course, I reacted at once.

'Or a combination of all three factors of course', the author echoed my impulsive reaction. 'Because the price effect of a price change doesn't only have its origin in a higher or lower benefit of the money spent on a certain product, but also in the benefit of the money of a substitute product. And if that substitute product's price changes in its turn, it will have consequences for the sale of the first product and others too. But this competing effect is not restricted to clearly provable substitute products, for in reality all products compete with one another. Thus a holiday trip by train doesn't only compete with a bus trip, but also with a new LCD TV or a luxury coffee-maker for instance. It sounds a bit farfetched, but the purchase of a luxury coffee-maker cuts down the remaining budget for a holiday trip. Most people are forced to make such choices owing to their limited income. And besides they can't do everything at the same time because of lack of time.'

Stress of choice, I thought, it sounds familiar.

'After having made clear that a price change of a product not only effects the product's sale itself, but also those of other products, an elasticity standard can be attached to it, namely the *cross-price elasticity*. The word 'cross(wise)' meaning that a price change of one product influences the sale of another product. This crosswise (mutual) influence can go both ways dependent on the interrelationships of these products. Two or more products can actually be mutually *substitutable* or *complementary*. Examples of substitute products are coffee and tea, car and bicycle or public transport, and like in the example above flowers and plants. Complementary goods are for instance car and petrol, bread and filling, and a printer with inkjet cartridges and paper. Now the question will be which effect a price increase of coffee for instance will have on the sale of tea. These products are mutually substitutable to a certain extent ...'

Well, not for me, I thought, for I don't like tea.

'..., but not entirely, as there will be confirmed coffee drinkers too of course who will never switch over to tea, whatever coffee may cost. But in general a higher coffee price leads to a reduce of the sale of coffee and an increase of the sale of tea. So the crosswise relation between the price of the coffee and the sale of tea is positive. When coffee gets more expensive by 10%, it may lead to 2% extra sale of tea, which means a positive cross-price elasticity of +1/5. With complementary goods this elasticity is negative, because if for instance petrol becomes more expensive and causes people to drive less, the car sale may be influenced negatively as well.'

Well, I'm not sure about that as more expensive petrol may also lead to an extra sale of economical cars. And then this cross-price elasticity is positive, isn't it?! What clever thinking of me. But the author didn't pursue the matter.

'After this brief analysis of the price effect or the substitute effect, we need to talk briefly about the income effect of a price change', he ignored my car-version. 'Price increases generally include a lower real income, meaning that we can buy less goods with our present income. Looking at the changes in the price level of all the total goods and services, we are speaking about inflation or deflation. These macro-economic terms will be dealt with extensively in chapter 8 and 9. Here we will restrict ourselves to the micro-economic income effect of a certain price change, and wonder what will be the consequence for instance of an increase of the gas price. Will there be less consumption of gas? There probably might be, but how much and by which cause?'

In that case we will turn down the thermostat a few degrees, I thought, but not too much or I will freeze and be forced to put on a warmer pullover - but isn't this just an ordinary price effect?

'That's a tricky question to answer. Are we consuming less gas owing to the price effect or owing to the income effect of an increased gas price? Or both?'

It will be both, if he puts his question this way, I thought.

'By both probably, but both causes cannot be easily separated in actual practice. If you don't turn down the gas heating after an increased gas price, but it makes you buy less steak, you might conclude that the price elasticity of gas is 0 and the income elasticity is positive.'

What? Positive? You buy *less* steak owing to the price *increase*, don't you?

'Why positive?' the author repeated my question. 'Because the increase of the gas price is the same as a *decrease* of your real income and this decrease leads to *less* consumption of steak. A minus divided by minus is plus, as we were taught in primary school.'

Okay, all right, you made your point, I gnashed. Have we finished this pliable purchasing behaviour, this weighing up and this irrational money mind, by now?

'This will be it for now on the cult of the rationally calculating animal. In the next chapters we will come across this animal once more, because his mind is a kind of calculating slot machine, trying to conjure up similar symbols of fruit in order to fill the till. But whereas 3 similar fruit symbols in a slot machine in the amusement arcade will be enough, you will need a few extra in real life. As we have seen in Gossen's second law. This law can be applied to the super slot machine of life, where you have to get an equal marginal utility per pound in all possible directions of spending in order to fill the till with money utility as much as possible.'

My till with money utility? Somewhat feeble this metaphor, I thought.

'Seen like this, Gossen's second law is a kind of instruction for handling the slot machine of life, but the chance of the uncountable marginal money fruit ever getting really equal, is minimal. But we never stop trying. Weighing the pros and cons. We are continuously calculating value judgments, whether or not consciously. Judging is a human habit, hard to get rid of. It's our nature. And as soon as we possibly can, we add a figure to each value judgment. Preferably in the form of an amount of money, a price, for it's easier to compare priced value judgments with each other than unpriced ones.

Thus judging and calculating is part of our nature, it's our second nature. Parallel to it this nature tries to gain possession of more and more on all fronts. In the next chapter we will go over a special case of this calculating and possessive nature with a fine-tooth comb. There we will ask ourselves how natural it is to want our possessions to grow constantly. Because everyone wants to have more and more, as we posed in chapter 3 referring to Mandeville, Schopenhauer and Hobbes. And this desire for more shows itself too and perhaps particularly in our longing for more and more money. A well-known way to get more money, is to make it grow by lending it out at an interest. But how natural is this? Is money a natural, fertile product that can grow just like a plant? This question and the related question whether charging interest is fair, caused many philosophers and clergymen to fly at each other in the past.'

Notes

1. Robert & Edward Skidelsky, *How much is enough? - Money and the good life,* London 2012
2. Douglas K. Smith, *On value and values - Thinking Differently About We in an Age of Me,* chapter 7, New Jersey 2004
3. Michael J. Sandel, *Niet alles is te koop- De morele grenzen van marktwerking* Utrecht 2012 (*What Money Can't Buy. The Moral Limits of Markets,* New York 2012)
4. Jaap van Ginneken, *Gek met geld- Over financiële psychologie),* Antwerp 2010
5. Written on among others by: William Poundstone, *Priceless - the hidden psychology of value,* chapter 16, Oxford 2011

The answer to the imaginative practical example of Mary Cameron
In the empty columns we have to fill in the course of the marginal utility and the marginal utility per pound. MU = Marginal Utility; MU/P = Marginal Utility per pound. (In the savings column this fraction has been omitted, as the last saved pound is the marginal utility of that pound too by definition.)

FLOWERS				PLANTS				SAVINGS		
Number of Bouquets	TU	MU	MU/P	Number of plants	TU	MU	MU/P	Number of pounds	TU	MU
0	0		0	0	0			0	10	
1	54	54	18	1	75	75	15	1	19	9
2	99	45	15	2	135	60	12	2	26	7
3	129	30	10	3	175	40	8	3	29	3
4	138	9	3	4	200	25	5	4	31	2
5	141	3	1	5	215	15	3	5	32	1
6	138	-3	-1	6	220	5	1	6	32	0

Mary Cameron has got £40 at her disposal. She aims for maximum benefit at the spending of this budget. How must she spend her money?

According to Gossen's law she must try to equate the marginal money utility of the last spent pounds on both flowers and plants as well as the saved pounds, because only then she won't get a higher total utility by further shifting of her budget. She buys x bunches of flowers at £3 per bouquet and y plants at £5 per plant and she saves z pounds at 'a price' of 1 pound per saved pound. So her pattern of spending is $3x + 5y + 1z = £40$.

Gossen's second law says that MU/P has to be equal for these three spending categories in order to get a maximum total utility.

After some searching we find in the schedule that she has to buy 4 bunches of flowers and 5 plants and has to save £3. In that case her budget of £40 will be totally spent: $3 \times 4 + 5 \times 5 + 3 = £40$. Then her total utility will be $138 + 215 + 29 = 282$ utility units.

7 (IN)FERTILE MONEY
On natural and unnatural growth and the interest prohibition.

'I'm not made of money or do you think that money grows on trees in my garden? We use these expressions to indicate that you can't always get what you want financially. Besides there aren't trees like that at all. Money isn't a natural product, it doesn't bear young if you plant a coin or a banknote. It won't result in a plant or a tree. Nor in animal offspring like a pig, a piggy-bank at the most. Money doesn't have reproductive organs, *Aristotle* said. This remains to be seen however, if we believe *Michel Foucault* saying that " *it was established by divine providence when He put gold and silver mines in the ground and made them extend slowly, just as plants are growing on earth and animals are multiplying. Among all things man may desire or need and those glittering hidden veins in which metals are growing in the dark, is absolutely a connection.* "[1] We have to bear in mind that he said this as part of the 'episteme' that applied to the 17th and 18th century.'

Episteme? I vaguely remember having heard it once, but don't ask me …

'An episteme can be described as *"an entity, to be dated per period, of conscious and unconscious presuppositions, which, as a driving force, enclose a broad process of thought and action"*, according to the course 'Epistemology' of the (Dutch) Open University'.[2]

Rather broad this definition, I thought. A bit of a reservoir term like that.

'But within this scope of thought of the 17th and 18th century, Foucault poses here that precious metals grow in a natural way just like plants and animals. And as money has often been linked to those metals, the conclusion can't be but money being able to grow in a natural way too. This thought may probably have been strongly denied by Aristotle. But why actually? He must have known about the existence of gold and silver mines too? And in his own time he could have seen for himself that gold and silver stock were constantly growing, couldn't he? Would he have thought that a certain, fixed gold and silver stock was circulating in the world? Unlikely. But if he knew that the world stock of precious metals could grow owing to natural causes, why this dogmatic assertion on the unnaturalness of money? All the more since money was associated with these metals to a considerable extend in his time as well.

Unlike pigs, horses or land, money is infertile by nature, so *Aristotle* said. By 'land' first of all arable and dairy farming areas were meant. But what about mining areas? How did he view the extraction of minerals? In those days gas and oil were unknown, but many natural products were used: sand, gravel, clay, loam, limestone, natural stone and there was even bronze and iron, to mention a few things. And of course gold and silver. Did Aristotle consider these products fertile or infertile? That's an important question, because if he would have judged them 'fertile', money as a derived product of those materials should have been labeled 'fertile' as well in my opinion. Hence our conclusion that the amount of money can definitely grow owing to natural causes, even when most growth of money isn't from natural origin nowadays and is steered or adjusted by (central) banks.'

But can't money grow in a different way? I threw in. Isn't it possible to put it in the bank, invest it in stocks and shares or invest it otherwise?

'What we call return or growth of money nowadays, is of quite a different order than the natural (in)fertility mentioned before. Our growth of money is artificial, synthetic, it hasn't got anything to do with natural processes. At the most you might say that growth of money is connected with the growth of economic factors like production and consumption. But even this is only partly true, because Central Banks are free to pump money into society without the need of anything productive as compensation. We will enlarge on that later. Now we will concentrate on the question whether money is a fertile or infertile product by itself. This question has exercised many minds in ancient times and in the middle ages, as asking interest for a loan is or isn't morally condemnable depends on the answer to that question.

The English verb 'geld' means to castrate or to cut. But it's unclear whether the resulting infertility has any etymological connection with the Dutch and German word for currency 'geld' and the old English word 'gild', which means payment and sacrifice. It seems easy to prove by experiment that money is infertile by putting it in the ground as a kind of seed and wait and see what will happen: as said before, there won't shoot a money tree or bush from it. And a planted gold coin won't result in a gold vein either, nor will a silver coin result in a silver vein. But all of this isn't proof for the infertility of money. The natural growth of precious metals, Foucault referred to, although being a process of many years, is nevertheless a kind of proof for the fertility of money. In the past people used to bury pots filled with coins, but not for the reason that they believed these coins would multiply themselves into fruit bearing plants. Money pots were buried for the protection of plundering and theft. For the lack of banks or a safe, you had better find a good hiding place for your coins, which meant burying them in your garden or on your land. In those days there weren't any metal detectors the enemy could use to trace and rob the gold and silver. In archeological excavations beside loose coins these brimful pots were sometimes found.

Hereafter we will return at length to this hoarding and dishoarding of money, because it's of importance for the understanding of the idea of money growth. But first something more on this monetary fertility discussion.

Following Aristotle, *Thomas of Aquino* (1225 - 1274) wrote in his *Summa Theologica* that coins can't bear coins *(nummus non parit nummos)*. This supposed infertility of money was connected with his idea that money is a consumable good and not a durable consumer good.[3] Different from durable consumer goods like land, house and horses, consumable goods will perish when appropriated, Thomas of Aquino said. In itself this difference is accurate, but his proposition that money must be considered as a consumable good is doubtful. In chapter 3 we described that the value of consumable goods will disappear after consumption, as these goods themselves no longer exist after consumption. But that doesn't imply that money used for consumption will be gone as well! Thomas of Aquino seemed to believe however that together with the consumed good, the money used to pay for it will be 'consumed' as well. You can often hear people say that you have to keep an eye on your spending, as each pound can only be spent once. This may be true on a micro-economic level, but not in a macro-economic sense, as in reality the same pounds are circulating again and again. It's true not immediately in your own purse, but in society as a whole. The same pound is spent again several times each year. It's called velocity of money (rate of circulation). So money is reused again and again: paper money and coins are replaced when the issuing authority considers them worn-out. Would it be a consumable good then or a durable consumer good?'

Okay, but is it right to say it one-to-one like that? I wondered. I mean, is money itself actually a good? Surely not? It represents an undefined claim on goods and services, but a claim in itself isn't a product, is it?

'And besides it's the question whether money is a good at all, even when it has a price.'

Aha, see, the author agrees with me here: money not being a good.

'As it happens money can't be two things simultaneously: money and a good. It's one or the other: either it's money, or a good. These two functions that exclude each other even apply to commodity money. As soon as a good serves as money, it's withdrawn from the commodity cycle and ends up in the money cycle that runs in the opposite direction in the diagram of the money cycle. Remember the distinction between proper and improper use of products we came across in chapter 2. Aristotle gave the example of a pair of shoes actually meant to be worn, but which can be improperly used as means of exchange too. In the first case the shoes are goods and in the second case money. Goods transferring from proper to improper use were called the metamorphosis of commodity by Marx, as mentioned in chapter 2, he considered this a kind of alienation. Those two functions an object can have, even apply to a product like gold. When gold is worn as a jewel or used in a gold lighter for example, it isn't money but a good. When these objects are being remelted in order to make coins of it, they change their character and become money.

But that still leaves us with the question whether money is a consumable or a durable consumer good. It's true, money isn't a good that belongs to the commodity cycle, but as we said before, it is used again and again, recycled you might say. Regardless of its form, each pound or dollar circulates several times a year. This phenomenon is known as the velocity of money (rate of circulation). When this velocity increases, the volume of the cycle of money expands too, the flow of money increases. It's unclear if Aristotle or Thomas of Aquino & co have implicated this velocity of money in their ideas on the growth of money, or that they only looked at the amount of money. Did they know the difference between *quantity of money* and *flow of money*? Did they know that the flow of money could grow by a higher velocity when the quantity of money remained unchanged? Did they link up the velocity of money and the supposed infertility of money? Because coins may not be able to bear coins as Thomas of Aquino thought, but the same coins can be passed from hand to hand more quickly and in this way make the flow of money distend.

Hereafter we will return to this question of the flow of money being able to grow without the increase of the quantity of money. For now we will stick to Thomas of Aquino's idea of money being an infertile consumable good. Hence interest being unnatural according to him, because interest is money, born from money and this presupposes that money is a fertile consumer good, comparable to land, horses or a house. This thought was the root of the medieval ecclesiastical prohibition on interest.

In order to get a better understanding of this interest prohibition, we will look in a different way at Aristotle's ideas on what he thought 'natural' and 'unnatural'. In doing so we will use a diagram, as described by *Arend Th. van Leeuwen,* among others, in his book *De nacht van het kapitaal (The night of the capital).*[4] He summarized the monetary - moral dilemma the Greek struggled with and linked Aristotle's ideas to Marx's. This diagram presents a historical development based on the 'myth of the barter', resulting in:

NN	N	NP	P	PP
		W – (G) – W	G – W – G¹	G – G¹
oikonomikè	krètikè	allagè, kapèleia	chrèmatistikè	tokismos
home economics	gathering	exchange, trade	creation of	lending
	possessions		money	at interest

The diagram has been made up with two characters, N and P. N is the symbol of 'normal', 'natural', P is the symbol of 'abnormal', 'unnatural', in accordance with the first character of Greek *para phusin*, un-natural. So both characters indicate a contradistinction. In between is the transitional stage of exchange and trade, which is just morally acceptable, according to Aristotle.

But what does the word 'normal' or 'natural' mean to Aristotle? In his opinion the natural form of gathering wealth is a capable control of house and land (this was originally interpreted as economics by the ancient Greeks: *oikonomikè = home economics*; a synonym still used for the discipline 'economics' is 'home economics'). The methods of self-supporting accumulation of property considered 'normal' by Aristotle, are quite different from what we think normal nowadays. Those methods depend on the way of life: nomadic, agricultural, piratical, fishing, hunting or a combination of them. The piratical way of life is considered condemnable nowadays, but to Aristotle the conquest of a country or slaves was a 'natural' and 'legitimate' way of obtaining possessions: *"They simply live the life that their needs compel them to (...) This means, that even warfare, which hunting is part of, is a natural way of gathering possessions. And this means must be used both against wild animals and humans who are destined to be obedient by nature but refuse to be so. For this is the kind of warfare that is right by nature."*[5] The present plague of piracy might be considered normal by Aristotle: *"Some lives will get happy by a combination that corrects the deficiency of one way of living by adding a second one where the first one failed. Combinations like that are the nomadic life with piracy, agricultural life with hunting, and so on."*[5] Piracy was a great problem all over the Mediterranean sea in the fourth century, nevertheless, *"because everyone having the power to hijack a ship had a right to do so - even Athenian ambassadors on an official mission were known to profit from some quick extra earnings once in a while when they came across a ship with a valuable load"*⁶, relates *Michael Scott*. This piracy was an important cause of the coming into existence of banks. At the start of the fourth century B.C. in the whole Greek world coins were used, but the Greek cities of those days, like West-European countries before the introduction of the EURO, minted their own coins. These domestic Greek city-coins were usually only accepted as a currency within their own borders, which forced traders to change them again and again in each city. They got help from money-changers who placed their tables in every port and soon started to take charge of the money of the traders. These money-changers were the precursors of banks. The ancient Greek word for table is *trapeze*, which is bank in New Greek.'

Very funny, this piracy, but our V.O.C (Dutch East-India Company) guys weren't averse to this either, if you ask me, I thought, which made me think of a former Dutch prime-minister who without blinking referred to this superior V.O.C.-mentality.

'However morally reprehensible, also judged by modern standards, wealth gathered like this, is limited by a kind of natural border. But this doesn't apply to wealth earned with trade and especially with creation of money (phase P) and with lending out money at interest (phase PP), according to Aristotle. This is also connected with the idea the Greek had of their world as a closed, round system. Creation of money opens this closed world into *"a never-ending movement"*, Van Leeuwen says, *"it crosses the border of the ancient polis and the closed **oikonomia**, it leaves the magic circle of the classical world and like space travel it proceeds into the infinite universe."*⁴ The aversion of the ancient Greek to this boundless creation of money was therefore partly based on fear of infinity. Ancient universe was closed, modern universe of never-ending creation of money is infinite. More on this later on.

On the left of the kind of economic organization and accumulation of property (N) that Aristotle considered normal, we see the ideal situation he preferred of the self-supporting household (NN), we spoke about. Not only the family household is meant by it, but also the larger community collectives like tribal relations and village communities. *"But they aren't completely able to support themselves either"*, Klever observed.[5] *"Complete autarky (self-sufficiency) is only achieved in national connection, the pursuit 'by nature' of all individuals and households."*

NP, the middle position in the diagram, is an economy in which exchange and trade takes place, whether or not with the help of the medium money as a means of exchange. This situation is acceptable as long as money has no other function but a means of exchange and calculating unit and this function not being disturbed by hoarding money. Plato was of the same opinion. He didn't object to the use of money, but he thought that money shouldn't have another function than facilitating the daily exchange among households. The other function he meant, is the function of hoarding money, that is to say the possibility offered by money for unlimited accumulation of capital, for limitless gathering and storing property. "Money is there to be spent", might be his standpoint in a nutshell. He wanted to forbid the possession of gold and silver for the same reason, as wealth and luxury would generate bad qualities that would endlessly reinforce greed and striving for profit. *"The more money, the more worries / and hunger for more"*, Horace (65-8 BC) wrote more than three centuries later in his *Odes*.

The idea that accumulation of capital is at the expense of the equilibrium of nature, can later be found again with John Locke (1632 - 1704). Before money was invented there was a kind of state of nature according to him, where scarcity didn't exist. There was enough land for everyone to be cultivated for ample means of sustaining life. Taking more than you needed for support was useless, because the increased yield of your land was of no use. Moreover, the law of nature forbids products of the earth to rot and decay, as God ordained them for consumption. This means that in the state of nature *"anybody's possession was limited to a moderate part, that is as much as he can appropriate without harming others. In that time people ran more risk to get lost in the vast wilderness of the earth when they had lost their companions, than being in the disadvantage of lack of land for cultivating."*[7] This idyllic situation ended by the invention of money, which caused human society to change into: *'The realm of scarcity',* Hans Achterhuis quotes Locke again in his book of 1988 with the same title: "*I dare boldly affirm, that the same rule of property that every man should have as much as his making use of it, would hold still in the world without straitening any body; since there is land enough to suffice double the inhabitants, had not the invention of money, and the tacit agreement of men to put value on it, introduced (by consent) larger possessions, and a right to them".*[7]

Hence by the introduction of money, scarcity came into being, according to Locke. The fact is that money makes it easier to gather more possessions than one needs. Before that time there wasn't "*the temptation to work for more than man needs*" - we had better say that the technical possibility (hoarding with the help of money) was lacking for the greater part. In his opinion the introduction of money changed "*the intrinsic value of things*", which is the value that "*completely depends on the useful purpose things have for man*". By this way of looking at *intrinsic value* he meant, in contravention of the standard definition, the *utility value* we've also seen with Aristotle or Marx (the metamorphosis of commodities). According to Locke this is the value depending on "the **utility** of things" which is based on a subjective value concept, being the value that springs from human needs. In this connection Adam Smith speaks about the "*value in use*", the utility of a certain product in use - Aristotle called it the *proper use*. As opposed to *improper use*, which is called *"value in exchange"* by Adam Smith, or the *"power of purchasing other goods"* - the *exchange value* by Marx - in which our idea of purchasing power may be recognized.'

The latter part sounded rather familiar to me. The author may have mentioned it a few times before, but at the moment I'm not in the mood to look it up.

'Both Plato and Locke thought that money should exclusively have a mediation function, so nothing else but an exchange function. But in contrast with Locke, Plato thought that it didn't have to have an intrinsic value itself - it might as well consist of a valueless piece of paper or metal by consent. Considering that the first banknotes didn't appear until the 17th century, Plato's opinion on money may be called modern. Plato proves himself to be an explicit monetary functionalist, whereas John Locke took up the position of a true substantialist. This question of substance and function, the intrinsic and nominal value of money will be dealt with extensively in the next chapter 8. Inevitably we will come across the idea of 'value' and once more we will ask ourselves where the seat of value is situated: in the physical reality or in our minds.'

Well, I'm quite confident in guessing the right answer to that question meanwhile.

'But let's return to the diagram now!' the author brought me into line.

The diagram? Which diagram? Oh yes, the diagram of Aristotle and Marx, it almost slipped my memory.

'In the diagram two more symbols are added to NP, the characters W and G. These symbols introduced by Marx, and especially the combinations made with them, are fundamental in his analysis of the economic process. W = goods, goods for exchange (German: Ware) G = money (German: Geld). The transitional stage from G to G^1 indicates the transitional stage from money to more money, the growth of the quantity of money. It also explains why these symbols aren't present yet on the left side of the diagram. For there isn't any exchange going on there and not until being in the process of exchange does the concept of 'goods' (German 'Ware') change its character: from goods for use (utility value) to goods for exchange (exchange value) and from there to the next goods for exchange (exchange value), whether or not with the help of money: (W - (G) - W). In the chapters 1 and 2 of *Das Kapital (Capital)* Marx analyses this different character of goods and the 'ideal or imaginary form' in between: money. Exchange of goods, circulation of goods, basically implies the possibility of money as a means of exchange: hence the G in brackets.

With the adjoining category P we end up in the so-called *chrèmastistikè* (money creation). In the language of symbols of Marx's analysis, here the change from goods circulation into money circulation takes place, aimed at accumulation of money. In this change the birth of modern capital can be seen, Marx says. In the last category PP the climax of this process is symbolized by the combination G - G^1: accumulation of money with the help of money.

In the diagram the successive stages of exchange can be recognized:

Goods exchange: W (shoes) - W (food)

Exchange with money as neutral means of exchange: W - G - W

Exchange with money creation as a result of commercial activities: G - W - G^1

Exchange with money creation without commercial activities: G - G$^{1'}$

Whew, I thought, what does this remind me of? Hasn't the author written about this before? Let me leaf backward. The matter of the shoes sounds familiar - ah, there it is, chapter 2, under 'exchange or use'.

'In this respect Marx speaks about *"the metamorphosis of commodities"*, and also about *"a social metabolism".*'

See, chapter 2, I said aloud to myself.

'We already extensively explained it in chapter 2, when we raised the matter of the difference between exchange value and utility value. But now the diagram above gives a summarizing picture of how both Aristotle and Karl Marx viewed the historical development of the economic organization of society, with an implicit moral verdict.'

Hence, moralists, both philosophers, I thought, but aren't all of them, basically?

'Right from the central position in the diagram, the economy appears where money creation can be found. We can see Marx's symbols change places here too: the mediating exchange function of money in W - G - W changes into a function of money as an aim. In the language of symbols of Marx's analysis the turn from goods circulation into money circulation, aimed at money accumulation: from G into G^1. In this case still by means of commodity trade, but frequently merchants and traders used to have a rather dubious reputation, because it couldn't be understood how this trade could cause an added value and consequent creation of money. We often come across this idea of principally unproductive trade activities in history. We pointed out to this idea before in chapter 3, where some people thought that exchange couldn't be a source of value. As an example we named Benjamin Franklin saying: *"War is robbery, trade is deceit".*'

Oh yes, it came back, and Marx agreeing. By the move from simple goods exchange (with the help of money as means of exchange) into trade (by which money is earned), barter had developed into the creation of modern trading capital, as the author mentioned above. And this development wasn't considered productive by Marx, as trading capital couldn't cause any added value in his view, if I had understood correctly. Hadn't I read it in ... let me leaf backwards to chapter 3 ... ah, here it is: *"Turn and twist as we may, the fact remains unaltered. If equivalents are exchanged, no surplus-value results, and if non-equivalents are exchanged, still no surplus-value. Circulation, or the exchange of commodities, begets no value".* Pretty smart remembering this, even if I say so myself, I thought self-congratulatory.

'The creation of modern trading capital in the phase W - G - W^1 can, according to Marx, only be traced back to the double deceit of the merchant, who worms his way like a parasite between the buying and the selling party.'

Ah well, I thought, the trader as a parasite, the idea appeals to me. So, not only bankers, but also all kinds of merchants, basically don't add any value to society. But at the same time I had to shake off this thought, for where would we be without all those traders? Purchasing agents, salesmen, importers, exporters, distributive traders, wholesalers and retail traders, market dealers, shopkeepers - all these traders do have a function in the process of attuning demand and supply as well as possible, by delivering the producer's goods at the right customer in the right place and by doing so they create value. Products often must be transported from one part of the world to the other and someone has to organize it. Nonsense therefore, that all trade is parasitic and unproductive, I concluded. Strange, those people having such black-and-white opinions on it.

And then this other thing I didn't quite understand, which I hadn't come across before, namely the exact meaning of the word 'trading capital'. What did Marx mean by it? The working capital of a company? The word in its modern meaning is the capital needed for the operational management, say the working capital or the liquid assets used for the financing of supply, cash and buyer's credit among others. But besides working capital the company surely needs capital for investments in permanent assets like machines and buildings. Could any of this be traced back in the diagram of

Aristotle and Marx? Not by me anyway. For the central part was only about exchange and trade. Where were the investments and the investment capital? The author obviously had no intention as yet to give an explanation, as without mentioning it, he continued from trading capital to usury capital:

'Anyway, right from the economy with money creation (P), detested by Aristotle and Marx, lies the even more terrifying realm of the money economy in which money seems to fecundate itself when it is lent out at interest (PP). Then the trading capital changes into usury capital: $G - W - G^1$ will be reduced to $G - G^1$, as the link of the goods trade has disappeared. Money is traded for money and increases without the intervention of goods. Here Aristotle's *'unnatural reversal'* is complete, which we mentioned before in chapter 4. It's the present-day situation of money being traded with the only purpose of earning money by it. It's the financial world of hot money, inter-bank trade and monetary derivatives, the derived financial products sometimes no longer understood by hardly anybody.'

Oh yes, the financial duds that caused the bank crisis of 2008 and the subsequent misery, I thought.

'This obscure trade could prosper well within the endless creation of money. It's true, basic derivatives like *options* and *futures* are in general still relatively easy to understand. Options give you the right to buy (call option) or sell (put option) something during a certain term at a fixed price, shares for example. Futures are standardized forward contracts that are traded in the stock market. Originally futures were related to agricultural and cattle breeding products as an insurance for failure of the crop and epidemics in meager years. By the way, the very first known forward contract dates from the sixth century B.C. when the pre-Socratic philosopher *Thales of Miletus* once earned a lot of money by a transaction like that'.

Ah, yes, the story of the olive-presses, I thought, sounds familiar - what was it like?

'As he used to live in poverty, it was concluded that the philosopher served no useful purpose. But because of his knowledge of the stars he predicted in the middle of a severe winter that next summer would yield a rich olive harvest. As he didn't possess a lot of money, he gave securities for all olive presses of Chios and Miletus, which he could rent for low prices as nobody else wanted them at that moment. The olive harvest of that summer appeared to be very large indeed, which caused a sudden great demand for olive presses. Thales could let them for much money, by which he showed the world that the philosopher could easily become rich if he wanted to, but that his interest was orientated differently.

But nowadays forward contracts don't only refer to physical basic products like corn and oranges, but also to various financial values and a series of raw materials: foreign currencies, money market interest rates, bonds, gold, oil, copper and so on.

The problem with modern derivatives however, is that they have been made up of different kinds of other derivatives and that they can refer to a combination of different underlying values with different price movements and different conditions, which confuses the perception.

Xenomoney

The question is to what extent all those derivatives can be considered as money. They are values referred to as **xenomoney** by *Brian Rotman* in his book *Signifying nothing, The semiotics of zero*.[8] Xeno means foreign, but xenomoney isn't the same as foreign currencies, as these are foreign kinds of money. The dollar is a foreign currency for a European, but isn't foreign itself. When travelling to America, we change our Euros into this foreign currency. But according to Rotman xenomoney is a kind of money that gets its value by mere thought experiments in the money markets: *"Money governed by purely financial dynamics, (…) independent from the physically determined constraints of underlying trade"*.

True, but wait a minute, I thought, what's so special about it? Wasn't this the very issue of the whole book? I mean the author's proposition that money is always a mind thing? Meaning that in fact any kind of money is a thought experiment? Independent of the material reality?

'Rotman's remark on the *"physically determined constraints of underlying trade"* raises some questions on what he assumes to be the nature of money, as he seems to suggest that (real) money can only exist when representing a trade transaction, so with a transaction of goods or services as compensation. This is the traditional idea of exchange represented in the economic cycle, in which money streams in the opposite direction of goods and services. In other words: Rotman actually claims that money is only (real) money when there is a certain covering in the form of trade transactions. The total of all those trade transactions in a country during a year might roughly be called the national product. And this point of view on covering has much to recommend it, as money represents purchasing power and this purchasing power can only be realized when there is something there to be bought. But what money can buy is more than just goods and services. You can buy all kinds of rights for example, like the options mentioned before or CO_2 emission rights.

Options and futures however, are not meant to be actually enforced at the end of the term, that is to say to change them for physically underlying goods, but only differences in interest, price and rate are meant to be settled. This makes them more like insurance products than physical transactions, but there is a risk in the possibility to speculate with them, simply an solely on the basis of these price signals separated from real values: "*The strategies provided by options and futures for speculation and insurance against money loss caused by volatility of exchange and interest rates, become an inextricable part of what determines those rates*". Thus a kind of circular movement is created of self-affirming 'signs', characterized as postmodern by Rotman.'

Postmodern? What does that mean again? Let me look in *van Dale* (Dutch dictionary of Dutch language) - mmm, '*a term introduced by the German philosopher Rudolf Panwitz in 1917*' it says. Panwitz? Never heard of.[9] Let me check Wikipedia on postmodernism ... what's this? Do I read it correctly? They say that the word 'postmodernism' was introduced by a *John Williams Chapman* as early as 1870 to indicate a certain painting style following French expressionism. What should I think of that? Well, Wikipedia, you shouldn't believe everything written there, but a fact like that can't be made up, can it? I used to think that it belonged to some French intellectuals: Derrida, Barthes, Foucault, Lyotard, Baudillard, people like that. Let me return to *van Dale*: firstly it says, that it has got something to do with architecture, with '*the trend in the architecture of the eighties to get rid of the rigid functionalism of the last half century ..."* and secondly a philosophical meaning, *'... manifest in ignoring the distinction between high and low art and anarchistic combination of elements from various movements, genres, styles, techniques and media: Philosophic postmodernism is of the opinion that man is largely ruled by uncontrollable forces and therefore not capable of controlling the world as philosophers of the Enlightenment thought.'* But what is actually meant by *'ignoring the distinction between high and low art'*? A kind of eclecticism? Wait a minute, I must have a booklet on postmodernism somewhere, let me look for it ... ah, found it ... but an unambiguous definition can't be found there either ... it says somewhere that there is an essence of *"intense irrationalism"* with various *"ways of interpretation"* and that *"the term 'postmodernist' itself refers to a mixture of an historic period and ideological implication"*.[10]

Rather confusing, if you want my opinion. Let's continue. In the beginning of the next chapter it says that *'a lot of postmodernist theory is based on a skeptical attitude: and in this respect the contribution of philosopher Jean François Lyotard is essential.'* See: Lyotard, that's the one I meant. Wasn't he the real father of postmodernism? He was the man who attacked the 'great narratives', according to my booklet, like that of *'the progressing emancipation of mankind'* and *'the triumph of science'*, as those narratives had lost their credibility according to him. In his book *The postmodern condition* he says it like this: *'Simplifying to the extreme, I define* **postmodern** *as incredibility toward metanarratives'*[11] Extremely simple? Well, for now I'll stick to the postmodern idea that absolutely true narratives don't exist any more and that everything is some kind of fiction. This conclusion may be similar to the idea in this book I'm reading right now, that money basically isn't a great narrative either, but a kind of fiction in our mind.

'So xenomoney, that's what we were talking about. A kind of imaginary money, you might say, intangible and unverifiable. Intangible because its value is unrelated to the physical world according to Rotman and completely determined by financial signs. Unverifiable because it's different from all national types of currency and it's unguarded by any monetary supervision. Rotman mentions the Eurodollar as a specific example of this. They are deposit units denominated in US dollars with a term up to six months, which are kept in banks outside the United States. Hence they are unguarded by supervision and regulation of the American Central Bank, the Fed (Federal Reserve System). We won't enter at length into the historic background and development of the Eurodollar market here, nor into the further implications of this market for investors and borrowers of Eurodollars. The conclusion will do here that a rampant mega money bubble in this billion market is circling the earth, which actually is largely beyond the control and regulations of monetary authorities and is also circulating separated from the foundation of goods and services. The 'signs' that determine the value of xenomoney no longer directly refer to the economic foundation of the underlying cycle of goods and services, but to other signs which are chiefly related to financial expectations. They might be seen as a kind of chain of imagined values which show themselves in monetary values and symbols.

This xenomoney's independence from the limitations of physical trade transactions, as observed by Brian Rotman, might be called an example of postmodern deconstruction', my author on money continued. 'Deconstruction is a contraction of destruction and construction and here it means that (xeno)money has largely been separated from reality. This view goes well with the theory of the founding father of Deconstruction : French philosopher *Jacques Derrida*.'

Derrida? Not Lyotard? Well, whatever, the one a father, the other the founding father, what difference does it make.

'Considered like this xenomoney suddenly becomes far less frightening, as it's nothing but one of those nominal values separated from immediate reality, which from a great distance may be retraced to some real value, although often with many links: a value derived from reality, and therefore indicated as derivative. And indeed: the value of those derivatives seems to be determined by financial powers only and hasn't got anything to do with physical reality. That is to say not with the physical reality as it used to be in the past. Because the value of many financial instruments and especially derivatives of which the greater part often consists of the value of expectation, meaning the value that the instrument is expected to have at the expiry date. It's as if the postmodern manifestations of money point *"back into the future"*, as *Pierre Guillet de Monthous* once said: *"By creating new financial instruments like futures and options postmodern deconstructionists believe money to create and guarantee its own value."* [12] Trade is carried on in purely financial products instead of goods, but are pretended to be autonomous 'goods' instead of mere price contracts in the secondary market. And within these price contracts prices are agreed on which will be settled in future. With this we have discussed at least two characteristics of this so-called xenomoney: first the by Rotman assumed independence from physical trade transactions and second the by Guillet de Monthoux observed reference to future values.'

Expectation values, in fact, I thought. Not hard to imagine with the often heard slogans like consumer and producer confidence and their statistics in mind. Economic optimism and pessimism, all being a matter of an almost religious future dimension.

'But the first of both characteristics may be questioned. The by Rotman assumed xenomoney's independence from physical reality is deceptive insofar that there has to be a real underlying source somewhere, as concluded before: a goods and services transaction, or a certain real asset, even when this source is hardly recognizable and the whole construction of derivatives looks like a waterhead or a pyramid upside down, with only a hint of reality at the bottom and for the rest largely a financial bubble.'

And when this bubble has been inflated too far and blows to bits … well, history has shown us, I gloomily thought, because I had paid my lesson meanwhile. But, never mind.

'We think that the rest of his view on the independence between xenomoney and real trade transactions, is contestable as well, as he only looks at historically realized economic transactions and not at future ones. *Pierre Guillet de Monthoux'* cryptic indication that postmodern money points '*back into future*', is spot-on in our opinion: modern money's value depends mostly on how we expect it to be of use in future.'

Perfectly clear, I thought. As for the vague postmodern monetary deconstructionism, its vagueness had become a little less vague by now.

But it leaves this question of the '*circular movement of self-affirming signs*' as the author had called it before. This phrase was rather mysterious to me, as I wondered what exactly was meant by 'circular movement' and which 'signs' were meant. He had said one or two things on those signs, but that explanation didn't go well with what I thought to be monetary signs and with how the author had explained them before.

The circular movement to start with. That movement is likely to be nothing but a kind of economic cycle, I thought, except that the circulating signs no longer refer to economic flesh and blood, so no longer to goods and ordinary money, but to almost occult financial spheres.

Signs are symbols, as I remembered from chapter 5. Images on coins and banknotes are signs. Those signs represent a certain value and often refer to the monarch or the authority guaranteeing the value. In the past symbols of money used to refer to the underlying value of its origin, like corn or cattle. The author had explained this before. The purpose of all these signs was to support faith in the currency.

But now he spoke of 'self-affirming signs' related to xenomoney. Were they different from the ordinary financial signs like currency signs, interest and discount percentages, sum of money and account number? This was about 'purely financial dynamics' according to Mr. Rotman and he especially referred to derivatives, if I had understood it correctly. But well, embroidering away on it: what are 'purely financial dynamics'? it refers to prices, interests and rates, which Rotman claims to be unrelated to the 'physically determined constraints of underlying trade', but the author had already questioned this, as he thought that there had to be a real economic transaction in the end. For if this shouldn't be the case: would there be anything this merry-go-round of purely financial dynamics is *not* separated from? Suddenly it dawned upon me: from our mind! From our interpretations and expectations! So from our economic optimism or pessimism. Will it all be a matter of psychology? It's often said, that the whole economy is nothing but psychology, like human behaviour, whimsical and unpredictable.

Our future, apart from the certainty that all of us are mortal, is uncertain by definition. This uncertainty involves risks. And we try to protect and insure ourselves as well as possible against these risks. That's the reason why derivatives have been invented, which circulate as xenomoney in a postmodern cycle. Derivatives are rather to be seen as insurance products than as physical transactions according to the author. Okay, this may be true, but what's wrong with an insurance? Is there actually a lot of difference between a fire insurance and an insurance in the form of futures against the price increase of oranges? Isn't it essentially about ruling out and limiting risks, even when they are speculated with? And risk trade is trade as well, with the difference that there isn't an 'object' on the counter, but only a contract with a signature, by which just a lot of money can be earned.

And there was something else that surprised me: Mr. Rotman called options and futures examples of xenomoney, but why 'money'? You couldn't pay with this kind of derivatives, could you? You needn't try this in a shop: can I pay here with Shell or USBC options? Or may these derivatives be seen as a kind of money one way or other? 'The question is to what extend all these derivatives can be considered as money', wasn't it the first question with which the author started the chapter. Well?

'But first we have to dwell on the question of xenomoney and the question whether this is money and what can or can't serve as money,' he took up my thoughts at that very moment. Sometimes it looked as if I had a conversation with myself.

'Our proposition is that essentially anything can function as money, a lot of examples of it may be found in history. Various concrete, physical things from shelves to cigarettes, from salt to gold and from cattle to corn beside intangible symbols like marks on a tally-stick and numbers in a computer. So why not derivatives like options and futures? A few important reasons are the whimsical value development and temporary character of most derivatives: these are contracts with an expiration or settlement date, so with a limited duration. They will become worthless afterwards. As a consequence they can't be used as money, because money must have a long-lasting relatively stable value to function as such. That's why xenomoney is unsuitable as currency for daily use. But in the financial world it's enthusiastically used for trade and speculation, and derivatives to a certain extent count as means of financial security for other transactions, so within the financial cycle they can be looked upon as a kind of money.'

No real money therefore, I concluded, what a relief.

'But even when xenomoney can't be used as ordinary money outside the realm of the financial world of derivatives, that world has a tremendous effect on the real world and the financial bubbles that regularly come into existence in derived markets may cause tremendous shock waves in the real world - just look at the financial crisis of 2008 and its consequences.'

I'd better not react, I thought, let it pass, and pay attention to the lesson.

'To put it differently: postmodern monetization force deconstructs the idea of money representing something. Following Simmel, it may be called an example of the '*Principle of saving energy and substances*'.'

Simmel again, of course.

'That principle leads to a growing extensive use of '*representations and symbols*', without any agreement with respect to the content of what they represent. Money as a pure symbol fits into this development too. According to Simmel this '*way of life*' presupposes not only an increase of psychological processes - just think of the complicated psychological processes needed to understand the idea of 'banknotes security' - but also an upgrading (improvement, extension) of those psychological processes: a principal change of culture towards intellectuality.'

Banknotes security as a number of complicated psychological processes? I didn't grasp the deeper meaning of this sentence right then, but never mind that, because:

'We will go into the background of all these psychological processes in chapter 8 and 9', the author announced almost as a rescue.'There it will become obvious how even nowadays many modern human beings are still struggling with this idea of security and getting anxious by a seemingly unsecured currency. They can't understand and accept that money is nothing but a contract, as Aristotle stated before.

And perhaps unnecessarily: the postmodern deconstruction idea of the value of money as well includes that it depends less on what money represented in the past than on what we can do with it in future.'

Rather obvious, I thought: money is purchasing power and this purchasing power refers to the future by definition, doesn't it, to what you can buy with your money tomorrow. So, nothing special. Or had I become a streetwise postmodernist by now, not to see any problem here?

I groaned, money, xenomoney, imaginary money, not far from being monopoly money - but what's the substantial difference between money and imaginary money, I wonder? All money is imaginary essentially, wasn't it the message of this book? All money is just an idea after all, isn't it? It's a mind thing, isn't it? And what about fertility and infertility of money? Is some currency more fertile than an other? But I was too impatient again:

Natural monetary creation?
'After having gone astray, it's about time to return to the main road of this chapter, which is the question of fertility and infertility of money. In Aristotle's and Marx's diagram xenomoney is situated in the far right corner of the unnatural reversal of end and means, where money is supposed to make more money without the medium of goods transactions: $G - G^1$. Money apparently multiplies itself, by which it suggests to be an extremely fertile material. It's the present-day situation in which money dealing by far surpasses fundamental goods and service trade and the original economic cycle diagram is no longer relevant. In this cycle the monetary streams are real and neatly contrary with an exchange of goods (and services) for money. This exchange has been inflated now with a huge amount of monetary air frequently disrupting the economic system, like a kind of central heating in which an air bubble blocks the circulation of real hot water.

The question we ask again now, is whether all this monetary air is only causing unnatural growth. That is, only more growth of money, without any real growth. In Georg Simmel's time (1900) this financial air bubble hadn't been blown up as much as nowadays, but even then, compared to goods circulation, money circulation regularly happened to expand extremely and cause inflation. And shortly after Simmel's death in 1918, as an after effect of the First World War, Germany had to cope with a very high inflation rate, when because of an overloaded currency press measuring the circulation rate had become almost impossible, which made the price index develop like this:

1913 100
1922 147,479
1923 75,570,000,000,000

(Already in 1919 *J. M. Keynes* warned us about this in his *Economic Consequences of the peace,* when the conquerors imposed reparations to Germany which would be impossible to finance.)

Simmel thought though, that an increase in the quantity of money <u>always</u> has real effects - even in case of full employment and no increase of production in the short term. We have to bear in mind though that he wrote this long before the nineteen-twenties, when the German money flow caused a price explosion. But in more normal circumstances he distinguished the following three *"Dienste des Geldes"* in case of an increase in the quantity of money:

1. Simplification of trade
2. Improvement of mobility
3. Condensation

<u>Ad 1.</u> Money simplifies commercial trade and therefore more money means more and quicker exchange of goods and services.

<u>Ad 2.</u> This money-service resembles the previous one, but by 'improvement of mobility' Simmel means that more money also involves extra stimulation of economic activities that didn't exist before.

<u>Ad 3.</u> Condensation means concentration of greater sums of money owned by less people, in other words creation of capital. This creation of capital enables extra investments and new enterprises.'

Item 1 and 2 might make some sense to me, but the third item shocked me. Wasn't it just a veiled justification of unequal distribution of income and wealth? And this distribution had become more distorted than ever before nowadays, at a high speed becoming a lot more unequal, in a way that 1% of the richest people in the world own 99% of the wealth of the world. It's a bloody shame and the cause of much social unrest which may end in digging up the guillotine for a new kind of 'French Revolution'. Speaking about unnatural money, I thought, unnatural and infertile … Don't get tensed up, I said to myself, take it easy.

'It remains a debatable question whether this concentrated creation of capital by a few people is fertile or infertile and whether it might frustrate a natural well-functioning of money. There are solid indications that from a certain level, a distorted distribution of income is contra productive and unsettling to society. Economic growth will be unbalanced and unnatural then, irrespective of the answer to the question whether money itself is or isn't a natural product. So, is money principally unnatural and infertile or may it possibly become an unnatural self-abusing monster by a wrong economic organization and income abuse? Aristotle considered money infertile from the start, but this infertility becomes a kind of self-abuse, which enlarges the unnaturalness and the quantity of money by artificial synthetic growth stimulaters. In Aristotle's and Marx's diagram our present-day economic organization is to be found in this last stage, in which money creates money (G-G^1).

Aristotle & co may have thought money to be infertile by nature, they didn't consider money itself a discreditable product though, when its use should be limited to a means of exchange. So it's an unnatural and infertile product, but not a problematic one as a lubricant to make trade easier. Not until it's going to be used for hoarding, do problems start, as shown in the legend of king Midas. But as long as money is just a neutral means of exchange and the money stream stays in line by growing proportionately to trade activities, the growth of this money stream can be considered normal (stage NP in the diagram with money as an optional means of exchange: W - (G) - W).

A great part of present-day money growth isn't directly linked to trade activities though, and is artificially 'created out of nothing', like credit granting in banks (more on this in chapter 11). But we think this may be the flaw in Aristotle's argumentation on infertility, as this 'creation out of nothing' is certainly a human creation! And if we assume man to be part of nature, we can assume money created by him having a natural source as well, can't we? Doesn't it undermine the whole discussion on the difference between natural and unnatural money growth, and turn it into a mock fight?'

So, everything man comes up with is supposed to be natural? I grumbled. Warfare and pollution included? Isn't it a load of nonsense?

'We believe to strike at the roots of this discussion by denying the principal difference between human and natural growth activity. Because, if this difference doesn't really exist, as human activities are part of natural activities, the claim will be untenable that there must be a difference between natural and unnatural money growth. We will return to the implications of this when we consider the medieval ban on interest, but first we will return to the diagram of Aristotle and Marx, who also condemned moneylending at interest (= stage $G - G^1$ on the right side of the diagram). Remember the gradual transformation from absolutely natural into absolutely unnatural in the diagram, from NN into PP. It meant an implicit moral judgment of a transformation from a 'good' to a 'bad' economic organization of society. As we have seen before, the characters N and P are symbolic indications of a gradual development: NN = absolutely natural; N = natural (or normal); NP = natural-unnatural; P = unnatural; PP = absolutely unnatural. This gradation can also be expressed in report marks: NN = 4; N = 3; NP = 2; P = 1; PP = 0. Or when evaluated: NN = excellent; N = good, satisfactory; NP = satisfactory-unsatisfactory; P = unsatisfactory; PP = failed, totally discreditable.'

Ah well, a nice example of awarding marks, I thought, I'm sure the author will make comments. And indeed he did:

'It's another example of how we like classifications, which we like to award with marks. In the previous chapter we described the human inclination to quantify in order to get a better grip on the matter. We have seen that Aristotle and Marx disapproved or even rejected an economy with money creation and moneylending at interest, but modern man isn't satisfied with it, he has to award it with a school mark between 4 and 0. By using marks, we get the impression that it's a factual, objective scientific phenomenon, but in reality it's a purely subjective judgment of a social organizational form, a moral judgment on the organization and functioning of economic life.'

Ethics masked by marks, I thought, making it look like laws of nature. It reminds me of an article by *Bas Heijne*, on a "*disenchanted world*"[14], quoting *Johan Huizinga*: "*Modern society pushes thinking more and more into the perspective of quantitative rating of relations, only to be expressed in a number. This shift in the way of thinking is full of dangers, especially in respect to the intellectual product, named history. The number makes the story go under and no picture will be created.*"[15] But I also remembered my disagreement with the last conclusion. I can't deny that we started thinking in numbers more and more, but I didn't believe in this 'no picture will be created' nor in 'the number makes the story go under'. On the contrary, as these numbers helped me to get a better picture of the situation, whether it concerns weather conditions, maximum speed or growth percentages for example. A story like 'it's awfully cold' means less to me than 10 degrees below zero and a wind-force of 8. This information makes me feel cold. But nevertheless, morality expressed in numbers - that's another matter, of course. Meanwhile my thoughts had wandered off so far that I had totally forgotten what the author was talking about. Ah yes, about numbers of course and their use in respect to the economic organization of society.

'But this diagram isn't beyond reproach', the author continued, without saying more on our inclination to express everything in numbers. Apparently this item had been dealt with more than enough, in his opinion.

'Firstly the diagram suggests that the 'economy' started as home economics. The term dates back to *Xenophon* (430/425 - 355 before Christ), a retired general who retreated as a gentleman farmer. He wrote *Oeconomicus* or *Oikonomikus*, a treaty containing economic advice to Athens. *Oikos* means house, which explains home economics. However: this treaty was in fact a reaction to the extensive international trade in those days, which had made the cities largely dependent on foreign suppliers and the like. And because of the many, almost continuous wars, cities became dependent and supplies vulnerable. The treaty was a plea therefore, for 'back to basis' and for autarky! A plea for a return to the farms of the good old days, in which every farmer could supply himself. In short, at first the real economy used to be very international in Greek time, but became more 'national' out of protection …

The second point of criticism, like said before, is that the diagram shows an implicit development from autarky by way of barter into trade by means of money. And according to *Graeber* & co, this barter never existed, it's a myth in his opinion.'

Two fairly major points of criticism, I thought. So what's really the value of a diagram like that, I wondered. Just a kind of thinking model? Economists rather like them, so don't worry about the quality of its reality. It's just a steppingstone for your thoughts, or a scaffold to support your story. What would be the opinion of postmodernists on this? Would they dismiss this 'great story' to the realm of fantasy? And say that a linear historical story like that is a myth? Looked upon it like that, David Graeber would fit into the picture of the postmodern tradition rather well too, I thought - however, postmodern tradition …, isn't this a contradiction and cursing in the postmodern church? Because if we consider the postmodern movement a tradition, it will have become a historical story too. Phew, what a turmoil. But, life may be fictional and fragmentary, capricious or eclectic without much to hold on to, we nevertheless long for some structuring of our values, I had read in chapter 3. We like to look upon our lives as a kind of ongoing and coherent story, I thought. But I'd better stop my speculations, as the author appeared to see no problem, I mean in spite of his criticism on the diagram, because:

'In spite of all these possible points of criticism on the diagram, it gives a fairly good picture of different stages of economic organization, in which money plays a smaller or larger part', he explained. 'And for a better understanding of how people used to think about borrowing money and asking interest, it's quite enlightening.

Quantity of money and money stream
But there is one other question in respect to this part of money that has to be enlightened, namely the difference between the quantity of money and the flow of money. We paid some attention to this before, but didn't go into the implications thorough-

ly. When explaining Aristotle's and Marx's diagram, we used these terms mixed up for convenience sake, as in Aristotle's theories and in the diagram this distinction between quantity of money and flow of money wasn't explicitly made. It was about money and money growth without any specification given. In the diagram a connection was shown between the economic organization of society and the growth of the quantity of money, whether natural or not, but what exactly was meant by this?

As said before, Plato was well aware that 'money should roll', and king Midas's legend made clear that a process of exchange that needs to stream will be stopped and that money will turn into stone in case of too much accumulation of money or an immense hoarding up. Then the velocity of money will have become zero. Circulation will have stopped and the economy will completely have come to a halt. Contrary to this at the other end of the spectrum is the situation in which the velocity of money has run wild and we want to get rid of our money as soon as possible, because it will lose value by the minute. (Like during the German hyperinflation circa 1923.) It's the question now whether Aristotle & co involved this velocity of money in their ideas on money growth from G to G^1 or whether they exclusively thought of the quantity of money.

The quantity of money is a stock variable and the flow of money a flow variable. In the cycle diagram in chapter 5, the money cycle represented a flow of money, so the product of the quantity of money and the velocity of money. Let's call it monetary exchange. Compare it to car traffic: it's the product of the quantity of cars and the quantity of driven kilometers by car. That is the total traffic flow. And when we drive more kilometers with the same quantity of cars, the quantity of traffic will increase. Like this the monetary exchange will increase when we spend our money quicker and more often. Based on this idea the American economist *Irwin Fisher* (1867-1947) developed his famous *equation of exchange*. It places monetary exchange opposite exchange of goods. On the economic highway these two traffic flows drive in opposite directions and when passing each other, separate vehicles constantly get other owners. Such an individual money vehicle is a unit of currency like the Euro or the Dollar. But which money vehicles, or types of currency or forms of money, should be part of this exchange of money, we will comment on later. We will go into this in chapter 8.

Hence the money flow consists of the product of the quantity of money and the velocity of money. A Euro will usually be spent more than once in a year. When the same Euro will be passed from hand to hand 5 times in a year for instance, this one Euro will actually represent 5 Euros in that year. The velocity of money will be 5 then. If there is a quantity of money of let's say €50 billion in a certain country, the flow of money in this country will be €250 billion when the velocity of money is 5. Following Fisher, economists represent the quantity of money by the symbol M (of Money) and the velocity of money by V (Velocity of circulation). Its product, MV, represents the annual money flow. That's the money cycle in the cycle model.

Opposite the money flow is the goods flow. And what does this consist of? In the first place of the quantity of traded goods and services. This quantity is usually represented by T (of Trade). These goods and services will be sold at a certain price. The average price of all this merchandise is called P (of Price). Its product, PT, represents the total value of all sold goods and services in a year. With what are they paid? With money. Therefore the only conclusion can be that the total money flow is equal to the total goods flow: $MV = PT$. (This is a necessary identity or tautology; that's why it is sometimes written as $MV \equiv PT$). This equation is called the *Fisher Equation.*'

The economic exchange of goods and services heading towards monetary exchange in a kind of ring road, but en route constantly changing ownership, I imagined it like this - Marx's metamorphosis theory represented as a cycle metaphor.

'It may be the question whether Fisher was the first to come up with his 'law', the author put the equation of exchange into perspective, 'as in 1867, Fisher's year of birth, this connection was also mentioned in *Das Kapital* by *Karl Marx*:

$$\frac{\text{Total price of goods}}{\text{Quantity of circulation of the same coins}} = \text{Quantity of money as means of circulation}$$

In the left part above the line PT can be recognized and below the line V; And behind the = the quantity of money M.'

Wait a minute, I thought, is this the same? Let's have a look: 'the total price of goods' PT divided by V = M ... ah, yes, M times V must also be PT, of course. Basic mathematics, how quickly it has gone.

'What does this elementary 'law' show us? An almost 'mechanical' connection between money flow and goods flow. For instance: when the quantity of money increases (M ↑) and we keep spending money as quickly as before (V constant), without an increase of the available quantity of goods (T constant), it will lead to inflation (P ↑). This type of inflation is called *monetary inflation*, as it's caused by a growing amount of money. But inflation will also occur when the amount of money doesn't increase (M constant) and people start spending money faster (V ↑). In that case it's called *demand-induced inflation*.

It's an example in advance of chapter 8 and 10, in which the phenomenon of inflation will be dealt with extensively, but to explain why money growth may have two causes, namely a growth of M and/or a growth of V, it's useful to juggle with these symbols just now. And what is the reason why?'

Well, why indeed, I thought.

'Because it isn't clear whether or not Aristotle & co involved velocity of circulation in their idea on the growth of money. On the one hand it's obvious that they know what hoarding may lead to, this 'unlimited desire for wealth' which blocks the money flow and caused king Midas to starve, but on the other hand Thomas of Aquino gives the impression by his idea of money as a 'consumable good' that it can't be used again. His conclusion is that the velocity of money circulation is 1: it can only be spent once, by which it will have been consumed. Like said before, this is a micro-economic view, but in the macro-economic view the same money is simply passing from hand to hand. And the quicker, the greater the velocity of circulation, and the larger the flow of money: growth of money without growth of the amount of money. We would like to ask Thomas whether this thought has crossed his mind in relation with his 'coins that don't bear coins'. That the same coins can circulate more often or faster, by which their productivity or economic fertility increases.'

Well, it depends on your definition of fertility, I thought. If you only look at the *quantity* of money, Thomas might have a point - apart from the natural growth of the silver and gold supply, Foucault referred to. And, if all human activity is considered to be part of nature, because man is a natural product as well, the entire world of money is eventually of natural origin.

Functional money
'In relation to the preceding discussion on money being natural or not, we mustn't forget an important underlying question of the difference between the substance and the function of money. We considered the matter a few times before and will come back to it in the next chapter. The substance of money is related to the quantity of money, regardless of the material quality of this quantity. Money can have any form, as we said before: cattle, salt, shells, gold, paper, virtual IOUs, and the like. Nowadays, having coins, banknotes and transferable money, this substance hardly ever has got intrinsic value. It isn't a problem for us, as we use money based on trust, which makes it functional.

Money gets its function when we use it, pay with it, calculate in it and save it. Without function substance is nothing. King Midas's gold had completely lost its function, it had become dead money, substance without any value. Money that doesn't circulate, with zero velocity of circulation, and for exactly that reason it isn't money at all. Money that doesn't circulate hasn't got any function and therefore loses its fertility. 'Money is there to be spent', is the proverb. And this circulation should take place into all directions, as an accumulation in only a few pockets will lead to a similar stagnating effect as with king Midas.

Marten Toonder described this in a beautiful Bumble Comic Strip: in 'The superbosses'[16] all money flows into the safe of a small society of superrich people, in which it literally coagulates into an immovable money ball and blocks the rest of the economy. The solution comes from a simple invention by Kwetal the 'brain-boss': an energy feeder that can turn incessantly and which makes an end to *'the centripetal power of the big capitalists by the centrifugal power of Kwetal's wheel'*. The money ball explodes with a big bang and the vault bursts, making its content rise up like a golden ground swell, *'sweeping away the superboss and the poor'*. The result is that money starts circulating again among the people and that the economy gets back to normal.

The better money circulates into all directions, the greater its function will be. But circulating too fast isn't good either, as it will lose its function by too much inflation. Steering a middle course between too much and too little takes a lot of skill sometimes. More on this art of navigation in chapter 10 and 11.

Traders in time
But let's go on with the ideas on interest of the ancient Greek and early medieval men, who had to cope with the ideas above, on the (un)naturalness and (in)fertility of money. Thomas of Aquino thought that money was infertile, by saying that coins can't bear coins. Moreover he thought that If money had been spent, it had been used as well. Both ideas on money - infertility and a consumable good - are connected: we have seen this before. But money might be used in a fertile way, that is productively and yield a lot of money. Evidently, Thomas didn't see the difference between money being used consumptively and productively, that is the difference between money as a means of consumption and money as capital.

According to Simmel, there wasn't a proper understanding of the notion of productive capital causing the invested money to return a capital yield or profit, until late in Christianity. Until then borrowed money mostly wasn't used productively but consumptively. This lacking understanding of the difference between consumptive and productive money can also be seen in the diagram before, in which Van Leeuwen draws the successive economic stages of development according to Aristotle (and Marx). This diagram merely dealt with 'money' without making room for money as 'capital'. It appears to implicate that money used to be looked upon as an exclusively consumptive consumable good in ancient Greece. And because Thomas of Aquino made Aristotle's ideas contemporary, it may not seem odd that he didn't pay any attention to productive, fertile aspects money could be used for.

Money was mainly used for consumptive ends in ancient Greece and during early Christianity. This was also the case in ancient

Rome where money was acquired in unproductive ways (wars, lootings, 'tributes', 'levies') and used for unproductive and excessively luxurious consumptive goods. The latter is sometimes connected to the moral decline of the Roman empire. The Romans often blamed corrupt Greek and Oriental influence for this moral decline of the Roman empire and considered the Roman armies serving in Asia responsible for bringing in the first luxury goods, like bronze benches, precious coverlets, bed curtains and other textiles, and marvelous furniture like tables with one leg and sideboards.

If people borrowed money, it was often used for consumptive ends. And because these weren't 'fertile', nor productive, they couldn't bring forth new money. The borrowed amount had to be paid back later, but meanwhile this money hadn't been used for a productive profit, nothing had been earned with it, no extra money had been created, so why should you return more than you had borrowed? Why should you pay interest for your borrowed money? Only because the person who had granted credit couldn't use it for a while? He didn't need it himself during this time, did he? Did he want money for this time? The time that isn't his but God's? You couldn't sell or let God's property, could you?'

Wait a minute, I thought, who actually is the owner of time? An artificial figure like God? He is, isn't he, as he is only existing in our fantasy, so how can an invented figure like that own anything? God is a human concoction, we invented Him, He is in our minds just like money, and maybe the idea of time as well - nothing but conjectures …

'Early medieval Christians considered asking interest for a money loan sinful and against God's will, because it was seen as a kind of theft, a theft of God's property: time! Because actually the lender sells nothing but time going by between the moment he lends his money and the moment he wants his money back with interest. So the usurer is a thief of His time. Besides, the way in which interest on money is being calculated, doesn't care about the difference between working days, Sundays or holy days. Interest calculated on money, which was called usury in the past, is always going on and is continuously producing new money, also on Sundays and holydays, even while asleep. The usurer therefore doesn't respect time rhythm, the natural order God enforced on the world and our body. This assembly line of usury is a crime against nature, and 'nature' is God, people started thinking from the twelfth century.'

Time thieves, I contemplated, stolen time, it reminded me of this famous jazz track of saxophonist *Oliver Nelson*, from 1961: *Stolen Moments*. Would he have thought of the time we are stealing from God, whereas in fact it can only be borrowed? Aren't we living on borrowed time? Do we pay a price for it? Questions, impossible to be answered.

'By Thomas of Aquino's translation the Christian ban on interest in the middle ages was connected to the ancient Greek idea that asking interest is unnatural and pernicious. The Church never condemned all kinds of interest, though. Usury only occurred when a money loan wasn't linked to production or exchange of goods. It means that usury was actually only linked to money loans without any connection with underlying goods transactions. In the diagram following Aristotle or Marx, it's the last stage G - G^1 in particular, with pure currency dealing without any exchange of goods. Though in the beginning within this exchange of goods a difference was made between consumptive or productive use of money, as we have noticed before. Besides the official ecclesiastical texts actually were about usurers *who exaggerate*, according to Le Goff [13].

Hence, the attitude of Church and society in the early middle ages towards usurers was mainly determined by the height of interest rates in comparison with the daily market interest rates. This interest was considered a natural price and its height was and is also an indication of the economic development of a country: in general the higher the economic development of a country, the lower the market interest rates. So the market interest rate was considered a just (fair) price and the higher usury interest rate was a sin against this fair, natural price, a sin *contra natura*.

To the ancient Greek however asking for interest irrespective of its height was put in a bad light anyhow because of the supposed infertility of money. 'Usury' was any kind of lending money for interest according to Aristotle, and not exclusively lending for extremely high interest, like in the middle ages and nowadays. The natural way of gathering wealth was prudent management of home and land, as we have said before. For wealth gathered in this way there is a limit, but not for wealth acquired by money trade. And the ancient Greek were rather afraid of the infinite, as we know. Interest was looked upon as a form of limitless birth of money from money out of principally infertile money, which disgusted them. Aristotle said: *"The most hated sort, and with the greatest reason, is usury, which makes a gain out of money itself and not from the natural object of it. Because money is merely a means of exchange, but not to increase at interest ... Of all modes of getting money this is the most unnatural.."*

Nevertheless lending at interest existed even in ancient times. *Robert Beutels* observed about this: *"The archeologists of the science of economics find traces of the interest loan in cuneiform tablets from the beginning of the Old-Babylonian period (± 2000 BC). Harley used to be lent at 33⅓ % and silver at 20%. In Greek ancient times the interest loan had been completely accepted. Apparently Aristotle's 'infertility of money' wasn't taken account of. Yet it is known that both in Babylonia and in Greece the interest practice was socially disapproved of. In the Roman Empire the legitimacy of interest charges wasn't doubted, although Roman jurisdiction pragmatically tried to suppress exaggerated interest rates."*[3] The rates mentioned in this quotation may sound absurd to us ...'

Well, quite so! I snorted. Aren't they sharks!

'... and Aristotle's negative judgment of interest may have something to do with it. In his time some banks in Athens gave credit at the considerable interest rate of 12%. These by banks offered possibilities to get credit weren't used much though. We have to bear in mind that these banks were quite different from our present-day banks. These first Greek banks were a kind of cross between an exchange bank and a pawnshop. They also accepted money on deposit, but probably didn't pay any interest for it.'

What?! I thought, it means an interest margin of 12%?!

'Nowadays when having deposit interests of about a mere 3% or even 0%, it would yield a nice interest margin, but granting credit wasn't the main task of the first Greek banks, as we have seen before,' the author immediately corrected me. 'What they offered was in fact a safe depository, a kind of vault especially useful for merchants passing through Athens who had no other place to store their valuable possessions. Those who wanted to borrow money, preferred to do so from their friends or relatives. Most credit transactions were of this personal nature; to ordinary civilians banks were mostly only 'lender of last resort'.

But credit was given indeed, originally to landowners for instance who had to bridge periods between sowing and harvesting.'

Wait a minute, I thought, isn't this using money productively? No kind of investment? As an agricultural credit like that can hardly be called consumptive, can it?

'Nowadays we may say that a short-term credit like that is an investment credit, productive money, but it wasn't seen like that then. It was just a bridge between expenses and income, a simple form of liquidity management. Those credits usually weren't granted by banks, but especially by merchants. Here we come across an important conflict of interests between debtors and creditors, which explains much of our attitude against interest. It's obvious why debtors disapprove of paying interest and creditors defend charging interest. And because the ancient Greek philosophers often were employed or paid by landowners, it's hardly inevitable that they defend their bosses interests. Philosopher *Bertrand Russel* clearly formulated this in his standard work *The History of Western Philosophy*, from which is the following quotation.[17]

" *From Greek times to the present day, mankind, or at least the economically more developed portion of them, have been divided into debtors and creditors; debtors have disapproved of interest, and creditors have approved it. At most times, landowners have been debtors, while men engaged in commerce have been creditors. The view of philosophers, with few exceptions, have coincided with the pecuniary interests of their class. Greek philosophers belonged to, or were employed by, the landowning class; they therefore disapproved of interest. Medieval philosophers were churchmen, and the property of the Church was mainly in land; they therefore saw no reason to revise Aristotle's opinion. Their objection to usury was reinforced by anti-Semitism, for most fluid capital was Jewish. Ecclesiastics and barons had their quarrels, sometimes very bitter; but they could combine against the wicked Jew who had tided them over a bad harvest by means of a loan, and considered that he deserved some reward for his thrift.*

With the Reformation, the situation changed. Many of the most earnest Protestants were business men, to whom lending money at interest was essential. Consequently first Calvin, and then other Protestant divines, sanctioned interest. At last the Catholic Church was compelled to follow suit, because the old prohibitions did not suit the modern world. Philosophers, whose incomes are derived from the investments of universities, have favoured interest ever since they ceased to be ecclesiastics and therefore connected with landowning. At every stage, there has been a wealth of theoretical argument to support the economically convenient opinion."

Looked upon it like this, Aristotle's ideas and others' take on a different aspect. As we know, because of the supposed unnaturalness and infertility they considered trade itself a morally dubious source of income, as according to them the traders' main aim was making money. The question is whether this main aim is only typical of traders. Landowners, the employers of many Greek philosophers were also striving for wealth, though not directly in the form of money. But is there an essential difference? Nevertheless, in the diagram above trade is graded a meager satisfactory. Aristotle gives a rather negative position to not only money itself but also to trade and merchants (not his employers). Merchants weren't respected much and in *The Republic* Plato links commercial activities to *'those who are the weakest, and unsuitable for other work'*.

But as long as this trade serves the necessary satisfaction of needs there isn't any problem. But if people use trade for gathering more wealth (stage P in the diagram), Aristotle considers them to be no longer engaged in productive but in destructive trade, which makes *'the good life'* in a satisfying social scope impossible. Destructive trade is merely about money, and Aristotle detests wealth gathered by this kind of trade, because it's unnatural.

This distrust of commercial activities is a recurrent phenomenon in history; as we have seen before. The Church in the Middle ages for instance was suspicious of trade and markets, because the profession of merchants was closely connected to the cardinal sins greed and desire (avaritia).'

Oh yes, the seven cardinal sins, I thought, I learned them at school once. Now, what were they called? Let me 'google': 1. **Superbia** (pride and vanity); 2. **Avaritia** (greed and avarice); 3. **Lux-**

uria (impurity, desire, voluptuousness); 4. **Invidia** (jealousy, envy); 5. **Gula** (intemperance, gluttony); 6. **Ira** (anger, revenge, wrath); 7. **Acedia** (laziness, idleness, flabbiness). When I look at this list, they are my sins once in a while too, I thought. Oh dear. But here we merely have to do with the the avaritia of traders and the greed of merchants.

'That's why merchants were of low standing and why theologians were openly discussing whether they could become part of divine salvation.'

Or whether they would end in Dante's hell, I thought.

'French historian *Jacques Le Goff* argued that in the twelfth century the purgatory had been created partly for merchants and usurers.'[13]

Ah well, there it is the gate of hell, I smirked.

'The most important reason for it was that asking interest became more and more common. The purgatory was meant for the interest-sinners as a kind of unpleasant clearing-house to heaven.'

To heaven? Not to hell? I must admit that my knowledge was rather inadequate in this matter.

'But anyone who did take usurious interest against the explicit ecclesiastical ban, and didn't show remorse or do penance, would quite definitely end in hell. This possibility to do penance by buying masses and indulgences in order to cut short the way to heaven, was a financial benefit to the church...'

Smooth customers those Church Fathers, I thought.

'We mentioned usurious interest above, but usury and interest are different matters. Usury only occurred when there wasn't any production of goods or their material exchange, says Jacques Le Goff[13] (the stage of PP in the diagram above, where money creates new money without the intervention of goods transaction: $G - G^1$). We have paid attention to this a few times before. So for Christians in the (early) Middle Ages lending money at interest without a connected goods transaction used to be a sin. 'Proof' of this could be found at several places in the bible. "*(...) lend out to them without expecting to get anything back*", for instance ('mutum date, nihil inde sperants' - Luc VI.35). In the Old Testament it says: "*If you lend out money to one of my people among you who is needy, you shall not be like a moneylender to him and you shall not exact interest from him"* (Exodus 22, 25). By means of councils the Church tried to curb the increasing flood of usury in the twelfth century when commercial economy arose: the second Lateran Council (1139), the third Council of Lyon (1274) and the Council of Vienna (1311).

But what concerns us in this connection is that there were double standards, because in the Old Testament book Deuteronomy it says: *"Do not charge your brother interest, whether on money or food or anything else that may earn interest."* And then: *"You may charge a foreigner interest, but you may not charge your brother interest (...)"* (Deuteronomy 23, 19-20). Quite a clever escape clause for moneylenders, Jews as well as Christians. In his book *The Ascent of Money, Niall Ferguson* explains why in the 14th century Venetian merchants had to go to the Jewish ghetto when they wanted to borrow money:[18]

"For Christians, lending money at interest was a sin. Usurers, people who lent money at interest, had been excommunicated by the Third Lateran Council in 1179. Even arguing that usury was not a sin had been condemned as heresy by the Council of Vienna in 1311-12. Christian usurers had to make restitution to the church before they could be buried in hallowed ground. They were especially detested by the Franciscan and Dominican orders, founded in 1206 and 1216 (...) The power of this should not be underestimated, though it had certainly weakened by Shakespeare's time. (...) Jews, too, were not supposed to lend at interest. But there was a convenient get-out clause in the Old Testament book of Deuteronomy: 'Unto a stranger thou mayest lend upon usury; but unto thy brother thou shalt not lend upon usury.' In other words, a Jew might legitimately lend to a Christian, though not to another Jew. The price of doing so was social exclusion".

Oh yes, *Shakespeare*, I thought, *The merchant of Venice*, the famous play, now what was the story like? Shylock, I remembered, a rich Jew who lived on the Rialto bridge and who was a moneylender. Next, Bassanio hopelessly in love, who needed money to conquer beautiful Portia's heart. This money, three thousand ducats, are lent to him at an interest by Shylock. Bassanio's friend, Christian merchant Antonio, acts as guarantor for the loan. But this guarantee was a problem, because although Antonio's boats sailed all over the world, he didn't have any liquid capital. That's why Shylock demanded a pound of flesh of Antonio's body as a surety. This harassment was meant as a revenge for Antonio having insulted and accused Shylock of exploitation. Antonio took the risk, as he was convinced that he would have earned 'three times three' as much as the principal debt in time. Which didn't happen, but after a lot of goings-on, Shylock got the blame and Christian morality prevailed, something like that I believe. Nice story, and this Jewish ghetto wasn't a paradise either, of course. I've been there once - somewhat depressing this district, almost sinister.

'Nowadays in our western culture we don't consider asking interest unnatural any longer, as we, being modern, try to make our savings as fertile as possible and are well aware of risk and return in doing so. As seen before, money's fertility can be motivated by looking upon it as a derived product, a kind of derivate of commerce and investments of goods and services: so, money as a production factor and not as a consumer good. And in financing this commerce and investments various risks are being run. Like for instance a *credit risk*: being the risk that a moneylender won't get a return. Or an *inflation risk*, in case the money you lent out has decreased in value meanwhile, with the result that when paid back the spending power returned to you is actually less. Moreover there is an *interest rate risk* or *risk of a fall in prices* if money is invested in business giving a fixed interest rate. Like bonds for instance, for when market interest rates increase, money stuck in bonds will have lower interest rates compared to the new ones and will therefore have decreased in value. Next to these and some other risks there also is the matter of having no access to the money lent out during the whole term of this loan, owing to which it can't be used for something else. Not for interim other desires or chances, nor for possible damage that has to be paid for.

All these risks were no reason to dispense with the ban on interest at first, even when there were numerous exceptions. Not until the sixteenth century did Flemish *Leonard Lessius* (1554 - 1623) liberate the interest commerce from its scholastic straitjacket, says Beutels.[3] In his treatise *De Justia et Jure* Lessius mentioned some reasons why interest should be justified. According to him interest was rightful as compensation for lost profit, in the sense of opportunity costs, because the lent money couldn't be used meanwhile for other profitable business. As compensation for sacrificing liquidity an interest payment was allowed. As an explanation he mentioned three motives for keeping liquid assets, which are quite familiar to us nowadays: the transaction motive, the speculative motive and the precautionary motive. Nowadays we are taught the 'liquidity preference theory' of J. M. Keynes, but it was actually thought up by Lessius 300 years before.'

Keynes falling short, I thought. Or would he have read this old Fleming?

'Keynes made no secret of it in his *General Theory* that he had read the 16th century scholastics,' the author confirmed my assumption, 'and according to Beutels " *bibliophile Keynes almost certainly implicitly refers to our Lessius , the Jesuit.*" [3]

Demanding interest payment for lending out money isn't unnatural to us anymore. We know that granting credit involves risks and missed alternatives for which a compensation is due.'

Well, the Islam obviously doesn't share this view, I thought, as according to this religion asking interest for a loan is still prohibited.

'Interest still is a taboo in the Islamic world', the author guessed my thoughts again. 'Riba is the Arabic word for interest or usury. The Islamic interest prohibition has been derived from some Koran verses. The motives for this prohibition show similarities to the motives of the ancient Christian interest prohibition as laid down by Thomas of Aquino and others. "Coins can't give birth to coins", he used to say and according to the Islam, money created 'out of nothingness' isn't allowed, as man acts like God then. According to the Islamic Theory money is only an instrument to measure the value of other things, but with no value itself - not fertile by itself, Aristotle and others said. But interest was also prohibited by the Islam for a more practical reason, namely to discourage usury. Many usurers charged extremely high interest rates which made it impossible for debtors to pay back their debts. This was certainly the case in Mohammed's time. The consequence and even the aim of usury loans like that was that the debtor eventually lost his possessions and freedom and ended up being a slave. We won't go into the ways in which the Islam deals with the interest prohibition nowadays and will only mention that its interpretation isn't univocal in the Islamic world.

Concluding we may observe that when speaking of fertility or infertility of our money in our western society, we often refer to the profit gained by our spending, savings or investments. The ancient Greek or medieval Christian moral implications of the words fertile and infertile connected with money have almost completely disappeared in our modern world.

Notes:

1. Michel Foucault, *De woorden en de dingen - Een archeologie van de menswetenschappen (The order of things - An archeology of Human Science*, chapter 6, London 1966)
2. Drs. C. Widdershoven-Heerding and others, *Wetenschapsleer (Epistemology)*, Open University course, Heerlen 2003
3. R. Beutels, *Over de usura-doctrine of het kerkelijk renteverbod*, Monthly Economy / volume 54, 1990, p. 316-326 *(On the usura-doctrine or the ecclesiastical interest prohibition)*
4. Arend Th. Van Leeuwen, *De nacht van het kapitaal*, Nijmegen 1985 *(The Night of the Capital)*
5. Dr. W. N. A. Klever, *Archeologie van de economie - de economische theorie in de Griekse oudheid*, Nijmegen 1986, Quotes from Aristotle's *Politica (Archeology of the economy - the economic theory in Greek antiquity)*
6. Michael Scott, *Het wrede ontwaken van de nieuwe wereld - Ondergang en herrijzenis van het antieke Griekenland*, Amsterdam 2010 *(From Democrats to Kings. The Brutal Dawn of a New World from the Downfall of Athens to the Rise of Alexander the Great*, London 2010)
7. Hans Achterhuis, *Het rijk van de schaarste - van Thomas Hobbes tot Michel Foucault*, Baarn 1988 *(The Realm of Scarcity. From Thomas Hobbes to Michel Foucault)*
8. Brian Rotman, *Signifying Nothing; The Semiotics of Zero*, California 1993
9. Rudolf Pannwitz was a German author and philosopher (1881-

1969), who wrote *Die Krisis der europaïschen Kultur*, Nürnberg 1917
10. Christopher Butler, *Postmodernisme - De kortste introductie*, Utrecht 2004 *(Postmodernism. A very short introduction*, New York 2002)
11. Jean-François Lyotard, *Het postmoderne weten,* Kampen 1987 *(The postmodern condition: A report on Knowledge*, Minneapolis 1984)
12. Pierre Guillet de Monthoux, *Monetarisiering und organisation. Eine Geschichte des imaginären Geldes für Erwachsene*, essay in *Georg Simmel's Philosophie des Geldes - Aufsätze und Materialien*, Frankfurt am Main 2003
13. Jacques Le Goff, *De woekeraar en de hel. Economie en religie in de middeleeuwen*, Amsterdam 1987 *(Your money or your life: economy and religion in the Middle Ages)*
14. Bas Heijne, *Zo'n onttoverde rationele wereld roept verzet op*, NRC Handelsblad, 14/12/2013
15. Johan Huizinga, *Vormverandering der geschiedenis*, 1941. Source: *Geschiedwetenschap / hedendaagse cultuur,* Verzameld werk VII (Collected Works VII), Haarlem 1950
16. Maarten Toonder, *De bovenbazen*, Amsterdam 1978 *(The superbosses)*
17. Bertrand Russell, *Geschiedenis der westerse filosofie (History of Western Philosophy,* London 1946)
18. Niall Ferguson, *Het succes van geld - Een financiële geschiedenis van de wereld*, Amsterdam 2008 *(The Ascent of Money. A Financial History of the World*, London 2008)

8 What any fool will pay for it
On the value of money

Dagobert Duck's money warehouse is always filled with gold coins and with a few scattered banknotes sticking out of the money mountain. He can dive and swim in it at his heart's content. Walt Disney and author Carl Barks made the expression "swimming in money" into a world famous icon. But uncle Dagobert not only daily swims in his money, he is also constantly thinking of it. He wakes up with it and goes to bed with it. Day and night it keeps him occupied and he is scared stiff of even losing a penny.

But why are there so few banknotes in the money mountain? Doesn't he like swimming in paper money? Doesn't it look like real money? Does it itch his feathers too much? Or doesn't he trust this bank paper much and is this the reason why he doesn't put his gold coins in the bank? Is he afraid that they will run off with his money? Because when he would bring all his gold coins to the bank, he wouldn't be able by his daily dive to check if it was still there. Don't you often hear stories of grabbing bankers who pocket the money of their clients? Uncle Dagobert obviously rather deals with big-time-crooks going for his money than with bankers. He knows what he is up to with these big-time-crooks. They are not the cleverest and easy to recognize by their black masks covering their eyes and their traditional operations with wrecking-bars and explosives. And their wicked plans always turn out badly. They will be arrested and transported in a Black Maria, which makes them disappear behind bars for a while. This hardly ever happens to bankers. They mostly can do as they wish and hardly ever take the blame themselves for the damage they create.

But although uncle Dagobert may have little faith in bankers and paper money issued by central banks, he won't light his cigar with it. You may come across this once in a while: someone lighting a cigar with a banknote. Hardly ever a cigarette. Cigars obviously belong to people who like to show their wealth. The Norwegian-American economist and sociologist *Thorstein Veblen* (1857 - 1929) analyzed the extravagance of stinking rich Americans in the end of the 19th century, who lighted their cigars with a 100 dollar banknote to show their wealth.[1] it's a kind of display of power often associated with cynical bankers. But someone like Amos W. Steinhacker, AWS in short, an extremely rich upper boss in the story *The Upper Bosses* by *Marten Toonder*, didn't do this. This magnate did smoke cigars, it's true, but like Dagobert Duck he wasn't able to make use of this kind of waste. And persons for whom money is no object like Oliver B. Bumble, aren't liable to make a show of it like that. Besides, this gentleman didn't smoke cigars, but a pipe. He didn't have piles of money lying about in his castle, although he did have a safe, which the crooks Super and Hieper were after. In this safe were bags with gold and in the story *Bombom de geweldige (Bombom the great)* neighbour Doddeltje's service as well. In a bomb explosion of the safe by both crooks this service was broken and both gold bags stolen. So once again: gold, like uncle Dagobert's.

Gold appearance and gold reality
From way back the outstanding symbol for wealth is gold. But why? Why does a bar of gold give many people an idea of wealth in preference to the same amount in banknotes? Because gold represents a material real value and a banknote doesn't? Because gold is more stable in value than banknotes? On close consideration these answers only seem to provoke more questions. For what might this 'material, real value' be and what does 'stable in value' mean?

In chapter two and three we have discussed the idea of 'value' in detail within a more general connection. But in this chapter we will go into the value-idea more specifically. Because like any kind of value, the value of money is basically nothing but a human idea.'

The central idea of this book, I nodded resignedly: money that is merely in your mind eventually.

'As we have seen before, the concept of value is rather complex with objective as well as subjective elements. When looked at it objectively we may conclude that gold has a number of important industrial applications, but its value has mainly been derived from the subjective importance or the status we attach to it. This status can be expressed for instance by wearing gold jewelry, an interior with gold vases or showing off with a gold bathroom in an oil sheik's luxurious yacht. If there are a lot of people who like gold jewelry, vases or bathrooms and want to possess these things, their demand for these articles will influence the increase of the price of gold. But will this influence its value as well? Only when we assume that 'price' and 'value' are synonymous - which needn't be the case. We have discussed this elaborately before.

Let's ask ourselves first whether there is a difference between a real or an essential value and an unreal or illusory value. If we accept such a difference provisionally, in which of these domains should the use of gold for jewelry be placed? In the domain of appearance or of reality? A question asked in such a suggestive way may be answered rather quickly by most of us as: 'decoration' rather belongs to appearance than to the essence of life and things. At least this was the standpoint of Austrian architect Adolf Loos (1870 - 1933), who hated decoration for decoration's sake, and therefore designed unadorned buildings. But decoration may be functional, like with parties, anniversaries, or fashion. A gold ring may have emotional meaning for someone. For this person the emotional value of the ring is much greater than the gold value expressed in money. The same with the golden frame containing the photo of your sweetheart. This 'emotion' may be a subjective value concept, but attaching the label 'appearance' to it, would be heartless. Which makes the difference between appearance and reality less obvious than it appears to be at first sight.

To uncle Dagobert the love for money was part of his being. Without his billions he is irretrievably lost, even the loss of a penny causes a nervous breakdown. He is the prototype of the miser we referred to in chapter 4 with the means - end chain. That's why he was originally called *Scrooge McDuck*, referring to *Ebenezer Scrooge*, the skin-flint in *Charles Dickens'* classical story *Christmas Carol*. The name *McDuck* refers to Dagobert's Scottish descent, a conscious choice of *Carl Barks*, the creator of the comic strip, because of the proverbial thriftiness of the Scots.'

McDuck I thought, what happened to this Mc?

'A reader of the Donald Duck once asked why Mc had disappeared from McDuck. The answer was that Dagobert himself removed this Mc, because it saved a lot of ink! So rightly a thrifty Scot, the duck for whom the means had become the ultimate end, just like king Midas, a personification of Aristotle's perverse reversal of end and means. To him his money mountain represents a value by itself. There being so few banknotes in this money mountain, gives a clue about his concept of monetary value: he is a definite fan of intrinsically valuable money, money with a tangible material value. Uncle Dagobert has complete confidence in the material value of his coins, which makes him an almost pure substantialist. Almost, because there are some odd bunches of green bank notes sticking out of the mountain.'

Green? I thought, green? I never noticed. But it makes sense, because this Duck is an American product, so they must be American greenbacks: dollars.

'So, uncle Dagobert loves money with a substantial, intrinsic value. His gold mountain proves it and so do the hardly ever mentioned bank accounts in the stories of the billionaire Duck. Did uncle Dagobert have a bank, anyway? He did according to his saying in the story *The recluse of McDuck Manor*[3], because there he says to Donald, who is scared by the store of money in the warehouse: *"Don't talk nonsense. This isn't all my money. I've got possessions and bank balances all over the world"*. But you can't swim in those bank balances obviously. They lack body and are just spirit, expressed in numbers in bank accounts and sometimes in computers in more recent stories as well. But the odd thing is that uncle Dagobert doesn't seem to worry whether the coins' value agrees with the value printed on them. Evidently, he implicitly trusts the intrinsic value of his gold mountain and those scattered green banknotes are more like decoration than money to him (or actually to the graphic designers). It doesn't mean that he has no faith at all in banknotes and bank balances, in that case he wouldn't have them, but he mainly believes in the intrinsic value of the money body, in his case especially the gold value. About time to bring the relation between this intrinsic value and the exchange value or nominal value of money into focus.

Intrinsic and nominal value - the monetary dualism of money body and money spirit

By the *intrinsic value* of money is meant the tangible value of the material it is made of. The *nominal value* of money is the value given on the coins or banknotes. The nominal value may be considered the same as the *exchange value* and nowadays that value differs a lot from the intrinsic value - think of the negligible intrinsic value of a banknote as opposed to its nominal value.

If looked at the contrast 'intrinsic' versus 'nominal' philosophically, we will recognize a familiar kind of dualism: body and spirit, in this case money body and money spirit. And in the course of history it has become clear that the money spirit can do well without the money body, because money has begun as 'spirit', namely as credit, as we have told in chapter 5. Originally people just made an agreement on claims and debts, at most confirmed by mnemonics like yap stones and wooden tally sticks. *David Graeber* among others clearly justified this in his book *Debt - the first 5000 years*, as mentioned before.'

Ah yes, the man of the myth of the barter, I remembered.

'In his book *Money - The Unauthorized Biography*, the development economist *Felix Martin* described the long-term use of wooden tally sticks in the English Treasury (more than six hundred years - from the twelfth until far in the eighteenth century).[4] These wooden tally sticks were used by Henry II (king from 1154 till 1189) to register tax arrears, as we have mentioned before in chapter 5. They were a bookkeeping aid, an administrative system to put the Treasury on record. They weren't sticks with an intrinsic value, they were only used as a registration system to register the nominal receivables and debts. They weren't used as money either in the English time, but they could be used as a means of exchange: as they weren't actually related to a name, but were comparable to a bearer cheque - the person who owned such a notched vertically sliced half stick, had a credit or a debt to the holder of the other half with identical notches. A kind of two-sided memo to guarantee that essential trust wasn't betrayed in a physical or nominal credit transaction. But this trust itself is in fact the basis of money, which essentially is nothing but a mutual trust relationship: a credit agreement or a mutual acceptance of debt, as it's called in textbooks on money and banking.'

So just an agreement, I thought, a promise - a promise-to-pay to be exact. An IOU, or an *I Owe You*. So nothing but a nominal promise of value without any intrinsic quality - money spirit without a money body - wasn't this what the author meant?

'Looked at it like this, the history of money did start in a purely nominal way and only later for memory's sake money bodies have been added in the form of tangible 'things'. In the beginning these money - things, these money products were supposed to need an intrinsic value comparable to the nominal or exchange value. That's why originally people wanted goods that were desired so much by everyone that they could serve as money. For this purpose products like cattle, beads, shells, rice and salt were used, the so-called *goods money*, as we mentioned in chapter 5. Some words in our language remind us of this: the Latin word for money is *pecunia*, derived from *pecus* (= cattle), and our word 'salary' has been derived from the Latin *sal* (= salt).'

It rings a bell, I thought, money salt. And the author had also mentioned slaves used as a means of exchange! The slave trade as a flourishing business, the Dutch were good at in the 17th century. Wasn't this the Dutch golden century? But we could refer to the Bible, in which Genesis 37: 28 states that at the beginning of the second millennium before Christ merchants removed patriarch Joseph from prison and sold him to Ismailian merchants for twenty silver coins. And as a witness for the defence Aristotle appears to consider keeping slaves to be quite natural, because he classified slaves as personal possession, the author had mentioned before. The Greek philosopher who considered fundamental human inequality the most natural thing: *"The one being a ruler and the other being ruled is inevitable as well as useful."* All of this in chapter 5.

'So, goods money,' the author continued his argument, 'these money goods had a substantial, intrinsic value with at the beginning a value mostly similar to the exchange value, but not everywhere. Hence goods money wasn't an adequate standard of value, because the goods used as money differed much in value in various regions.[5] These money goods were economic goods, which could also be consumed, which didn't happen as long as they circulated as money! For instance during the time that salt was used as money, it wasn't consumed, but kept circulating as money salt. And in the Somali coast region blue cotton pieces used to circulate as money, pieces that weren't used for clothing or the like kept circulating as money. The same applied and still does to gold and silver, as we have mentioned before: as long as these precious metals are being used for technical ends or adornments, they can't be used as money. Only by withholding gold and silver from their other utility functions, will they be able to function as money. This goes for the opposite situation as well of course: as soon as gold and silver coins are melted down for other ends, they will loose their money function.'

That's right, he had mentioned this before, even more than once, it almost made me yawn.

'Related to this, Georg Simmel has been quoted in a chapter before on the evolution of the *"Substanzbedeutung des Geldes zur Funktionsbedeutung (Meaning of substance of money for the meaning of function)"*.'

Certainly, in the chapter on symbolic money and the like, if I remember correctly, I yawned. Let's have a look, wasn't it chapter 5? Well, whatever.

Substance and function
'Let's put under the microscope the circling line of reasoning between substantial and functional monetary thinking. According to Simmel the concrete, substantial idea of value is related to a materialist philosophy (spirit is matter), whereas the functional idea of value is of a transcendental philosophical nature (*"auch die Materie ist Geist (also matter is spirit)"*, as he put it).'

Wait a minute! Matter as spirit? Let me return to this obviously rather essential chapter 5 - let me have a look - oh, yes, the second diagram in this chapter: it shows this transformation movement going up and down from spirit to matter: on the one hand an abstraction process from money-thing to money-thought (from money matter to money spirit) and on the other hand a concretizing process from money-thought to money-thing, from money spirit to money matter. Body and spirit mutually influencing and creating each other. Am I right putting it like that?

'This ongoing spiritualizing of matter and at the same time the opposite movement of spirit to matter, or from idea to product, is also responsible for the enormous increase and diversification of financial products like options and futures, we have mentioned before in the section on xenomoney: postmodern imaginative 'signs'. These imaginative monetary signs appear to be the end now of the circling historical thread of the development of money.

Let's resume the thread once more at the tip where the history of money started according to supporters of the myth of the barter: with goods money. This side of the thread is mostly considered the beginning of the development of money in traditional textbooks on economics: generally desired goods that started functioning as money, material substance that got a monetary function. In practice however not all these generally desired goods were suitable to serve as means of exchange. We discussed this at length in chapter 5: cattle and agricultural products being perishable, the irregular harvests or means of exchange that could be collected too easily, like shells and salt. In that chapter we have stated as well that the most suitable means of exchange had to be durable and had to represent great value in comparably small quantities. Moreover, it had to be impossible to increase their quantity that much that their exchange value decreased quickly (= inflation). After many experiments with the use of various kinds of goods money, it was eventually decided that the precious metals gold and silver were the most suitable means of exchange. The reasons were *durability, stability in value* and *higher value in small amounts,* as mentioned before in chapter 5.'

It sounded extremely familiar - but this might be so because I remembered this trio from my earlier schooldays. Just like this matter of the "stability in value" of precious metals, which appeared to disappoint in practice because of the exploitation of new mines and the import of gold, which caused a dramatic decrease of the gold price. But hadn't this been discussed in chapter 2?

'By displacing various kinds of goods money by gold and silver the *goods standard* disappeared and the *metallic standard* was created, we also concluded in chapter 5. In addition we should pay some attention to the intrinsic and nominal value of these precious metals. What about the relation between money body and money spirit connected with these precious metals? Which motives do explicit supporters have of the one value or the other? To what extent do *substantialists* oppose *functionalists?*'

Good heavens, the man repeats himself rather often, I thought, hadn't he mentioned these substantialists and functionalists before in chapter 5? And after that once more? Is he doing this on purpose, these repetitions, as a didactic principle, or did he plainly forget he wrote on this before? Well, he might be regularly referring to his own sources in previous chapters, but it turns out to be a menu of repetitions on the reader's plate. The reader has to find out for himself where and in which form he consumed this meal before. He obviously is supposed to be able to distinguish and value the subtle differences of taste this author-cook dishes up. But such a didactic culinary method sometimes looks like a senile form of self-plagiarism, I thought.

'You might say that the first users of precious metals as money were real substantialists: people who considered the value of the money and the value of the material it was made of as completely coinciding. The initial use of these precious metals, especially silver, goes as far back as the 24th century before Christ in Mesopotamia! And in the pharaohs' time in Egypt all kinds of silver objects like ingots, rings and threads were used as money. This silver was weighed at every transaction and this weight defined the payment value. So, purely material, clearly substantial. This used to take place not on 'markets', but was arranged by the authorities. An economic system like that is called a 'centralized redistribution', a technical term for the primary process of goods distribution: agricultural products and craft goods were collected from the population by the authorities (kings and temple priests) and then redistributed according to social status and profession. Bear in mind what we have said about this in another connection in chapter 3. There we mentioned the coming into existence of money on the sacrificial place: the sacredly sacrificed cattle which was divided 'according to each one's honour and merit', so exactly like the pharaohs' system of centralized redistribution according to social status and profession.

In such a centrally planned economy it used to be the king who set the standard weights of precious metals and the prices of a series of goods, including the fines, as seen in the following curious example:[6] *According to the laws of king Eshuna in northern Mesopotamia (at the beginning of the 2nd millennium before Christ) the fine for biting* *someone's nose was 1 mina silver (about half a kilo), a considerable sum of money, while a smack in the face cost the offender 10* **shekels**, *a sixth of 1* **mina**. (A mina was a weight and currency unit in Mesopotamia; 1 mina was 60 shekels. Mesopotamia is the region between the rivers Tigris and Euphrates, central area of Iraq.)

In the beginning people paid with nuggets of precious metal, which had to be weighed to determine their value. In order to avoid this unpractical weighing, people started to produce nuggets with standard weights. In chapter 5, we quoted Aristotle (from his *Politica*: "*The amounts were first determined by size and weight, but later by printing marks on metals*").'

Isn't it almost senile, all these repetitions?

'Gradually the authorities started to take care of the production of these lumps of metal. In order to discourage deceit with structure and weight, the authorities took the production in hand, mostly in the form of flat metal slices, bearing a stamp to guarantee weight and calibre. This is how the first coins came into existence. The word 'mint' has been derived from Latin *moneta*. The temple of goddess Juno Moneta (the Warner) in Rome, the place of the Mint in the Roman Empire. The first coins had been made before that (not 'minted') in the beginning of the 7th century before Christ in Sardis, the capital of Lydia in Asia Minor, in western contemporary Turkey. These coins were made of electrum (an alloy of gold and silver), gold and silver. Afterwards copper was also used, with tin and bronze or with zinc alloyed to yellow copper. Originally the coins used to be irregularly shaped, but became rounder later on, although oval and rectangular shapes exist as well.'

I had seen pictures of them somewhere, if I remember well. Money from ancient China, I guess, octagonal coins and sometimes also coins with a round or square hole in them in order to be able to string them on a rope for transport convenience sake.[5]

'When the exchange value of a coin is the same as the exchange value of the metal it has been made of, it's called a fully fledged coin.[6] The intrinsic value (the value of the metal) is equivalent to the nominal value. Coins like that actually have the same function as sheets or nuggets of gold and when the market price of gold or silver changes, the value of such fully fledged coins changes as well.

The most well-known Dutch coin of this type is the *gold ducat*, much in demand with collectors, but not used as a currency. The South-African *Krugerrand* and the Canadian *Maple Leaf* are some other examples. The market value of gold determines their exchange value. As these coins don't serve as currency, no nominal value is printed on them. They are just gold products cast in the shape of a coin with a certain weight and gold content to make them attractive for collectors. The fully fledged gold and silver coins with a nominal face value, meant to be used as money, often started disappearing from circulation, which may be easy to guess why.'

Is it? I thought. Let me guess ... It must be connected with the gold and silver prices ... but in what way exactly? But no need to think it over as the author gave the answer right away:

'The reason why is simple: when the market price of the precious metal the coins have been made of exceeds their nominally legally determined face value, these coins will be remelted and sold to gold and silversmiths, or exported. This was happening during many decennials in England for instance since the beginning of the seventeenth century. In those days the market price of rough silver regularly exceeded the legal exchange value of silver coins, which caused the contemporary circulation of money to decrease more and more.[4] Besides the kind of coins that continued to circulate were of a lesser quality: they had become worn from daily use or their edges had been grinded off with a knife to gain some extra silver dust. This so-called 'clipping' of coins occurred more often with gold coins - in the section below we will go into this matter. Anyway, this crumbling away of coins had serious consequences, which we will discuss in connection with substantialist John Locke.

But before, as a kind of intermezzo we will look at a special kind of coin standard that had been invented to handle a possible shortage of precious metals or the flow of circulating fully fledged coins, but which appeared to be difficult in practice because of 'Gresham's Law': the double or bimetallic standard.

Intermezzo: the double metallic standard and Gresham's Law
In many countries the so-called *double* or *bimetallic standard* has existed for a long time. In this gold and silver were both standard coins and the

value of all coins was conversed to their gold and silver value. In the Netherlands for instance the gold tenner and the silver guilder had a fixed quantity of gold or silver, equivalent to the value of these coins as a currency. So the intrinsic value (material value) was the same as the nominal value stamped on the coin. The double standard had one irritating disadvantage however: if one of both kinds of metal decreased in value compared to the other, everyone held on to the relatively more expensive metal and the overvalued metal kept circulating. 'Overvalued' means that the officially, legally determined value exceeds the market price of the precious metal. For instance: if the market price of silver decreased in value, people held on to gold coins, while the silver coins kept circulating. Gold was used to buy silver, of which coins were minted and in this way the difference between the intrinsic and nominal value was cashed. (This difference is an example of arbitrage profit). In this case silver currency was called *overvalued* and gold currency *undervalued*. The English merchant and financier Sir Thomas Gresham (1519 - 1579) observed this and based on this he formulated his famous law: **"bad money drives out good money"**. (This quote was written by him in a letter to the queen in 1558 and not until 1857 did H. Macleod call this *Gresham's law*.) Practically in respect to the double standard sometimes the one sometimes the other metal circulated - and therefore it was also called an *alternating standard*. Mostly silver kept circulating, as its price compared to gold fairly decreased. This double standard had a lot of adherents in the past in America, as it had advantages too. In chapter 9 we will tell a nice story about this with the help of *The Wizard of Oz* and the *'crime of 1873'*.

Who likes to rack his brains by calculating an arbitrage profit as mentioned above, might derive some pleasure from the puzzle below:

Calculation example: arbitrage advantage as a result of Gresham's law
Suppose that both gold and silver are standard coins while the legal value relation between equal weights of gold and silver has been set on 15 : 1 and the market relation is 18 : 1. Which percentage of maximum advantage will this arbitrage give?

The answer to this little brainteaser can be found at the end of this chapter.'
All right, I thought: a sum, and I rememberd myself sitting in that bare schoolroom with the hard desks, where I rather looked out of the window than at the blackboard. How on earth could the author

imagine that I would 'derive any pleasure' from it ... I'd rather keep silent on how often I stayed down a grade. But come on, let's have a go: can I figure out this arbitrage puzzle? Well ... let me have a look at the end of the chapter ... well ... nearly correct.

'In this situation of the double metallic standard it turned out that people held on to the intrinsically more expensive currency and that the intrinsically cheaper currency kept circulating as an instrument of payment. But actually this is a common phenomenon. If we no longer trust the value of a certain currency, for instance because we expect it to decrease in value, we try to get rid of it by changing it for another currency we trust more. This happens internally as well as externally, thus both for domestic currency and foreign currency. We will go into this matter of internal and external value of money later on, but first we have to wind up this case of substantialists versus functionalists.'

Of which I know which side you are on by now, I spoke out loud, as if the author was in my room.

'A notorious substantialist was John Locke. Why notorious? Because with his substantialistic ideas his monetary advice given to the English government in 1695 caused a financial mess the year after.[4] He claimed that money was nothing else but (the value of) the silver it was made of. A pound was therefore simply an objective reference to a certain weight of silver: exactly 3 ounces, 17 pennyweight and 10 grains. He considered the gradual decrease of the pound's silver content a crime wave unparalleled in English history. *"As money was nothing but the value of the silver it was made of, it meant nothing else but robbing the unfortunate users of coins in broad daylight"*, Felix Martin summarizes Locke's belief.[4] He considered the silver reduction a criminal devaluation and pleaded for the return of the official weight of silver for the mutilated coin. And unfortunately: with his prestige and political influence John Locke was successful in his action. In January 1696 Parliament decided that from June the same year imperfect coins were no longer a legal currency. Till then damaged and worn coins could be used to pay tax or to buy government bonds. The imperfect money collected in this way would be re-minted, but this time with the right weight, for which the Ministry of Finance had to supply the desired extra silver. The person who hadn't handed in his imperfect money to the Mint in time, had to take his loss according to the difference between the intrinsic and nominal value. This happened to many poor and ill-informed citizens who hadn't handed in their coins in time, which caused a lot of disturbance. The government reacted with a partial financial compensation, but for our story it's more important now that a lot of extra silver was needed to finance the entire exchange operation. The money collected in coins was £ 4.7 billion and when they had been re-minted, only £ 2.1 billion in new coins was put in circulation.'

What? Wait a minute, how is this possible? What happened to the rest?, I thought.

'This was caused by the old coins having a lower silver content than the new ones. From the total quantity of silver brought in by the old imperfect coins, fewer new perfect coins could be minted. And the Ministry of Finance appeared to have not enough extra silver to fill up this shortage.'

Well, of course, how stupid of me, I reprimanded myself.

'Owing to this exchange operation less money came into circulation and a shortage of coins was the immediate result. This led to a higher silver price and deflation, meaning that the price of goods and services decreased (because of the value increase of silver money), which resulted in a stagnation of trade.'

Stagnation? I thought, trade stagnating because of a price decrease? Isn't it more likely that a price decrease incites people to buy more? Or isn't it?

'This may be surprising, trade suffering from decreasing prices, but this is the usual consequence in a situation of deflation. And why? Because people postpone their purchases, as expectations are that things may be even cheaper tomorrow. Hence deflation curbs spending. This caused confidence in the English economy to disappear, which resulted in a decreasing growth to zero or even to negative. So this was sacrificed on the altar of Locke's monetary philosophy.'

So this is the result of the philosophy of monetary substantialists, I repeated to myself and suddenly I imagined Locke as a swimming duck stuck and splashing in a big layer of shining duckweed of precious metals, like uncle Dagobert in his money mountain.

'Confidence therefore is the keyword in every monetary system, in any shape whatever. Because without confidence no monetary system will function and the economy will come to a grating standstill. As confidence plays such a crucial part both in money's internal and external value, we will devote a special section to this straight away, a section on *"guarantee and devotion"*. Before that we need to know the difference between internal and external value of money.

Internal value: purchasing power and inflation

By the internal value of money is meant the value of one's money in one's own country. This value is the currency's purchasing power, the amount of goods and services we can buy with it. This purchasing power decreases by inflation. Inflation is a general price level increase which may have been caused by overspending (demand-induced inflation), too much money supply (monetary inflation) or by cost increase (cost inflation). These kinds of inflation have come along in chapter 7 with the Fisher traffic equation (MV = PT).

Inflation is calculated with the help of *price index figures*. They present the average price level of a package of goods and services for a certain situation (time or area) compared to a base situation. Starting point is the amount of goods and services in a base period and this package's value is put on 100 (100%). The value of this package will be calculated in the current period and will be expressed as a percentage of the base period. For instance: if in the current period the prices will have increased with 10%, the price index figure will be 110. But does this also mean that the purchasing power will have decreased from 100 to 90? Or in other words: will our old € 100 in fact be worth € 90? Just think about this question … the answer can be found at the end of this chapter.'

Ugh, I thought, another sum! Let's have a quick look at the end of the chapter … what, it's a bit different from what I had expected.

External value: rate of exchange and purchasing power parity

'The external value of money is the purchasing power of a national currency abroad. This value changes by an alteration of the exchange rate. If the euro's value increases compared to the dollar, it's an *appreciation* of the euro and a *depreciation* of the dollar. (In this case **not** *revaluation* and *devaluation*, because nowadays it's no longer a matter of an alteration of the exchange rate determined by central banks, but an exchange-rate alteration determined by free market processes of demand and supply.)

For a better understanding it won't hurt to do a little calculating exercise.'

Oh no! Not again, I moaned, but I couldn't' get away with it:

'Suppose the euro to be worth 1.50 dollar one day and the euro to appreciate with 10% in a next period. How many dollars will the euro cost thereafter? And will the dollar be depreciated with 10% compared to the euro? The answer again at the end of the chapter.'

I couldn't help shivering ... let me have a look ... well.

'It's true, the purchasing power of a certain currency at home or abroad is not that simple as we might think on the face of it. In fact this purchasing power is rather different regionally, even within our own borders. Just think of the difference of house prices between London and Littlehampton for example. And when comparing The Netherlands to Germany, we'll see that prices for similar goods often differ. The same goes for the country itself. Life in the big city is more expensive in certain fields, but cheaper in others. Price comparison is often difficult to do owing to very different living and working circumstances - as represented in the housing market. But for identical products that are sold everywhere, you might expect prices to be much the same everywhere. As a rule a carton of full-cream milk in a supermarket in Amsterdam or The Hague has the same price. And considering the open borders in the EU this price can hardly be different in The Netherlands from the one in Germany, one should think. Because if milk will bring in much more in Germany than in The Netherlands, it won't take long before Dutch milk will flow towards their eastern neigbours, and this will continue as long as prices will be equal again.'

A picture of an economic system of communicating vessels forced itself upon me.

'The differences in price which nevertheless do exist within the EU for identical products, are caused by differences in cost and VAT.

The purchasing power of the euro in the EU can easily be determined, but how do we determine this purchasing power outside the EU? What can we buy in America with our euro? In order to determine this the exchange rate is needed. In principle the exchange rate reflects the *purchasing power parity*, that is the relationship between foreign and domestic price level. If the euro is worth one and a half dollar, the same product should be one and a half times as expensive in America. If the carton of full-cream milk costs €0.50 in our home country, it would be $0.75 at a perfect purchase power parity. But in reality it doesn't work out in such a precise way. If we travel abroad, we will soon notice that one country is more expensive for us than another and that some products are more expensive and others cheaper. This might be related to matters like the difference in labour costs, energy costs, taxation, transport costs, insurance premiums, legal regulations, cultural customs and demand and supply. Besides price comparison of a single product makes no sense; it's better to compare inflation figures, as they consider the prices of a whole consumption package of goods and services, the total price level.

The renowned magazine *The Economist* offers an annual comparison of the purchasing power parity in various countries with the help of the 'Big Mac' of Mc Donalds. This *'Big Mac parity'* must be viewed with a wink of course, but the idea behind this is obvious: The Big Mac is an international standardized product, which in principle when converted must have the same price all over the world. Do you fancy another nice little sum to illustrate this Big Mac parity?'

No! I screamed almost desperately, but what's the use?

' All right, here we go': it sounded too roguishly. 'Suppose that the Big Mac costs €5 in Amsterdam and $5 in New York. The exchange rate is €1 = $1.50. Question: Is the euro on the basis of the the Big Mac parity undervalued or overvalued? You can find the right answer at the end of this chapter again.'

Let's do it right away, I thought, let's get it over with ... Ah well, what shall I say ... But I'm sure that I'm going to mix up these terms 'over and undervalued' again next time.

'After this roundabout along the concepts internal and external value, it's time now to pay some attention to this rather important trust, no system can do without. Trust which should always be supported by government guarantees to stabilize the currency's value. Without trust any kind of currency and any monetary system is doomed to fail. More than that: money is actually nothing but a kind of trust - since it has its origins in credit!

Guarantee and trust
The gradual centralizing of the production of coins by the authorities was meant to guarantee the weight and proportion of coins. But the maintenance of this guarantee for a right intrinsic value was rather disappointing in practice. As it was very tempting to tamper with these coins for some extra pocket money. This tampering caused the circulating coins to deteriorate gradually: one had to cope with the practice of *clipping* and *sweating*. 'Clipping' was shaving small pieces from coins to get some gold or silver and then the coin with less weight was spent as usual. At first to fight this practice a circle was put on the coin for example, with a cross or image inside and a text outside. As long as the whole circle was visible, the coin remained acceptable. Later on, when coins were still thick enough, notches and edge inscriptions were added. Present ornamental edges are no longer meant to discourage clipping (since the intrinsic value of our coins is negligible), but they do remind us of this origin. The second way to win metal out of coins was 'sweating'. The coins were shaken in a hard sieve, an artificial form of abrasion. The sweater collected the gold or silver dust. With the current harder and cheaper metals sweating is no longer profitable.

Another reason for the deterioration of coins was that medieval moneyers regularly issued new coins with a lower percentage of gold or silver. The moneyers owned the rights of coinage - mostly monarchs, although the nobility or cities sometimes also appropriated coinage right - and determined weight, percentage and the outward appearance of the coins. However, when the demand for money exceeded the available quantity of precious metals needed for coinage, this demand for money could only be satisfied by remelting old coins into new ones with a lower percentage of silver or gold.'

It would have appalled John Locke, I thought.

'Besides, this extra coinage was attractive for the moneyers, because the mint master had to pay tax to his 'boss' (the moneyer) on the quantity of processed precious metal: the so-called *seigniorage*. This seigniorage often was an important source of income, which caused the authorities to be quite happy to cooperate in remelting old coins into new ones. It made the purchasing power of the coins decrease, owing to which the prices increased - hence inflation. During the reign of Henry VIII (1491 - 1547) of England for example there were ongoing coin deteriorations and the percentage of copper became so high that it wasn't long before copper became visible on the surface of the coins, at first on the king's nose. He got the nickname *Old Coppernose*. This intrinsic coin deterioration, which took place especially from 1542 to 1547, caused a tremendous inflation therefore. But what does strike us most in this story?'

Was I meant to have noticed something? Nothing in particular had attracted my attention; hadn't I paid attention carefully enough? What on earth was the man getting at?

'If we get to the heart of the matter in what has been stated above, it arrests the attention that in the opinion of the users the purchasing power of money appeared to depend on the intrinsic value of the coins! Nowadays this relation between intrinsic value and purchasing power has practically disappeared; hardly anyone worries about the intrinsic worthlessness of our current paper money and virtual bank money (besides gold fetishists perhaps, whom we will come across hereafter).'

Mr. Simmel would certainly welcome this and classify it as a major step ahead in our capacity for abstract thought, I considered. Wasn't this what my author on money had claimed?

'When the nominal value of gold and silver coins is equal to the intrinsic value, so when the value of the weight of gold and silver is the same as the value of exchange, sometimes other gold and silver objects may function as money in addition to coins. This happened in the late Roman empire for example since the middle of the third century. In the fourth century public servants not only received their wages in coins but sometimes also in other valuable objects of precious metal.'

Which at that moment (temporarily) lose their character of consumer item, as such an item can't have two functions at the same time, I remembered from the German philosopher on money. A gold goblet can be either a consumer item or an exchange item, but not both of them at the same time. That's the difference between utility value and exchange value. Yes, I did remember something, I congratulated myself.

'But then, we were talking about coins initially made of precious metals in order to guarantee their value. But which value exactly? In the first place the intrinsic value, because that value was initially considered the foundation for the value of exchange. If exchange value is interpreted as purchasing power, the purchasing power of the money will be derived from the gold and silver value of the coins. The value of bronze, copper or nickel coins which circulated later on was much lower than the nominal value, owing to which the link between the intrinsic value and the purchasing power of the coin was cut. From then on the money's purchasing power was only linked by the nominal value to the exchange value, meaning that the nominal value represented the purchasing power.

To encourage confidence in coins without any intrinsic purchasing power their value had to be guaranteed by the monarch or the authorities. To enforce this a reference to our trust in God was put on the edge of the guilder and likewise on the American dollar. An example of a coin which name literally shows the guarantee of the authorities was the English 'sovereign', a gold coin of £1 or 20 shillings, minted for the first time in 1489 during the reign of Henry VII and declared the standard coin when the golden standard was introduced. (No longer in circulation now.)

The above in connection to the example of the 'sovereign' once more raises the question where the actual exchange value of a coin is to be found: in matter or spirit.'

Same question, same answer, I riposted: in spirit of course.

'After having said all this on the preceding pages, the reader may not be surprised to learn that we don't believe in the value of the money-thing itself, as we think that ultimately all value is subjective originally. Like philosopher *Simon Critchley* we are of the opinion that money is legitimized by *"a sovereign decree or a sovereign guarantee that the money is reliable and isn't forged"*.[7] And in his words: *"It has generally been agreed upon that money - in normal circumstances - is worth more than the paper it has been printed on. We buy or sell in American dollars, or any other currency, trusting each note to fulfill its promise."*

So an agreement, just an agreement in the shape of a banknote, an IOU not to a registered owner, but to bearer.

'Philosopher *Michel Foucault* takes up a similar point of view in *The Order of Things* by saying that *"(...) it is because the process of minting them into gold and silver coinage has given them a utility and a rarity that those metals do not possess of themselves."* [8] By which he denies that the exchange value of gold money is based on the intrinsic value of this material! The full quotation goes: *"Gold and silver have very little utility - 'as far as their use in the house goes'; and, however rare they may be, their abundance still exceeds what is required by their utility. If they are sought after, if men find that they never have enough of them, if they dig mines and make war on one another in order to get hold of them, it is because the process of minting them into gold and silver coinage has given them a utility and a rarity that those metals do not possess of themselves. 'Money does not draw its value from the material of which it is composed, but rather from its form, which is the image or the mark of the Prince'. (Scipion de Grammont 1620). Gold is precious because it is money - not the converse. (...) money (and even the metal of which it is made) receives its value from its pure **function as sign**."* By this roundabout we have returned to chapter 5, to the section on symbolic money and the importance of the **function as sign** according to this philosopher.'

Another example of a didactical meandering cycle by our author on money, I thought, almost a touristic course set out with pickets leading along the same monetary sights, but always with a little different view.

'What in fact do you hold when you hold a banknote? What do you feel?'

Paper, I thought, just paper.

'Not newsprint, because this feels quite different. Nor 80-grams copying paper, because if a banknote is made of that, you will immediately know that it isn't real, a forgery.'

Aha, but our author on money makes quite a different detour now, I thought, namely the detour to the difference between 'real' and 'false' money - and I think that this is not the same difference as the difference between intrinsically perfect and imperfect money. As imperfect money may not have any or hardly any intrinsic material value, but it doesn't mean that it is false.

'What is called false money nowadays, is quite different from what it meant in the past when authenticity was closely linked to the purity of the intrinsic gold or silver value. The 'authenticity' of our contemporary euro notes for example is guaranteed by the issuing Central Banks, which gave these banknotes numerous authenticity marks, like watermark, hologram, a specific screen, gloss effects, raised print and an embedded dark vertical metallic thread. The banknotes are made of a special kind of paper, which consists of cellulose, synthetic fibers and a special kind of cotton. Owing to all these safety features this kind of paper is also called safety paper. This paper can't be easily forged, nor can the paper that is used for passports. Often artificially printed with a design of a famous designer, but nevertheless: paper.

A lot of work has to be done for the production of real banknote paper, but what is the value of one small paper like that? Is a 50 euro note worth five times as much as a 10 euro note? It is by the figure on it. But if the figure wasn't there or if you would close your eyes? Does the one note feel five times as expensive as the other? No, because the value of the paper of both notes isn't different: this value is immeasurably small, a lot less than a cent. And yet everyone accepts a euro note with a print of 50 euro for the value of 50 Euros.'

That's because nowadays we have the ability of abstract functional thinking, I reacted, one of the things I had learned meanwhile, I complimented myself. Mr. Simmel would have been proud on me.

'A banknote is actually a kind of voucher. Comparable to a book token or a flowers voucher. But in case of a banknote, a voucher with unlimited validity. The fact that anyone accepts a banknote as a kind of voucher that can be exchanged in any shop for things is related to the confidence we have in these money-vouchers. We count on it that any shopkeeper will accept them as a currency without difficulty when we want to pay at the cash deck. Just like you can pay with film vouchers in the cinema and with flowers vouchers in the flower shop. Because also vouchers like these have only a nominal value, as the paper the vouchers are made of costs almost nothing.'

Yes, you made your point, I thought impatiently, as his text started to look like a merry-go-round of words.

'This idea used to scare people in the past. The idea that a printed paper like that could serve as a currency. That's why in 1814 the first series of Dutch banknotes were bearing the signatures of the board of directors of The Dutch Bank (DNB)[9] to reassure the recipients. Nevertheless people suspected this novelty to such a degree that they often couldn't wait to hurry to the Oude Turfmarkt (The Old Peatmarket) in Amsterdam to exchange them for coins. (DNB resided in the Oude Turfmarkt from 1814 till 1976.)

The first Dutch banknotes were known as robins, because they were printed in red ink. For the same reason the American dollar bills are still called 'greenbacks', because of their green colour. The introduction of these greenbacks in 1862 caused a major anxiety psychosis in large parts of the population in America. They were afraid that by the creation of this paper money an inflation monster was born, because the floodgates had been opened for an unlimited creation of money.

The shadow of money

The possibility of having currency printed uncontrollably, which might result in a constant currency depreciation (inflation), also frightened *David Amis Wells* (1828 - 1898). His curious book *Robinson Crusoe's Money* was published in 1867. Wells filled the position of *Special Commissioner of the Revenue* in America from 1866 to 1869 under president Andrew Johnson. In this capacity he was *"asked whether he could manage to write an essay, in which important questions on finance and the currency system would be explained in plain words in a style that might incite the general public to pay attention to these abstract and over and over again discussed economic question"*, according to the preface by Mr. G. Vissering, president of The Dutch Bank from 1912 to 1932.

M.A. Woolf draw a cartoon for Well's book titled *A Shadow is Not a Substance*. The drawing shows to the point the author's opinion and fear: 'real' money consists of gold and silver and the paper 'greenback' is nothing but its worthless and even dangerous shadow. In modern language we might say that the author considered paper money a dangerous derivative of precious metal, a derivative of real money that could easily end up in inflationary smoke. This image shows the fear of the inflation bogy.

The subtitle of the Dutch translation of 1919 of Wells' book is: *"Populaire uiteenzetting omtrent den oorsprong en het gebruik van geld en ruilmiddel" (Popular explanation of the origin and use of money as a means of exchange).* In the preface Vissering expresses his approval to the drift of the story in which 'real' money is defined as a means of exchange which nominal value must be equal to its intrinsic value.'

Hence a pure substantialist, Wells as well as Vissering, I concluded.

'This intrinsic value is represented in the cartoon as a gold dollar coin, which material value is the same as the purchasing power of the coin. The shadow this hard gold coin casts on the wall behind is not made of gold of course. What we see, is only a dark shape without any physical contents. This dark shape depicts the American paper dollar, greenback in ordinary language, because of the green colour, as we have mentioned before. In this connection, Marx spoke of paper money as gold appearance of gold substance. Among this gold appearance he also included other money 'satellites' turning around the real money, like coins of copper or bronze.'

Money satellites, I thought - nice word that might also apply for all modern derivatives, for the whole collection of xenomoney.

'What caused this fear of paper money? For paper money is generally accepted as money nowadays, even when the material it is made of isn't worth anything intrinsically. It's no problem at all for us, as we mentioned before, as a dollar will be a dollar, no matter what it looks like. And we don't worry about there being only some figures on our (digital) bank statements - except when banks are getting in trouble. We accept these worthless pieces of papers and bank statements without any problem as the value printed on them and we are satisfied with this value sign, the nominal value. Without a thought we pay each other with scraps of papers on which some high authority printed a value sign. A banknote is nothing but a piece of paper with a symbolic sign on it and that's the reason why it is also called token money. It shows that we obviously trust the authority that put the sign on it. An almost blind trust apparently, as we have concluded before. But in Wells' days many people were scared to death believing that together with the disappearance of the money's material value the value of the money itself would vanish too. As if they were afraid that without a body the soul would die too. For how could the 'dollar's soul' exist in the shape of a dollar sign without a dollar body? In previous considerations on the dualism of money body and money spirit, this question of the abstract (money) sign that starts leading its own life without having an apparent physical (money) body has been discussed in great lengths.

Wells' curious story describes *"an imaginative community developing from the most primitive periods of society into a modern state"*. As starting point he chose the island of Robinson Crusoe, as having evolved for this occasion into an almost modern state with Robinson as president. The problem of this starting point is that he puts *'an imaginative community'* on the scene, a society made up by him. As in reality societies like that never existed, as anthropologist David Graeber has conclusively shown. In the island of Robinson Crusoe Wells describes, a monetary system develops from the inconveniences of barter trade.'

Ah, there will be the myth of the barter again, I sighed.

'David Wells' book follows this imaginary path without question. But before the story follows this path, castaway Robinson

Crusoe has to manage to survive on the island on his own. At the beginning of his stay he discovers in one of the chests washed ashore some pins, needles and thread, a pair of large scissors, ten or twelve good knives, about a dozen and a half white linen handkerchiefs and finally, hidden in a drawer of the chest *"three great bags of money - gold as well as silver."* But this money is no good to him: *"Oh, drug! I said out loud, what art thou good for? Thou art not worth to me, not the taking off the ground. One of these knives is worth all this heap. Nay, I would give it all for a gross of tobacco-pipes; sixpenny-worth of turnip and carrot seed from England; or for a handful of peas and beans, and a bottle of ink."* Shortly afterwards Robinson Crusoe gets the company of Friday who had escaped the cannibals and then of Friday's father. But even then they don't need money, as in this small community of three people there is close cooperation and all useful things are being shared. Shared: not exchanged! The process of exchange won't start in a society until the population has exceeded a certain limit, a limit by which personal relations gradually change into impersonal ones. The subjective relationships based on trust in which the credit system flourishes, change into more objective relations. In Wells' story this takes place when pirate Will Atkins arrives with a ship filled with English sailors and they settle on the island. The small-scale almost intimate relations on the island make way for a much greater network of connections and quite soon the barter trade appears to have become that complicated that a growing need is felt for a general means of exchange.

Wells declares the ailments of barter in a truly ridiculous explanation of the problems of exchange of tailor Twist, baker Needum, mason Pecks, farmer Diggs, and some workman who is paid with a ton of coal for his work, and some separate servants of a butcher, a blacksmith, a carpenter and the servant in a drapery, *"who for their day's work respectively received a sheep-skin, a dozen horse shoes, a piece of pine timber and two yards of red flannel."* All of them get very tired of searching and not finding the right trading partner: *"All were in no condition, through bodily exhaustion, to resume work on the next day and all clearly saw that their condition would not have been much improved if each had received an entire payment in either meat, drink, or lodging in place of coal, skin, lumber, horseshoes or cloth."* Eventually after a lot of carrying-on and toing and froing, encouraged by Robinson Crusoe it's decided *"To adopt some single commodity which all should agree to take in exchange for whatever of products or services they might have to dispose of; so that whenever any one had any thing to exchange, he might first exchange it for this commodity, whatever it might be, and then with such intermediate object purchase at such times and places, and in such proportions as he might desire, whatever he might need."* It had to be a valuable product, *"an article, which by common consent was given a universal and comparatively unvarying purchasing power."* By this 'unvarying purchasing power' a fixed standard of value was meant, a standard comparable to the standard of length and weight. And this fixed standard of value was called *"money, the equivalent for all other commodities or services as the measure of values."* With this (goods)money was born on the island. In choosing this kind of money everyone agrees that it must be a valuable product and not just some paper symbol. Hence, a product with its own, intrinsic value, equal to its exchange value or nominal value. And gold is the most suitable product for a product like that, is the opinion.

The inflation bogy
The main theme of Wells' book is the fear of inflation completely getting out of hand and disruption in society when instead of 'real' gold coins 'unreal' paper money is brought into circulation. By unreal money he means money without intrinsic material value, money as a mere 'token' printed on some intrinsically worthless bearer like paper. According to Wells the equalization of such a token of value with the value of gold is fundamentally wrong.'

Aha, there will be the Lockian vein again, I thought, or of those who are afraid of a nominal function without an intrinsic substance.

' To him it's like equating the picture of an apple with the apple itself. Or like *"a secretary for the interior part of the island"* in his book suggests to cover the deficiencies of cattle of the heathen by *"a large number of pictures of fine fat cattle"*. Because according to this secretary the imputation of the heathen that they didn't get all the cattle they were entitled to *"had no further foundation than the inability of the heathen to make the sense of completion harmonize with the sign of transmission"* And these *"pictures of fine fat cattle"* were in any case a clear proof of the transfer having been produced. It was up to the heathen now to harmonize *"their sense of completion"* with that. Further on in the story Wells gives another splendid example: during the war with the Cannibals the latter slaughtered a great number of cows. Besides numerous cows had also been *"put into requisition by the government for the soldiers"*. All these cows belonged to the *"Lacteal Fluid Association"*, which took care of the milk supply in the island. Plain logical therefore that the milk supply is inadequate at the moment, by which babies suffered most. But Uncle Dick, *"a highly popular and humane man and a special friend of children"* knows what to do: as till then the milk in the island had been distributed with the help of milk-tickets and it had been the custom that more milk-tickets gave the right to more milk, the solution was obvious: more milk-tickets had to be printed! And *"That night the babies were all supplied with milk-tickets in the place of milk. Milk-tickets hot, milk-tickets cold, milk-tickets sweetened, milk-tickets plain, milk-tickets with their backs printed green, and interchangeable with milk-tickets drawing cream skimmed from other milk-tickets. But, strange to say, the babies, one and all, with that same sort of instinctive perversity which induces children of a larger growth to refuse to accept shams for reality, and be grateful in addition, refused to take to milk-tickets."* It is not known whether the famous surrealist painter René Magritte has read Wells' book or whether he agreed with the general fear at that time for 'shadow money', but in his famous painting *Ceci n'est pas une pipe* from 1928 - 29 the same message can be discerned: the image of a thing is not the same as the real thing. This painting caused a lot of discussion on the difference of the concepts 'real' and 'unreal' and also attention was drawn to the danger of the combination of image and meaning as a variable that can be manipulated. And exactly this manipulation with paper money was feared by Wells and many others. His story describes how such paper can be printed limitlessly by which it inevitably loses its value and causes inflation. Eventually this inflation has a destructive effect on economic life and on society. And to think that in Robinson Crusoe's island virtual money didn't play a part at all. Whereas possible manipulation of our present-day virtual money has increased many times, which grateful use is made of.

Wells thought that gold was the best material for real money. He believed the price of gold to be rather stable over the years, because it is based on a fixed quantity of labour to mine a quantity of gold. It proves Wells' belief of the value of a product being based on labour costs. No question of demand and supply therefore, no subjective price factors dependent on necessities, but only labour costs determining the price of gold.'

Which looks suspiciously like the view of classical economists, *Adam Smith* and *David Ricardo*, if my memory serves me well. That was in ... let me have a look ... chapter 3, 'toil and trouble', or something like that, objective value completely resulting from human labour ... yes, there it is: *"The real price of everything, what everything really costs to the man who wants to acquire it, is the toil and trouble of acquiring it."* It's obvious that to create value a product must be generally desired, but however this certainly goes for gold according to Wells, in his view this desire is obviously of no importance for valuation. This places him in the camp of the *substantialists*. So, Wells, like John Locke, thinks from the concrete material, they hold the view of the materialistic value of money. They believe that the intrinsic or material value of money is its only value. Only this value determines the purchasing power of money according to them.'

Yes, you have already said it umpteen times, I thought. Enough is enough.

'The functionalists on the other hand think more intellectually, you might say, more abstractly. They believe that the value of money is simply determined by the token of value printed on it. If on a dollar-bill or dollar-coin has been printed that this piece of paper or metal is worth 1 dollar, then this will be its value, irrespective of the quality of the paper or the metal. Hence, to functionalists the thought or rather the token is more important than the material bearer of the thought - the material the currency is made of plays no part - or have we already said this once before?'

Once? A thousand times by now! I coughed.

'To them all money is actually token money. But we will resist the temptation to start the whole story all over again and with that we will close this chapter.'

At last, I sighed.

Answer to the arbitrage puzzle with Gresham's Law
Apart from the cost of minting and melting down the purchasing power benefit is
(18 - 15) : 0.15 = 20%

Answer to the purchasing power question
No, the purchasing power has not decreased by 10%, but only by 9.1%! How is this possible? Well, when we have bought a certain package of goods before for € 100, after an average price increase of 10% it will cost us € 110 now. But the purchasing power of our money will have decreased from 100 to 100/110 x 100 = 90.9. Or, our money will have decreased 9.1% in value.

Answer to the appreciation/depreciation question
Against the dollar the euro will increase 10% in value. For the same amount of Euros you will get 10% more dollars, or 110/100 times as many dollars. A euro will cost only 100/110 x 1.50 = 1.36 dollars (rounded off).
The depreciation of 1.50 to 1.36 dollars for one euro is about 9.3%.

Answer to the Big Mac parity question
Based on the Big Mac parity the exchange rate would be € 1 = $1. In the currency market, however, you will get 1.5 times more dollars for a euro. The euro will be overrated then and the dollar underrated.

Notes:

1. Thorstein Veblen, *The Theory Of The Leisure Class,* New York 1899
2. Marten Toonder, *De bovenbazen*, Amsterdam 1978 *(The Superbosses)*
3. Carl Barks, Walt Disney, *Oom Dagobert, avonturen van een steenrijke eend,* Haarlem, Amsterdam, Hoofddorp 1977 - 2006 (*Uncle Scrooge Adventures*)
4. Felix Martin, *Money: The Unauthorized Biography*, New York 2015

5. Catherine Eagleton, Jonathan Williams, *Money - A History*, New York 1997
6. Bert van Beek, Hans Jacobi, Marjan Scharloo, *Geld door de eeuwen heen - geschiedenis van het geld in de Lage Landen*, Amsterdam 1984
7. Simon Critchley, *Geld is de ene ware God waar we allemaal in geloven*, article in Filosofie Magazine 2010
8. Michel Foucault, *The order of things*, New York 1971
9. Frits Beutick, Cherelt Kroeze, *Kapitaal Nederland - 100 markante momenten uit de financiële geschiedenis van Nederland*, Arnhem 2011, *DNB 200 jaar*, DNB Magazine 2014 *(Capital Country - 100 memorable moments from the financial history of the Netherlands)*
10. David A. Wells, *Robinson Crusoe's Money; or, The remarkable fortunes and misfortunes of a remote island Community*, New York 1876

9 THE GOLDEN MISUNDERSTANDING
On gold shadow and gold substance

'Do you know the story of the gold island?'

Ah, Robert Louis Stevenson's children's book, I thought, or was it Treasure Island?

'We don't refer to R. L. Stevenson's book about captain Flint who had hidden a large treasure on a remote island and some pirates going after it. Nor do we refer to this other Gold Island in Elinar Kárason's trilogy, but to a fictitious remote island somewhere in the Pacific Ocean, where all gold reserves of the world are safely hidden away in caves. The island is inhospitable and hermetically sealed to prevent unauthorized entry. All monetary gold reserves have been brought there to protect them against robbers and terrorists. They are closely guarded and only once in a while a few conscientious bookkeepers are allowed to take a good look at the state of affairs. All this gold serves as coverage of the world's money supply and when the bookkeepers make their annual report and everything has been approved, the world heaves a sigh of relief and moves on to the order of the day. In complete confidence we let money do its job as lubricant of economic intercourse, uniform standard of value and storage device.

But one fateful day the island is hit by a major seaquake, which destroys the caves and the entire island together with the gold and drags the whole supervisory staff into the depth of the ocean. The annual audit check had been completed shortly before and the accountants had returned to their offices, had written their reports, signed as correct and had notified the financial world. Our question to the reader will be now, what is going to happen to the financial world by this.'

Well, if you put your question like that …, what the eye doesn't see the heart doesn't grieve over, I thought.

'Well?', the author asked, 'well? Nothing at all as a matter in fact! As you may have guessed. The world keeps on turning as usual and money continues smoothly performing its three functions. Nobody worries about the loss of the complete monetary world's gold supply, because everybody believes it is still there. The gold substance itself appears to be of no importance, as long as we believe it exists. But then ... people begin to notice that there hasn't been any contact with the island for a while now. At first they believe that there are technical problems, but when after a week they haven't managed to repair the connections, they decide to size up the situation on site. A group of specialists travels by airplane towards the island, but when the plane approaches the island, the radio signal can't be located and there aren't any images on the radar. At the spot where the island is supposed to be, an ocean extends out endlessly. After an extensive search it's obvious that the island has disappeared. The monetary and political authorities of the world assemble in an emergency meeting and they decide that the mystery of the disappeared gold island must be hushed up. But as always with mysteries: they won't remain secret for long and soon the news leaks to the press with alarming headlines like *"New Bermuda triangle swallows the world's gold supply!!"*

Once again the question to the reader is what he thinks will happen to the international monetary system after this news.'

It will collapse completely of course, I could predict with certainty - panic everywhere, the whole financial house of cards collapses.

'The answer won't be difficult to guess,' the author said without allowing me time to think it over properly. 'The stock market collapses, a bank run will follow and the economy sinks into the morass of a severe crisis. And why? Just because our human mind makes us believe that our money is no longer covered. Because the majority of those minds still believes that gold is the ultimate basis of value for our money. That money should be covered by gold, or at least part of it. But these people believe a myth, the same myth that turned out to become king Midas' fate. And as long as there are so many of them who believe in this myth, they will again and again undermine the financial system by their unstable trust. Because 'trust' as we know is the keyword with money and in fact it makes no difference, whatever mankind chooses as the monetary system's basis for trust: yap stones, tally sticks, shelves, gold or any other physical, spiritual or virtual product whatever. All these monetary bases of trust boil down to precisely this one keyword, trust. Trust in the counterparty's creditworthiness whose word we like to believe with the help of money. Money is a kind of belief, gold is a kind of belief, namely that it represents a certain value - and eventually all value is a kind of belief too, nothing but an idea.'

Again, this author on money reveals himself as a born supporter of the subjective theory of values, I concluded. Hence, for him no objective, in reality existing objective values. But I think that he had this kind of view before … let me have a look … already at the beginning of chapter 3.

'With respect to the position of gold, 15th august 1971 can be considered the date of the radical change of the idea of representativeness of value. What happened that day?'

Well, let me think … 15th august 1971? It didn't immediately come back to me.

'That day president Nixon decided to definitely end the exchangeability of the dollar for gold. According to French philosopher *Jean - Joseph Goux* it was a *"semiotic decision which meant a revolution for the concept sign or script, and for the customary subordination of the symbolic value in relation to reality."* [1] The 'monetary sign', the dollar, stopped representing the material underlying substance (gold) from that moment on, but got the status of substance itself, if you will. In other words: sign had beaten matter, or function had conquered substance: gold substance was officially declared subordinate to monetary function that day. It meant a radical change in the concept of the coverage of money: *"From then on the dollar banknotes (…) themselves are the guarantee, the coverage behind the bank signs."*, Joseph Goux concluded in his article. *"In other words, the sign and no longer the thing is the guarantee, the coverage."* He is of the opinion that *"this moment of schism and radical change (…) (might) be unambiguously handled as the start of postmodernism."*

What?! I called out in surprise, 15th august 1971 as the start of postmodernism? That's quite a remarkable historical date and interpretation of that question in relation with xenomoney in chapter

7, which hadn't been discussed at all there, if I remember correctly. Or had it? Let me leaf backwards ... That xenomoney was about 'sign' which often only referred to other signs, as a *'kind of chain of imagined values'* the author had called it and in this regard the symbolic dollar sign fits in. Oh well, all right then ...

'French economist *Jean Denizet* declared this date of 15th august 1971 one of the most important historical dates, *"not only of the postwar period, but of the entire human history"*, and he added that this was *"the monetary fiduciarisation of humanity"*.[1]'

Fiduciarisation? What kind of word is that? I thought. I knew the Dutch word 'fiducie', meaning faith, and fiduciary, meaning based on faith - and of course, fiduciary money: money that derives its value from our trust in the nation or institution that issues it. It's also called fiat money. Gee, had I learned this at school?

'Well, we doubt whether this road from gold to paper money and contemporary virtual money has been as straight-lined as suggested above.'

No, I guess not, I thought, because hadn't its course been circular or pendulating? Haven't you described this before in your book?

'In traditional economics books the road of the monetary standards are usually described as a road from goods money via metallic standards to a paper standard or a system without a standard.[2] But that road hasn't developed as straightly as those books usually suggest.'

See? Didn't I say so?

'But before we follow that winding road, we will take the traditional economic narrative path, from the (myth of) the barter via goods money to metallic standard and eventually the contemporary system without a standard, also called paper standard.'

A virtual standard now, I would say, I added. Because this bank paper hasn't been in the lead for a long time now, has it?

'And of course the term "paper standard" is outmoded as a matter of fact,' the author again guessed my thoughts, 'for the bulk of the payments is handled virtually nowadays, with cash card and computer. The myth of the barter has been discussed enough by us now and also the various kinds of currencies used as money in the past (and still are sometimes now) have been reviewed extensively.

Therefore we pick up the thread from the precious metals gold and silver, which have been predominant in the monetary spectrum for so long - and according to many still ought to be. These metals have covered a monetary road from the materials in raw form like bars, blocks, ingots, bears, threads and rings via coins into standardized bears in the vaults of Central Banks. These gold supplies in the vaults of Central Banks all over the world used to do duty as coverage of the money supply for a long time.'

For a long time? What is a long time, I thought, till when exactly? Did it stop having this duty? Don't these banks still have vaults filled with ingots of gold?

'This gold coverage of money has actually been abolished at the same time as Nixon's action in 1971, even though calculating a coverage percentage continued for years afterwards. Quite a lot of students of economics have had to break their brains over it.'

Yuck yes, I had repressed it by now …

'We won't bother the reader with it, but for 'education and enjoyment' we will get a nice didactical aid from the museum of economics, being the "inverted pyramid of credit".'

Pooh! No, there is no need is there?

'Imagine the following diagram: two triangles drawn on top of each other, standing on their tips and the one on top has been shifted for a great part over the bottom one. Have you got that?'

Brrr, Yes I've got that.

'You must demarcate a frog now in the lowest triangle by means of a horizontal line. Next you write *"Gold"* in this frog. Or even better: *"Gold and currency"*. We will go into its meaning later on. If you like you may colour or shade this frog. So, this demarcated lower frog represents the gold supply of a country, stored in vaults for example of the Central Bank, in The Netherlands therefore in the DNB, and in Great-Britain the Bank of England, the BoE. But also a lot of monetary Dutch and British gold lies in New York for instance. These vaults may be considered a kind of extension of the vaults in Amsterdam and London.'

I know them! I exclaimed joyfully. Not that long ago I've been there! Had a guided tour! A friend thought that I might like that. I had rather visited a museum, but all right. 'Liberty Street, please',

I told the taxi driver. 'Gonna rob a bank, sir?' he said. Wanted to be funny, that man. After a ride, much too long in my opinion, we held in front of a building that looked like a Florentine palace from the Renaissance with a kind of medieval castle tower on top of the roof: The *Federal Reserve Bank of New York*, quite a fortress made of limestone and sandstone, windows barred by huge iron fences. I looked around and felt closed in, as if I was standing in a great crevice. I had experienced this 'canyon feeling' before that week, but not as strong. The building of the FeD wasn't that big actually, but the skyscraper opposite seemed to fall over me. I got dizzy trying to get a view of the top. 'Chase Manhattan Bank', my companion informed me, 'built in 1961, sixty-five floors, almost twenty-thousand employees, the first office tower in the International-Style in Lower Manhattan. That's why, I thought, the International-Style, what else. Unimaginative straight tower blocks, functional but unimaginative. 'Now we will go thirty metres underground, fifteen metres below sea level', my companion announced when passing the arched entrance. 'We are lucky that I could get tickets yesterday, usually you have to order them a week ahead.' 'Sheer luck', I said, but I wouldn't have been sorry if they had been sold out. Admission tickets for the burial chambers of the FeD, I thought. 'Almost seven thousand tons of gold are still lying there', my companion told me, 'at least half a million gold ingots, about twenty percent of the world's gold supply. In 1973 twelve thousand tons were lying here.'

Once inside, we were added to a group for a guiding tour and a young blond guide led us to the shafts with the gold. Probably a student, I thought, someone who did this work as a job on the side. 'The vault door weighs about ninety tons', the student said with a weary face as if he personally had had to carry it downstairs. Behind the vault door, buried thirty metres deep in Manhattan's layers of stone, in bare iron cages with steel fences like the ones in prison cells, were the gold reserves of more than eighty countries, a number of foreign banks and international organizations, spread out in five underground floors. 'These countries used to handle their international debts by asking the FeD to carry some ingots of gold from one cage to another', the guide told us. And the next thing was that the boy started a lecture on economics, which made me conclude that he had to be a trainee of some school of business or economics.

'Formerly, during the golden standard - from 1880 till 1914 - countries with a deficit in the balance of payments had to pay their debts with pure gold', he started. The student told the well-known story of the international gold transports as a result of national surpluses or deficits. When a country imported more than it exported, it was at the expense of the country's gold supply, as deficits had to be paid in gold and fixed gold prices had been agreed on. Each currency represented a fixed weight of gold, owing to which there were fixed exchange rates. You have to imagine it like this', the student guide said: 'For example, when currency A has a value of 0.10 ounce of gold, while currency B has a value of 0.20 ounce of gold, 1 unit of currency B is worth twice as much as 1 unit of currency A. It meant an exchange rate of 1 currency B = 2 currency A.' And when country A bought more from country B than the other way round, country A had to pay country B on balance. With what? With currency A? This may be possible in principle, he said, but country A had the obligation to deliver gold to country B for a fixed price of 0.1 currency unit A per ounce of gold.

I still remember how it made me a bit dizzy, but nevertheless had recalled it apparently, or I wouldn't have been able to pick it up like that. But then, I had learnt it at school too of course.

How did it continue? Ah yes, country B changed the surplus of currency A for gold without hesitation, because what use was a supply of currency A to them when this currency couldn't be used to buy goods and services from country A? Gold could be used as payment all over the world and currency A only in country A. Hence, gold from the vaults of country A disappeared to country B. This loss of gold meant that the money supply of country A diminished, as the money supply was directly connected with the gold supply. That's how a deficit in the balance of payments resulted in a diminishing money supply by gold flowing out abroad, with all its consequences: deflation. After all less money in circulation led to a decrease of prices in country A, because money had actually become scarcer and therefore more expensive. On the other hand, those lower prices were favourable for the competitive position of country A, which caused the export to increase. At the same time the import decreased, because foreign products had become relatively more expensive for the inhabitants of country A. The increase of export and decrease of import made the deficit in the balance of payments gradually disappear and even possibly change into a surplus, by which the lost gold could be recouped. It made the money supply of country A increase again and eventually also the inflation, which caused the export to curb again and the import to increase until there were deficits again: the economic cycle in a nutshell. After that the guide looked around his group to see if everyone had understood his rehearsed lesson, about which I had my doubts.

But I still remember what happened next, as it was rather crazy.

'Sehr gut', someone said approvingly, 'man hätte es niemals … ich meine, it was the perfect monetary system.' These words came from a little German.

The whole group turned around and the guide said: 'Well, mein Herr …'

'Flick, Helmut Flick, Düsseldorf.'

'Well, herr Flick, don't you think the dollar is a better standard?'

The little German laughed sneeringly: 'Der Dollar? Soft like the butter in the burning streets of New York City, das ist ihre Dollar.'

'So that's why you visit us, because America is very cheap nowadays for your kind of people', the young guide reacted a bit malignantly.

Given his fair shortcut hair, he might have been of German origin himself, I remember myself thinking.

The little German didn't take it lying down: 'Yes, indeed', he agreed, 'aber warum is your dollar almost nichts mehr wert today, you think?'

'Because the euro is very expensive', the guide carped back.

'What kind of answer ist dass den? Natürlich ist der Euro sehr teuer for you Americans, because you Americans spend so much and save so little.'

There was a bustle in the group and for a moment everyone present seemed likely to interfere in the conversation, but apart from an unintelligible French-Japanese grumbling, nothing followed.

I nudged my companion and whispered: 'But all the same, that little German fellow is right. The Americans import too much, which causes their permanent deficit in the balance of payments.

And because the dollar has a floating exchange rate, and because of the deficits in the American balance of payments for years on end leading to a continuous supply surplus of dollars, the dollar is liable to depreciation more and more.' My companion frowned his brows and I remember how he gave me a worried look.

'Well, in a way you may be right, sir', the guide suddenly said accommodatingly, 'but you mustn't forget that the whole world wants our dollars.'

'Yes, das ist es eben, but makes that you people think that you can throw your dollars out of the window like water and make the whole world wet?'

A suppressed giggling sounded, but the young blond guide apparently was made to feel responsible. A little unseemly, he stated that this and that eventually could be blamed on the country that had thrown Europe into the second world war. That country had to answer for the devastation of the ancient world and only American dollars could bring salvation then. And yes, how much everyone wished to have them, he added with a forced smile.

The group looked at him in surprise. Why let he go himself like that, I wondered. Why was he offended like that? It can hardly be the first time that he has to drag along nagging tourists, surely? I took him to have some sort of rudimentary feeling of guilt, as may be seen more often with young Germans.

'Eine Scheißstory', the little German reacted. He wanted to say something else, but his wife pulled his sleeve: 'Helmut! Bitte!' Helmut grumbled a bit and kept silent then.

We continued our route through the underground vaults of the Fed, but it was obvious that the guide didn't like it any longer, as he finished up everything at a higher speed now and the accompanying comment was left out, as a result of which we were outside again in less than three quarters of an hour. That was quick, at least.

But where did I leave off? How on earth did I end up in New York? Ah, yes, gold. The monetary gold at the bottom of the frog of the upside-down credit pyramid. The gold corner that reminded me of the underground vaults in New York.

'And if this is going to sink in, you may be able to guess what the lowest triangle represents', I read.

Guess? Do I have to guess again? Just tell me.

'Well? The whole lowest triangle represents the monetary activities of the Central Bank. And when assuming that this supply of "gold and currency" at the bottom of the diagram serves as a coverage for the circulating amount of money of a country, what would be in the rest of the bottom triangle then?'

Well, what indeed? Actually I wasn't in the mood to think it over.

'To answer that question, you must think of the kind of currency the Central Bank issues …'

Banknotes, came to my mind.

'Paper money', the author said, 'so banknotes. Euro banknotes nowadays in the Euro zone. It makes the lowest triangle complete now: at the bottom a frog with "gold and currency" and on top of it the banknotes the Central Bank put into circulation.'

And do I have to colour or shade that part? I thought. Well, the author refrains from giving a clue on this, now.

'But that's not all, as we still have a second upside-down triangle, which is partly placed in the lowest one. And what may this second triangle represent, do you think?'

I don't think, I read, I sulked.

'This upper triangle, at least the part that rises above the lowest triangle, represents the amount of money that has been put into circulation by the full service banks. And what kind of money is that?'

All right, that will do.

'Bank money, as a matter of fact, or money of account, say, our collective bank accounts.

Yes, say. It may be just me that I'm rather fed up with this part, but what is the guy driving at, I thought.

'But there is another small frog of this upper triangle placed in the lowest triangle. What does that represent?

This frog is in the banknotes part of the lower triangle, so … that must be banknotes in the purse of these full service banks. A supply of banknotes not yet in circulation, but waiting to be withdrawn by us. From the cash dispensers particularly, nowadays. All right, by now we will have a complete idea of the inverted pyramid of credit. And our question is then: why is this thing called a pyramid of *credit*? And not just a pyramid of money for example?'

Because money is credit, I blurted out, without thinking it over.

'Because eventually our money is nothing but credit!', the author said with an exclamation mark.

Had hit the mark! I congratulated myself.

'And according to this concept of coverage represented in these inverted pyramids, this credit is based on the gold that a country possesses.'

And on currency, I at once remarked quite attentively.

'On currency too', the author repeated me, 'so, gold and currency. And in our case this currency for a large part consists of dollars …. So …'

So? So what?

' …. hence, the circle has been completed.'

Circle? Which circle? I thought that it was a triangle - excuse my corny remark.

'By this circle we mean that nowadays almost all over the world the supply of currency reserves consists of dollars (that is dollar credits) and that means that those dollars have taken up the leading part internationally in the coverage of the international money system. And this part was actually sort of forced upon the world from 1971 August 14th onwards.'

Forced upon? Oh yes, because from that moment Nixon stopped the exchangeability of dollars for monetary gold. Of course it's still possible to buy and sell gold on the free gold market, but from that date onwards the American government refused to continue the national gold pouring out abroad far below the market price - the money symbol had conquered the gold matter, if I put it right. And from that moment onwards the value of gold was determined by the dollar instead of the other way round, *Jean - Joseph Goux* had maintained, as a kind of postmodern reversal of cause and effect. A typical case of *"The medium is the message"* if you ask me. Would the Canadian philosopher *Herbert Marshall McLuhan* (1911 - 1980) have agreed with this proposition? He must have, as in this case the medium is the dollar and the message the greenback sends out is "love me, trust me, for I am the holy unit of value". Hence, this message of value completely coincides with the monetary dollar medium. The reasoning is watertight if you ask me.

'But all good and well, even when the dollar has the main part on the stage of the international currency reserves, it won't answer the question whether these reserves may or may not serve as means of coverage for a national currency. These reserves may be of importance to meet deficits in the balance of payments, but do they also function as the basis for the internal value of the euro? Or to put it differently: do we need dollars to bring the euro's purchasing power up to the required standard? Again the answer is yes and no, as is usually the case in economics. Yes, because a country's purchasing power is also dependent on the prices of the imported goods and services - and for The Netherlands they are quite a substantial part of their spending. Just think of oil internationally being quoted in dollars. No, because the value of a country's currency, like the euro, isn't directly dependent on a foreign currency, like the dollar, but on the total production of the country itself, like the euro area as a whole. Money derives its value from the amount of goods all of us produce. Or, the value of money results from the proportion between the total amount of money and the gross national product, in other words the total flow of money in proportion to the total flow of goods and services produced in a year. And once more by way of this approach we come across Fisher's traffic comparison: $MV = PT$, do you remember?'

Yes, I do. The economic cycle in a nutshell, if I remember well.

'So, what in fact do we need gold for? The gold supporters believe that this monetary relic represents some natural value in itself and by now it should be clear that we don't believe this.'

No, not objective, but subjective value, I added almost automatically.

'But how much trouble it has been to communicate this message in monetary history! And still is! The message that the shape of the money is of no importance. Gold isn't money, silver isn't money and paper isn't money, but money can be of gold, silver or paper. Or any product whatsoever.'

Or no product at all, I thought, for it is just based on an agreement.

'This may also explain why there has been such a lot of discussion throughout history on the shape of a currency or currency standard.

This will be the moment to return to the eternal misconception or maybe even the eternal feud between 'substantialists' and 'functionalists', as we have called them before in previous chapters. Money is a function, Simmel used to say, an abstract function, and we couldn't agree more. The chosen money matter is just a vehicle or instrument with which we pursue this function - we have discussed this in great length before. But it took a while before most people understood this concept of that function of money - or: re-understood, we might rather say, as originally money was nothing but a debt arrangement, for which at the most a mnemonic device was needed, like a tally stick.'

Repetition, repetition, the golden didactic magic wand, I daydreamt in an almost poetic impulse.

'This constant struggle with the choice of the shape and conditions a money standard must meet, may keep on haunting humanity for ever. Similarly the way to the international gold standard was much more twisting and unmanageable than is often thought. *Niall Ferguson* among others mentioned this in his book *The Cash Nexus. Money and Power on the Modern World, 1700-2000.*[3] There he tells about *"the yellow brick road"*, which has such a prominent part in *The Wizard of Oz*. This original book from 1900 by Frank Baum was actually a monetary allegory on the struggle for bimetallism in America at about 1890 and America joining the gold standard. Because, different from what temporary gold fetishists may think, there was a lot of protest against gold in America in the past. *"In the opinion of populists the gold standard was a British and/or Jewish trick to decrease the agricultural prices of the Midwest and enrich the moneylenders on Wall Street"*, Ferguson says by way of illustration. If we aren't mistaken many present-day European populists are of exactly the opposite opinion in their plea for the exit from the euro and a return to the gold standard, in addition to which they want a return of the national monetary gold from the foreign vaults to its native country.

Of course we can't compare the American populist movement at the end of the 19th century to the gut feeling connotations of the European populism in the second decade of the 21st century. Although fear of strangers did play a part in America (as shown in the quotation above), it was mainly a fight for the free coining of silver.[4] The democratic candidate for president William Jennings Bryan held an enthusiastic speech, titled *Cross of Gold*, in which he challenged the Republicans with the appeal: *"Thou shalt not crucify mankind upon a cross of gold."* This 'gold cross' was the gold standard which caused deflation and turned out disastrously for farmers, because agricultural prices decreased even more than the general prices. But why did this mono-metallic gold standard lead to price deflation, you may ask.'

I might ask that, certainly, I grumbled.

'It was caused by the insufficient increase of the gold supply in comparison to the real national product, or, there wasn't enough money in circulation compared to the goods and service trade. It made gold more expensive, which caused the prices to decrease. Between 1869 and 1879 for example the American money supply increased with merely 2.6 percent per year, while the production increased with 5.0 percent per year. This scarcity of money led to deflation.'

Aha, I thought, if beside gold, silver money could be allowed …

'According to the supporters of the bimetallic standard this scarcity of money could easily be met when beside gold, silver was allowed to be used as money too. But this had been made impossible by the **Crime of 1873**.'

The crime of 1873? Never heard of.

'The "Crime of 1873" was the demonetization of silver by the *'Coinage Act of 1873'*. As a result the double or bimetallic standard, which had existed for nearly a century, was put out of action. This standard had been established in 1792 under Alexander Hamilton and functioned fairly well. In practice this double standard actually turned out to be a single standard of sometimes gold and sometimes silver owing to Gresham's Law (see chapter 8), but it did make it possible to meet deficits of gold or silver. This flexibility disappeared from the system by choosing the single gold standard - from that moment onwards the economy was nailed to the "gold cross" according to populist ideas.

Amidst these monetary frictions the *Wizard of Oz* was created. The word 'Oz' refers to 'ounce' of gold (1 troy ounce = 31.1034768 grams), the basic weight for gold. Heroin Dorothy lives with her best friend, dog Toto, with her aunt Em in an impoverished farm in Kansas. The house is dragged away by a tornado to the country of Oz. This cyclone is a metaphor for the free silver movement, which in 1896 swept from the west and which shook the foundations of the Republican political establishment. The house lands upon the Wicked Witch of the East. The witch dries out completely, leaving her silver shoes behind - a reference to the silver component of the bimetallic standard. Dorothy gets the shoes to wear them at the Good Witch of the North. The silver shoes have magical power, which isn't understood by the inhabitants of the East (the Munchkins). The dried wicked witch of the East represents the business world and financial interest of this region.

Dorothy wishes to go back to Kansas and asks some friendly inhabitants of the country where she landed the way. They don't know the way, but advise her to go to the Emerald City. This *Emerald City* can be found at the end of *the yellow brick road*. This road symbolizes the gold standard and the Emerald City refers to Washington, D.C.

Thus the silver shoes and the yellow brick road are the primary symbols for both precious metals. On the way Dorothy is first joined by the Scarecrow, the symbol for the farmers in the West. He believes to have no brains, because his head is filled with straw. But he soon appears to be rather bright and shows that the farmers in the West are quite aware of their interest in the choice of the money standard. They are not going to be fooled by the so-called experts who tell them that only a mono-metallic gold standard will bring universal happiness, as they know from their own experience how such a simple standard may effect agricultural prices. After that they are joined by the Tin Woodman, Baum's symbol for the workman. This woodman used to be of flesh and blood once, but was cursed by the Wicked Witch of the East: while working, his axe slipped and chopped off a large part of his body. A tin butcher repaired the missing parts, by which the tin woodman could work like before. But he was unhappy now, as he missed his heart. This tin man was a populist and socialist metaphor for the idea that industrialization had alienated the working class, because independent and self-reliant working craftsmen had been degraded to cogs in a giant machine. At last Cowardly Lion joins the company. He represents William Jennings himself, the orator against the 'Gold Cross', depicted as a roaring lion. But why cowardly? It was because at the end of the nineties of the nineteenth century the world's gold supply started to increase, which made long-term deflation turn around into the direction of inflation. This was good for the agricultural prices and the economy as a whole, which made silver as second monetary standard metal less important.

Meanwhile the number of supporters of paper money had increased too. These "greenbackers" originally were followers of the *Greenback Party*, which existed in America from 1874 to 1889.'

So, starting a year after the 'Crime of 1873', I concluded - coincidence? For, if I remember well, in exactly the same year an economic crisis arose in America - railway companies couldn't settle their debts, if I'm right: the *Panic of 1873*. But the author didn't go into it.

'The party name refers to the American green paper dollars, which among others were issued in 1861 and weren't covered by gold.'

Not covered by gold, is this what I am reading, I thought?? Since 1861? While French philosopher Jean - Joseph Goux had characterized the disconnection of the dollar from gold by Nixon in 1971 as a … let me leaf backward … *"moment of schism and radical change"*. This 'schism and radical change' apparently also occurred a century before in history.

'This shows how history repeats itself', my author on money wrote too. 'We have said so before: history doesn't develop in a straight line, but in a meandering one. And if I'm allowed to add an outspoken proposition, following Goux we might interpret even 1861 as a kind of postmodern milestone: leaving behind the material coverage, and the monetary sign standing on its own feet in the shape of the paper greenback, without the support of gold.

But the cause of this decision of the disconnection in 1861 was quite different from 1971. As a matter of fact 1861 was the start of the American civil war, which lasted until 1865 and this war unsettled the entire financial system. Government spending due to this war was shooting up, while tax proceeds from the South came to a standstill. The illusion of a quick victory by the Federal authorities in the North turned out to be ephemeral and in view of the Southern victories it became more and more difficult to sell government bonds in order to finance the war. Soon it became clear that the gold supply wasn't nearly enough to finance the war and that the gold standard had to be given up. A bankrun in New York forced the banks to give up a large part of their gold reserves and at December 30, 1861 they ended the repayment of banknotes in gold. Banks in other states soon followed their example and even the U.S. Treasury itself stopped the repayment of U.S. Treasury notes (the American treasury paper money). This meant the actual putting out of action of the gold standard in America. But what to do next?'

Well, what indeed, I thought. Additional printing, I would say. They are doing this nowadays when there are shortages - aren't they?

'After a lot of commotion it was decided in 1862 to issue paper money that wasn't covered by gold, but by government bonds.'

Paper covered by paper, I sneered. How to fool people?

'This new American paper money became known as 'greenbacks' because of the bright green printing ink at the backside of the dollar bills. The acceptation of this money was purely dependent on the public's trust in the American government and this caused a huge problem initially. Because for some time this new paper money hadn't been the only currency in circulation: there were still gold coins and banknotes circulating, which had been issued by private banks and which seemed to be covered by gold. This dual money system soon led to a difference between the legal value and the market value of the paper government money.'

Aha, I anticipated: Gresham's Law will be active again here.

'For, while each dollar was worth as much as the other officially, quite soon the gold dollar coin became more valuable than the greenback in practice - in 1864 for example, 1 gold dollar could be exchanged for 1.85 greenback. And of course speculators and arbitration agents turned it to their advantage. An intolerable situation, which had to be ended and which caused a violent monetary struggle between Republicans and Democrats. The Republicans favoured a return to the gold standard, in which they initially succeeded with the "Contraction Act", which led to a large decrease of the circulating amount of paper money. And so, what was the consequence of this?'

Deflation! I called out loud, as I thought I began to understand it.

'Deflation and recession in 1867, but you might have guessed it by now. It will be the same every time: if there is less money in circulation, this money increases in value, which means that prices will decrease as you can buy more with this money. And who was going to be left holding the bag?'

The farmers, I exclaimed, not as loud as before, as I had to think of the neighbours.

'The agriculturists mainly, as again they had to deal with a decrease of their prices. And thus especially these farmers welcomed the ideas of the Greenbackers. This way money politics became a hot item in national American politics, which led to the founding of the Greenback Party in 1874. But already in 1889 this party was finished. And why? Among others because the Democrats had adopted the Greenbackers' standpoint and also started pleading for a larger (paper) monetary policy. For the rest the Greenback Party fell into oblivion, because the People's party had adopted their basic program. The supporters of that party were called Populists and were mainly socially conscious people.

But ....'

Wait and see what will come, I thought, the author will wipe the floor with his entire story, or he will turn it around, as he liked to do before, when looking at his text so far.

' .... If there can be too little money, there can also be too much. Too little means deflation and too much ...'

'Inflation! I almost shouted with joy, just a bit too loud for my neighbours perhaps. But I didn't shout with joy because I felt cheerful, as my eyes hurt and I had become thirsty. Let me go the refrigerator first.

'Well yes, as you may guess: inflation!' it sounded together with the carbonated pop of my bottle of water. 'Too much money in proportion to the production decreases the value of money, by which prices increase. And this was feared by quite a few people when the greenback was coming on. Those green bills could be printed additionally, just like that, couldn't they? Who was going to supervise it? Who was going to take care that politicians would keep their hands off the money press when they had to finance funny plans or plans to wage war? Unrestrained additional printing of money hadn't been possible with gold coins, at least only in a limited way, as gold had to be found and mined first. But from chapter 2 we may remember that also the gold and silver supply used to be very irregular in history, which caused money to have a fluid value. We gave the example of the gold and silver lootings by the Spaniards of the Incas after 1530. But *"What the Spaniards hadn't understood"*, says Ferguson, *"is that the value of precious metal isn't absolute. Money is worth what someone else is willing to give for it."* [5]

Yes, this message had come across loud and clear in the book I'm holding, I grudged.

'And *"An increase of the supply won't make society richer"*, he added.'

I had to think this one over. It seemed to be a rather essential proposition to me: more gold doesn't make a country richer, the man says. Is that true?

'Ferguson's statement is at odds with the ideas of an economic movement in the past, called mercantilism. This theory has dominated economic policy in Western Europe for a long time, from about 1500 till 1750. According to the mercantilists wealth was almost entirely the same as the possession of monetary assets like gold and silver. Hence, the more gold and silver, the richer we are. A simple thought, which reminds us of king Midas, for what exactly is the purpose of all this precious metal? What does a country need it for?'

To pay its import, I reacted impulsively.

'Practical to pay your foreign suppliers with it, is the general idea. And indeed, gold was and is used for that. But nowadays most international payments are made in dollars and the dollar's value is standing on its own postmodern feet since 1971 when it was disconnected from gold. This value is supported by those who for the time being fully submit to this green shadow. For the time being - as this dollar shadow can only last and grow as long as America's import exceeds its export, or as long as the world is eagerly willing to pay the gluttonous overconsumption of the Americans, that is to say is eagerly willing to pay the US - deficits.

And thus by way of this approach we have returned to the feared 'shadow of money', which we have discussed at length in the previous chapter. This 'shadow' represented the green American paper money, which many considered to be ghostly inflationary bogus money. The fear of the shadow and the inflation bogey, which David Ames Wells referred to in his book of 1867, was of course also caused by the civil war of 1861 - 1865, settled shortly before. Because in that war the money press was working at full speed. No need for a Greenback Party then, which wasn't founded until after the war when the monetary brake was used to control the currency flow of greenbacks - with the deflationary effect we are acquainted with.

What we also learn from this historical example, is that monetary history often repeats itself, or shows a picture of low and high tide: a too small deflationary currency flow alternated by rising currency waves and now and then a real currency ground swell, for which the floodgates are sometimes deliberately opened when the monetary captains fear that otherwise the economic ship will run aground. This did happen during the stagnation that embraced the world after the financial crisis of 2008. The monetary coaches opened all currency floodgates to get the vessel afloat again. We will go into that in the next chapter - for the long-term effects of this operation are incalculable yet.

Many fear a repetition of the German situation in the first years after the first world war. The German collective memory is still haunted by pictures of those years when paper money was cheaper than coal to light the fire with. But paper shadow money together with a much greater and at the same time vaguer money shadow pushed gold money almost entirely out of the monetary picture. This second vague shadow is the virtual monetary shadow. This shadow even no longer has a paper substance, and has to manage without a body. This virtual monetary shadow will be more visible in the next chapter.'

The monetary 'Invisible Man', I thought, when I put the book aside and rubbed my eyes. H. G. Wells might have been the right person to make good use of it.

Notes:

1. Jean - Joseph Goux, *Electronic money, or the fingers of the invisible hand*, article 1998
2. A brief outline can be found in: H. A. Frey and R. Widemann, *Geld & Internationale economie - Schematische kern en oefenboek*, Groningen 1991
3. Niall Ferguson, *The Cash Nexus, Money and Power in the Modern World 1700-2000*, New York 2001
4. Hugh Rockoff, *The "Wizard of Oz" as a Monetary Allegory*, Journal of Political Economy, Vol. 98, 1990, p. 739-760
5. Niall Fergusson, *The Ascent of Money - A Financial history of the World*, London 2008

10 THE CENTRAL BANK AS HORN OF PLENTY AND THE END OF SCARCITY
On the belief in monetary omnipotence

'Nowadays central banks are often seen as an endless source of money, like a monetary horn of plenty. The monetary symbol of this Cornucopia at the ECB in the second decade of the 21st century used to be the bazooka. The monetary bazooka is a symbolic horn in the shape of a straight tube which could shoot money limitlessly. A picture that matches well with our insatiable desire for wealth. This is also the theme of the grail stories, the medieval legend which may be inspired by older stories from the classical and Celtic mythology. According to *Marc Shell*, author of *Money, language and Thought*, these grail stories are the cradle of modern money.[1]

The desire for infinite wealth returns in many stories, among others in the one of the Holy Grail. The Christian myth of the grail may be a variant on the Celtic myth of a pot or kettle that gives eternal life or magic powers. Some, like *Marc Shell* in his book, connected the grail with the *Ring des Nibelungen* by Richard Wagner. In Wagner's piece dwarf Alberich steals the Rhinegold from the Rhine daughters with the intention to remelt it into the gold ring by which he strives for world power. In Marc Shell's view this treasure of the Nibelungen is a kind of Holy Grail too, an inexhaustible horn of plenty: *"Even if one had paid all the people in the world with it, it would not have lost a mark in value!"*.

It's important to notice that in the stories of the Grail and the Ring the material 'thing' (grail, ring) was still linked to the idea that represents the thing (wealth, influence, power)! This dates back from a time when purely symbolic signs (paper money, credit) weren't understood or accepted as bearers of value yet. People could hardly imagine another symbolic picture of abundance than something of concrete material: in this case especially gold. The material 'thing' is the valuable object here. We have discussed this at length in previous chapters.'

An example again of monetary dualism, if I'm right? The grail spirit coinciding with the grail body, correspondent with it, or even better maybe: locked inside and waiting to be freed to stand on its own spiritual feet without the support of material crutches? Or did I go overboard speculating like this?

'The most famous grail stories are the Arthur novels of the 12th century, like the *Knights of the Round Table*, but even today new stories are written. Think of the *The Da Vinci Code* by Dan Brown or the movie *Indiana Jones and the Last Crusade*. Shortly after the publication of the grail stories in Europe, new financial institutions like the banks of the Medici family in Florence began to *"challenge theories on production and representation"*, as Shell calls it. According to him these ancient stories were permeated with the monetary theme, or rather the tension between monetary spirit and monetary body, as we have called it before. This 'challenging' was done by the financial institutions by way of putting fiduciary money into circulation (paper money, bank balances), which caused the disconnection between the (gold) matter and the value (sign). It resulted in a gradually growing belief (trust) in a grail of plenty without the necessary material gold grail or ring. The new financial grail knights were no longer seeking such a material Grail, but only abstract kinds of value in the shape of signs. When reading this, what strikes us most?'

What struck me most? That I could be quite right in guessing that monetary dualism is implied in grail stories, I thought.

'Here we may hear Jean - Joseph Goux's voice from 1998 resonating. Or Shell's voice in Goux's, as Shell had written his book one an a half decade before. Goux explained that breaking the dollar - gold link in 1971 was a revolutionary step towards the reversal of causality between money - thing and money - symbol, between monetary body and monetary spirit, because from then onwards gold no longer determined the value of the dollar, but the dollar determined the value of gold. But according to Shell the link between gold (grail, ring) and value sign had been broken and reversed much earlier, namely from the moment onwards when the new grail knights no longer sought the grail thing but sought the grail spirit in the shape of value signs delivered by modern financial institutions. Both, Shell as well as Goux, thus observed that from then onwards the sign determined the value of the thing instead of the other way round, and here another voice resonates, the voice of this other French philosopher: Michel Foucault, whose voice was heard in chapter 5. For he said that money completely derives its value from *the sign's function*.

If we follow the line of these grail stories to our present time, we may wonder whether our central banks may have taken over the part of the grail. In any case, the metaphor of the bazooka suits the picture of a grail-like 'thing' that delivers value. That thing took a belligerent shape in the second decade of the 21st century. Whereas shortly before the material image of a 'money tap' or 'money press' was satisfactory, in view of the enormous magnitude of the money storm a heavier weapon had to be dug up - but still again a 'thing' with which the production of money was illustrated.

Nowadays the image of the money tap is mainly used for government spending and especially when it is turned off. In respect to the creation of money by central banks this tap metaphor is dug up again now and again when a rain of money is regularly irrigating the economy when it threatens to dry out, like the well-balanced hosing of a vegetable garden to stimulate growth. The money tap seems to be a useful instrument to evoke a positive image of fruitful monetary irrigation as long as it is used moderately. The money press metaphor is of a heavier, more industrial nature and depicts a machine which might easily fall into the wrong hands, that is in the hands of irresponsible political leaders. The only thing these leaders had to do was turn on the money press to distribute intrinsically worthless paper money around the country. This fear was depicted in John Cameron's cartoon of 1865, when the American money machine worked overtime.

RUNNING THE "MACHINE".

The picture shows a money machine which is operated by William Pitt Fessenden, 'United States Secretary of the Treasury' under American president Abraham Lincoln, in office from 1861 to 1865. The secretary of war under his predecessor James Buchanan had written an indiscrete accusatory letter to Lincoln's government, which had turned on the money machine for five months without interruption. This secretary, Edwin McMasters Stanton, wrote after the defeat of the Northerners in the battle of Bull Run in 1861: *"The imbecility of this Administration, culminated in that catastrophe (Bull Run), and irretrievable misfortune and national disgrace never to be forgotten, and to be added to the ruin of all peaceful pursuits and national bankruptcy, as the result of Mr. Lincoln's 'running the machine' for five months."* Seated at the table (clockwise from top left) are Stanton, Lincoln, secretary of state William H. Seward, Navy secretary Gideon Welles, and two unidentified contractors. Under the authority of Lincoln, William Pitt runs the money machine and says: *"These are the greediest fellows I ever saw. With all my exertions I can't satisfy their pocket, though I keep the Mill going day and night."* At left a messenger hands an envelope to Stanton announcing: *"Mr. Secretary! here is a dispatch. We have captured one prisoner and one gun; a great victory."* Elated over this minuscule achievement, Stanton exclaims *"Ah well! Telegraph to General Dix*

252

(Union general John A. Dix) immediately." Meanwhile, Lincoln is guffawing because he is reminded of "a capital joke." Seward, with a bell in one hand, hands an envelope for "Fort Lafayette" to a young officer or cadet, saying: *"Officer! I am told that Snooks has called me 'Humbug' - Take this warrant and put him in Fort Lafayette - I'll teach him to speak against the Government."* Seward was criticized for arbitrarily arresting civilians and incarnating them in federal prison at Fort Lafayette. Beside Seward, Gideon Welles ineptly works out a problem. *"They say that the Tallahasse sails 24 miles an hour! - - Well then, we'll send 4 Gunboats after her that can sail 6 miles an hour, and that will just make enough to catch her."* At the center bottom, the two contractors ask for more greenbacks.

This cabaret-like historical example is one among dozens. In the course of history numerous cartoons have been published on monetary blunders and evils, and also on supposed or feared mistakes in the money system, depicting the psychological fear of money without a substance. The cartoon in chapter 8 on the "shadow of money" is a good example of this. And the recent monetary metaphor of the money bazooka fits the tradition as well: it reveals again the fear of the inflation bogey which already casts its shadow ahead. If this money bazooka keeps on firing its money grenades into society this violently and massively, this bogey may be brought into being again, many people believe.

But what do these grenades look like? And what kind of explosive do they contain?'

What kind of explosive? Money of course, I thought, what else? But how to imagine this exactly ...

'The explosive is essentially money of course, but what kind of igniter could be used to fire this money and detonate it like a kind of fragmentation bomb in society? In the Bumble Comic Strips *The Upper Bosses*, which we mentioned in chapter 7, this happened with the help of the 'energy feeder' of brain boss Kwetal, which could make an end to *"the centripetal power of the big capitalists by the centrifugal power of Kwetal's wheel"*. But the ECB doesn't have a centrifugal mechanism like that unfortunately. Because this ECB doesn't have a direct line with the public, that is to say with families and companies. These contacts go by way of the general banks and if the

ECB wants to fire more money into society, these money grenades will land at the general banks first. The grenades the ECB used, to fire extra money at these banks, were the unlimited quantitative extensions and purchases of government loans by the ECB after 2011. The Fed and the Bank of England preceded them.'

Ho, wait a minute, I thought - unlimited quantitative extensions? What are those?

'Unlimited and quantitative expanding is actually nothing but the possibility for banks to get unlimited credit from the ECB. As part of this book, it would be getting too far off the subject to give more details of all these kinds of credit and conditions - we refer to a good monetary handbook.'[2]

Let me see which handbook the man recommends, I thought ... well, a work by himself!? But then, I'd done the same if I were him.

'But even when not discussing the various credit forms the ECB disposes of for the banks, it won't do any harm to briefly explain the basic technique of all these credit loans. Each credit loan by the ECB to a bank is principally handled in the same manner each time, namely by way of the method of the *mutual debt acceptance.* And this is actually the long and the short of each credit loan: a lender hands over an amount to a borrower at the agreement that the latter will pay it back in due time. In case of a private bank loan it means that client X is credited a certain amount in his account (a bank debt to client X), but at the same time he owes the same amount to the bank: hence, mutual debt acceptance. To the bookkeepers among us: the bank books it as *Debtors to Creditors.*'

'The consequence of such a bank credit loan to a family or company is an increase of the amount of money in society. Thus, there is creation of money, which isn't easy to grasp for many people, as money has to be taken from somewhere, hasn't it? Well that's the point: no, money doesn't come from somewhere, it's created at the moment the credit is granted. When the simplicity of mutual debt acceptance sinks in, you will agree with the famous economist *John Kenneth Galbraith*, who once said: *"The process by which banks create money is so simple that the mind is repelled."*

An individual general bank can't go on granting credit limitlessly however, as there has to be a certain liquidity coverage. This coverage is a buffer for those who decide to use their money of account for transfers to other accountholders in other banks or to use it for cash withdrawals. But this liquidity coverage will never be enough to meet a *bank run*, as about only ten percent of the total amount of current account credits is covered by cash and other liquid assets. Hence, when we all at once would withdraw our money, the bank can't by no means meet it.'

The word 'bank run' reminded me of an old western in which a bank averted a rush like that by placing a money-box in front of the window - but this box had only been filled with gold coins on the face, whereas in reality they had been placed on a pile of paper or rags to make it look like it had been filled with gold to the brim. But the cowboys felt reassured and with their trust in banking restored, they went home and economic life in the Wild West resumed.

'Generally speaking no one worries about the marginal liquidity coverage of money of account - as this money of account is money, isn't it? Money in the shape of acknowledgements of debt, that's all, IOUs. But if trust in banks has been damaged and clients will massively start withdrawing their accounts, there is nothing left to save. There are many examples of this in history all over the world.

Credit loans of the ECB to a bank principally don't differ from credit loans of a bank to a family or a company. Like said before, it's a matter of mutual debt acceptance. Because also when the ECB grants credit to a bank, this will basically be booked the same way as "Debtors to Creditors": bank A is granted an amount (debtors bank A at the ECB). A credit like this can only be granted on security however, like government loans, as the ECB is not allowed to grant blank credit to a bank. The exact names and handling of various credit forms the ECB grants the banks, we won't comment on, as said before. That would be getting too far off the subject in this book, but it's important to realize that these credit possibilities are actually unlimited!'

What? Unlimited? And a moment ago he said … well no, it holds for a private bank, as a bank like that must have a certain coverage of liquid assets. He means the Central Bank, here, the ECB, the Bank of England or the Fed in America. So an ECB might do this …?

'The Central Bank can supply banks with new money limitlessly and that idea is difficult to grasp. As it was hard for Marco Polo to understand in the thirteenth century that ' the great Khan' could change paper into money in China. It seemed a kind of alchemy to him. And I have to admit: the process of money creation does show some alchemistic characteristics. It looks like sheer hocus-pocus. By a few simple clicks on some computer buttons, millions or even billions of Euros of the ECB will be transferred into bank accounts within a few milliseconds, by which new money of account has been created.'

Fired into society, I repeated to myself. Only by entering some numbers into computer systems.

'So, limitlessly. The question is though, whether this can be done just like that, these unlimited quantitative extensions, or this limitlessly granting credit to banks. And the answer is simple: yes it can be done. But this doesn't mean that all this extra money which lands in banks first, will automatically find its way into society further onwards. As a matter of fact, in certain circumstances the banks can block the flow of money, like a kind of monetary beaver dam which disorders the monetary watercourse. This phenomenon happened with great intensity after the credit crises of 2008, when banks didn't use their almost free liquid assets as basis for private credit grants but sat on it like a chicken on its golden eggs. And why?'

Well, why indeed, I thought - greed? Bankers will be bankers, won't they?

'Mainly out of fear. As it happens, after the credit crisis they didn't trust anyone anymore, not even their fellow bankers. In the normal course of events banks give each other daily loans of many billions in order to make the money market run smoothly. Because alternately one bank has a deficit and the other a surplus and then they help each other out in the inter-bank money market. But in the period after the credit crisis they didn't dare to trust that their colleagues were going to pay back the money lent to them. And therefore banks kept holding on to their cash money, which stopped flowing. It wasn't put into circulation. These liquid assets didn't become 'real' money then, meaning that it didn't end up among people, it didn't circulate among families and companies. The money market was obstructed and the public money supply M_1 didn't increase, at least not enough.'

In this, brain boss Kwetal and his energy feeder might have been a way out, I thought. A clever dwarf who could get things going with a kind of monetary fly wheel. But what do I read now? Public money supply M_1? What was it again? I remember reading about this M_1, and I vaguely remembered that it was part of the lessons on economics at school, and that there was an M_2 as well, or something like it …

'This money supply M_1 might be confusing. Money is money, you may say, so why M_1? M is short for Money, so why is this 1 added? Is there a Money 2 and 3 as well perhaps?'

What a clever author to be able to guess his readers' questions again and again, I thought.

'And well, what is money actually? That is to say, what could be considered money and what couldn't, or not quite? You don't dwell on this question normally, as for most of us one pound is the same as the other, wherever it is: in our purse, in our bank account, in our savings account somewhere abroad or put away for a rainy day. And yet, there is a difference. Because, when you have stashed away a few hundred pounds in a fixed deposit with a term of say about five years, it isn't at your disposal during this time (or only with extra costs) and this means that you can't spend these pounds straight away. Hence, they aren't *primary liquidities*, as it is poshly called, no M_1, or no primary public money. Long-term fixed savings have been taken out of circulation for that time, you might say and are therefore not available for private consumer expenditure. This is different for short-term savings or for a savings account that can be withdrawn any moment; these short savings are nearly money, *near money* it's also called. It may not be primary money, nor primary liquidity, but it is certainly secondary liquidity.'

Aha, M_2, therefore! I concluded, but I was mistaken:

'This near money must be M_2, I could hear you say, but no, M_2 represents the entire primary liquidities + short-term savings + short-term deposits, so M_1 + both short-term savings. '

Ugh, schoolwork, I grumbled. Let's hope there won't be an M_3. But alas:

'And an even broader money definition is possible and that's M_3. That includes among other things IOUs (up to 2 years) issued by banks and government (treasury issues for example), and additional shares in money market funds, all of it as far as it is controlled by the 'public', that is by families and companies. We won't discuss it in detail here, but meanwhile it may have become clear that money can also take any shape that doesn't immediately circulate as a means of payment. The most important concept of money however, is the public quantity of money M_1.'

So, the primary liquidities, I repeated to myself.

'And this public amount of money hardly increased after the credit crisis of 2008, because the money pumped in as liquid means by the ECB got stuck in the banks. But this blockage caused a reservoir filled with potential money ... And, as said before, this reservoir filled with inter-bank liquidities stirred up the fear of the inflation-bogey in many people. According to them it was just a matter of time, we only had to wait for an increase in economic growth as an uplift from the cyclical valley. And once when this upward road had been taken, the monetary dam might break with great force causing the economy to drown in a monetary ground swell.'

A virtual flood of money in this case, I thought, no paper flood like the one in Germany around 1923, when they tried to control this paper tsunami by printing mega value signs on them like *Hundert Billionen Mark*. But could this happen again nowadays? I knew that there were still a few countries in the world with a screaming inflation, but not important countries like the US or China or the EU. I wasn't afraid of an inflation getting derailed and expected the ECB to prevent it. But by this I proved to have an almost blind faith in the monetary steersmanship of our Central Banks. Was this right, though? As there also were critics who maintained that Central Banks were busy destroying our money in a kind of continuous *Money Murder*.[3]

'But such a monetary ground swell is rather unlikely nowadays', the author reassured me, 'as Central Banks have various instruments at their disposal to dam it. These Banks aren't only capable of creating money limitlessly like a kind of modern Holy Grail, but they can also block the Grail before it boils over. Anyhow, this over boiling wasn't happening at the moment this text was written (2016), as at that time deflation was more feared than inflation.

That doesn't alter the fact that the ECB and other central banks can only function as contemporary transformations of the ancient grail concept as long as people trust it. It's the core of each grail and money story: trust, which at the same time is the weakness. The value of each currency ultimately depends on this trust, as we have repeated more than once before. The intrinsic value is unimportant and …'

There it is again, the sound of the echo of the monetary functionalist, a kind of verbal *Simmel* shadow, I heard someone say, myself in fact.

' … anyone who pays with paper money or cash card will agree. Sometimes an anxious note may be heard that our present sign money doesn't have enough 'coverage'. In the previous chapter we discussed gold coverage for example. But like the search for the Holy Grail never stopped being a quest, a search for meaning, which will never be completely found, the desire for an intrinsic money body is a grail illusion as well.

Money body and grail illusion
Although the Holy Grail gives the impression of a concrete horn or scale, it actually represents a spiritual source. The tricky bit for the Knights of the Holy Grail is to get to the bottom of the nature of this source. They are challenged to discern two sources of the grail illusion and to defy them: on the one hand the power of sensory impressions like appearances and on the other hand the power of desire. In Wagner's opera *Parsifal* the black magician Klingsor made himself immune by self castration. As a result he got magical power over desire (in the shape of Kundry) and got hold of the 'holy spear', which represents thought and viguour. Kundry is deployed to tempt Parcifal in order to get hold of the Grail, but it doesn't succeed, because a knight is meant to resist, control and ennoble the dark powers of desire. This ennobling means striving for 'higher' things, of a more spiritual nature, independent of material matters.

A problem of the quest for the grail is that 'thing' and 'symbol' coincide and Marc Shell therefore asks the question: *"how can some-*

thing be symbol and source of all things at the same time?" It leads to entanglement of (production of) things and the representation of things. By this entanglement it was at first unclear to many people whether metal money belonged to the collection of goods or that it was a symbol that merely represented this collection. Let alone that it could be both at the same time: money being merchandise as well as sign. Might precious metal money be a kind of economic body with a monetary spirit? And when this precious metal money could be produced limitlessly by some Holy Grail, is this inexhaustible source also a symbol of all things together? And yet … and yet … reading this, what strikes us then?'

Nothing struck me.

'A certain similarity will strike us between the grail as a creative instrument and the ECB as a money creating institution. With this difference that the creative power of the original grail is of a mainly spiritual or divine nature, and the ECB's mainly of an earthly origin. The more ordinary metaphor of the Horn of Plenty fits better in the picture of the activities of our Central Banks. This horn limitlessly creates purchasing power in the form of all kinds of imaginable goods including gold and the ECB creates it in the form of sign money. Again, we come across the monetary dualism of body and spirit and conclude that the present-day Central Banks only supply 'spirit' in the form of virtual sign money. They supply functional money without a substantial form. The ECB as a postmodern horn of plenty only presents us with numbers in a computer-controlled monetary bookkeeping system and almost everybody is satisfied with it. But those functional money numbers actually represent nothing but (a claim to) substantial products of a material and immaterial nature (goods and services), which the classic horn of plenty could create directly. What takes place on this postmodern money stage, is an abstract performance of a chameleonic Mammon, which can represent any desired form by means of monetary signs.

Having this postmodern Mammon in mind, we may ask ourselves whether the ancient horn of plenty only supplied substantial things or functional ones as well. Only all kinds of goods and services, or also the corresponding representative symbols. We are inclined to answer: both. For if we take a good look at what such a horn is capable of in the field of economics, the almost inevitable conclusion is: anything! The ancient horn of plenty didn't help us to relieve our material worries, but in the form of a grail it also presented us with spiritual food like salvation of our soul and religious impressions. It was an instrument that could remove scarcity in the broadest sense of the word. And if there were no scarcity, who would still desire money?

Beyond scarcity
Anything would be available with a horn of plenty, so who would still need a separate means of exchange, monetary unit and saving means then? An undefined means of purchase? Anything we need would be immediately supplied by such a grail-like horn. If we should have something like that, we might be able to return to the idealized state of nature, as defined by *John Locke*, in which scarcity didn't exist at all. According to him this situation existed before the invention of money. The introduction of money led to economic scarcity in his opinion. But if this were true, would more money also mean more scarcity then? If this would be the case, the Central Banks are creating scarcity by their continuing money injections. It appears to be a paradoxical situation, but it might have an element of truth.

Before the time when money didn't exist, there was enough land to cultivate for everyone with ample means of sustaining life, according to Locke. It was useless to take more than needed for one's daily life, as surplus produce was of no use. Besides the law of nature prohibits products of the earth to decay and waste away, as they are destined by God for consumption. This meant that in the state of nature *"every man's possession was confined to a moderate proportion, and such as he might appropriate to himself without injury to anybody in the first ages of the world, when men were more in danger to be lost, by wandering from their companion, in the then vast wilderness of the earth than to be straitened for want of room to plant in."* This idyllic state of nature was ended by the invention of money, by which society changed into *"The realm of scarcity"*. Once more Hans Achterhuis quotes Locke in his book of the same name of 1988[4]: *"I dare boldly affirm that the same rule of property - viz., that every man should have as much as he could make use of, would still hold in the world, without straitening anybody, since there is land enough in the world to suffice double the inhabitants, had not the invention of money, and the tacit agreement of men to put a value on it, introduced (by consent) larger possessions and the right to them."*

By the invention of money scarcity was created, according to Locke. Money makes it easier to gather more possessions than needed for use. Before that time there wasn't any *"temptation to work for more than one needs"* - or rather, the technical possibilities (storing and potting to prevent decay) were almost entirely lacking. In his opinion the introduction of money changed *"the intrinsic value of things".* He defines this *intrinsic value* as the value *"which depends only on their usefulness to the life of man."* By this idea of *intrinsic value* he meant, contrary to the common definition, the *utility value*, which we have seen before with Aristotle and Marx (in the metamorphosis of commodities). According to Locke the intrinsic value is the value that depends on 'the **use** of things' and thus he reasons from a subjective value conception, the value resulting from human needs. We have discussed this extensively in chapter 3. To brush up: in this connection Adam Smith spoke of the *"value in use"*, the usefulness of a certain product in use - Aristotle called this the *proper use*. Opposed to his *improper use*, which Adam Smith called *"value in exchange"* or *"power of purchasing other goods"* - Marx's *value of exchange*, in which we recognize our concept of purchasing power. Does all of this ring a bell?'

Yes sir, to a certain degree it does, I nodded obediently.

'Locke posed that scarcity didn't exist before the invention of money. In *An essay concerning the true original extend and end of civil government* he put forward both sons of Adam and Eve to support this proposition: *"At the beginning Cain might take as much ground as he could till and make it his own land, and yet leave enough to Abel's sheep to feed on."* But, says Achterhuis: *"Unfortunately Locke chooses the most unfortunate example possible. Because, in the story of Genesis, Cain beats his brother to death exactly because of a scarce good he didn't get. It concerned Jahweh's attention, the God to whom both made a sacrifice. God only paid attention to Abel's sacrifice and 'he ignored' Cain's. In vain God warns Cain not to compare himself to his brother, in order to control the sin of envy. Cain doesn't listen, though. He couldn't bear that Abel got something he didn't have. He lured Abel into an open field and killed him."*

The story of Cain and Abel indeed is the archetypal myth of scarcity, says Achterhuis and here he locates *"the social sources of violence"*. Like Hobbes before: *"Two people become each other's enemy, when they desire the same thing, which nevertheless they can't enjoy both."* In the Bible story it was God's attention. In connection to this Achterhuis refers to the central notion in the philosophy of René Girard: *mimesis*, imitation. In imitation the source of culture is to be found, but it can degenerate into *'mimetic desire'*: people preferably desire the same as someone else does. *"Who says mimetic desire, says scarcity"*, Achterhuis summarizes it. He also mentions a variant of the archetypal myth of scarcity: *"In exegeses from the end of the 19*[th] *century God didn't get the blame of Cain's mimetic desire, but a woman, namely a sister of both brothers, desired by both brothers at the same time. Because she chooses Abel, Cain kills him. The Bible story is said not to have mentioned this quarrel about their sister because of the incest prohibition."*

But back to our present-day money and the Central Banks like the ECB in their part of the horn of plenty. We may sometimes get the impression that those banks want to suppress or even abolish scarcity by their unlimited money supply in the second decade of the 21st century. Borrow money almost for free! A paradoxical kind of reversal of Locke's idea that money creates scarcity: pump as much money into society as needed to give people enough means to fight scarcity. In this connection Achterhuis points out: *"Just like the holiness in traditional societies, money in modern societies is a mechanism if not to conquer scarcity then at least to control it."*[4] Striking in this is that he compares money to 'holiness', to divinity, and he continues: *"In this sense money is also characterized by the ambivalence of the scapegoat. On the one hand it gets the blame for violence and scarcity, and on the other hand it is divinized because it offers a solution for it."* And the solution chosen by the ECB and other western central banks in the second decade of the 21st century is exactly this: fight the fire with more fire, let the money bazookas roar and the 'money press scream', like *Maarten Schinkel* once said.[5] But unfortunately, this didn't succeed in the second decade of the 21st century. And why not?'

Because the banks blocked the circulation of that money, didn't you say so above, I reacted.

'On the one hand because the financial system was blocked, but it wasn't the only reason. An other reason was that more and more people tried to escape from the traditional economic system. They did so in two ways: on the one hand by critically holding their needs against the light and reduce them and on the other hand by becoming more self-supporting. The first way is connected to the ancient Aristotelian idea of the golden mean, of knowing where to draw the line. Those who aspire this in the 21st century don't tackle the traditional scarcity concept *"Means / Needs"* at the numerator by increasing their *Means* (money), but at the denominator by decreasing their *Needs*. This honourable pursuit hasn't only been inspired by Aristotelian ideological motives, but has also been inspired by lack of faith in economic prospects. As a consequence of this people took it easy. In jargon this is called low consumer confidence and connected to this producer confidence left a lot to be desired too. The second way, pursuing more self-supporting, is connected to the prevailing money system itself. An increasing group of people wants to become more independent of the official money system, for instance by creating alternative means of exchange with the help of LETS (= Local Exchange Trading System). These alternative money forms mostly circulate in relatively small circles, which aim at using locally and regionally produced goods as much as possible. Alternative and additional money forms do have a long history though. Thus, in 1696 Quaker John Bellers suggested the introduction of labour vouchers to pay unemployed persons for the goods they had produced with the help of public facilities. The system became defunct rather soon though, but quite a few other persons tried to get something like that going, like philanthropist Robert Owen 140 years later, without success as well. But in 1814 in the American state Indiana the *Harmony Society* founded a fortress-like utopian little town named *Harmony*, later changed into *New Harmony*, in which Robert Owen among others was involved too. The New Harmony experiment with an alternative economic system started in

1825 and was on the rocks as soon as 1829 because of internal differences. And this is more often the problem with alternative communes idealistically pursuing autonomy with a currency of their own. But nowadays successful alternative money systems exist all over the world, among which the Swiss WIR - bank.'

And what to think of the *Bitcoin* and all other kinds of crypto money? I wondered? Are they going to last long? I had my doubts, as there had been various misfortunes with this Bitcoin in the past. But the author didn't go into it.

'For some years Belgian economist *Bernard Lietaer* has been fervourly arguing in favour of diversity in the money system, so parallel currencies, official and additional ones.[6] In the framework of this book it would lead too far afield to go into all these additional currencies, as in relation to our argument it's of no importance which currency is used - as all of them are mind-things.'

It goes without saying, I said aloud, as I nearly finished reading the book.

'But did all of this mean that people had less confidence in official money itself? Money that is brought into circulation by the government and monetary organizations?'

That seems only logical, I thought, but I was wrong again:

'No, strangely enough nothing seemed wrong with public confidence in money itself, as people held on to it in full confidence. Families massively put it in savings accounts, expecting it to keep its value, even though the savings interest rates were negligible. And many companies were rolling in cash, which in large numbers like that put in short term deposits sometimes caused negative interest rates!'

What!? Negative interest rates? I thought, pay money to store your money!? Who would do a thing like that? You had better keep it in cash, hadn't you?

'These negative interest rates were accepted, because keeping all these millions in your own safe was too risky, for example because of burglary or damage by fire, as extra insurances would be needed then.'

Luxury problems, I concluded. 'All this money in cash and savings makes clear that nobody feared inflation. Rather the other way round: expecting things to get cheaper in future seemed more evident than expecting them to become more expensive, deflation seemed to be brewing. And that was a bad omen in economics, as deflation or even the expectation of deflation often results in stagnation.

Owing to all of this the opening of the money sluices by the ECB wasn't of much help, as this money didn't circulate enough. For the greater part it got stuck as a kind of liquid mud behind the sluice gates of banking and the other part was saved or hoarded up. Keynes's old saying was applicable here: *"You can lead a horse to the water, but you can't make it drink"*.

To put it in terms of the cycle in chapter 5: this hoarding up made the rate of circulation of money (the V of MV = PT) relatively low then and never managed to increase, in spite of the Dutch prime minister encouraging us to buy a new car.

Thus the generous throwing of almost free money by the central banks didn't have the desired effect for a long time. The horses didn't want to drink it. Why not? Weren't they thankful? Weren't they thirsty?'

Less thirsty than before, you said before, I said aloud to the author. Because a number of people had returned to Aristotle's virtue, hadn't they? The virtue of the golden mean, of knowing where to draw the line?

'Of course they were still thirsty, as human needs are limitless, despite the waking up of a selective group that had been converted to Aristotelian virtue ethics. But they seemed to mistrust the monetary water. Water that reflected the shadow of monetary signs that had been sent into the world as smoke signals by the high priests of the money system, but what did they represent? What exactly was their message?'

Shop till you drop! entered my mind. Buy, buy, buy!! Rather banal. That was the message. But the public distrusted the monetary high priests and didn't believe in the wholesome effect of this fashionable horn of plenty, which from the ECB in Frankfurt preached the Glad Tidings of the monetary Manna.

'The message was that we had to learn to have faith again. Faith in a carefree economic future, to which a broad gold brick-road in a virtual shape might lead us. Did we still fear grim economic times? No need for that! We only had to become optimistic and spend money. This hanging on to this thriftiness was of no use. Stop being an egoist by sitting on your money! Or else you have to pay a fine!'

What? Pay a fine on your savings? Who the hell comes up with such nonsense?

'A fine indeed, it happens. We know the concept of penalty interest rates on early mortgage repayment and we also got acquainted with the phenomenon of negative interest rates on putting away too much cash by companies. And in the middle of 2014 the ECB determined for the first time a negative deposit interest rate for banks of 0.1%.

Anyhow, we haven't arrived at the point yet that public distrust in the high priests of money is punished by a fine on private savings accounts - although this is actually happening right now: a minimal interest rate of about 1% for the saver won't be enough to meet inflation and the (Dutch) taxation on the supposed return. And if on these savings additional wealth tax has to be paid, the poor saver will make a real sacrifice. Therefore once more the message of the Dutch prime minister and the money popes of the Central Banks of that time: do buy this new car at last, and preferably a new house as well right away, a new kitchen, a new … You don't wish to be also guilty of the crisis, do you? Follow the signs of money, follow the new gold.

This new gold consists of monetary signs distributed almost for free by the Central Banks. The Central Banks acting as generous donors who try to prove that Locke's scarcity ideas are bullshit by doing exactly the opposite of his theory: fighting the evils of scarcity by almost limitless money injections. It remains to be seen whether this will be successful, but the Central Banks create the strong impression of wanting to be the postmodern variant of the classic horn of plenty or even of the postmodern holy grail. Looked at it like this, seen from the other side we might consider the Holy Grail the very first kind of Central Bank!'

Good grief, this goes rather far, I thought. So far, I fairly understood the story on monetary dualism between money body and money spirit and considered it a reasonable and acceptable story, but this idea of the Holy Grail as the first Central Bank? Who might have been the first Central banker then? Christ himself perhaps? But the author ended the story here and after that he wisely decided that mum was the word.

Notes

1. Marc Shell, *Money, Language, and Thought*, Baltimore, London 1993 (originally California 1982)
2. See for example: Reinold Widemann, *Het Rentelabyrint - Conversaties over geld en interest*, Dordrecht 2012
3. Edin Mujagić, *Geldmoord - Hoe de centrale banken ons geld vernietigen*, Amsterdam 2012 *(Money Murder - How the Central Banks are Destroying Our Money)*
4. Hans Achterhuis, *Het rijk der schaarste- van Thomas Hobbes tot Michel Foucault*, Baarn 1988 *(The Realm of Scarcity - From Thomas Hobbes to Michel Foucault)*
5. Maarten Schinkel, *De gillende geldpers van premier Abe*, Article in NRC 20-5-2012
6. See for example: Bernard Lietaer, *The Future of Money - Creating new wealth, work and a wiser world*, London 2001

11 MONEY ART AND ARTIFICIAL MONEY
On the representation of money and value

"In exchanging art for money, we exchange one abstraction for another"
Daniel Spoerri

'I can't think of a more appropriate quotation to open this final chapter with than this one by Swiss artist *Daniel Spoerri* (born 1930, Rumania). He expresses the essential character of both money and art: *"both are symbol systems"*, says art historian and economist *Olav Velthuis*. *"Their value doesn't exist 'by nature', but is a social construction: their meaning is based on various social conventions and institutions (museums or banks for example), which add legitimacy and value to both art and money."* [1] Or in the words of American artist *Christopher C. K. Wilde* (born 1972, Madison Wisconsin) *"Art and money are cultural inventions without real value."* [2] But these statements of *Velthuis* and *Wilde* raise the question what exactly they mean by this *value by nature* or *real value*. Do such values exist at all?'

Ah, I sense the author's line of thought, I thought, as he had elaborately discussed this value question in a previous chapter - let me see - chapter 3 it was.

'The reader who persevered in reading this book, may remember the challenging introductory question of chapter 3: *"Do things have a value by themselves?"* And to give a crystal-clear answer to this question: *"No!!"*

With two exclamation marks, yes, I remember.

'Things and nature don't have any value by themselves, we posed, following *Georg Simmel*, although quite a few people might disagree. But we argued that everything that is considered valuable by man, has been given this value by man himself. We discussed objective and subjective value, seemingly objective costs and subjective utility, and concluded that when properly looked at it, eventually everything we label with value is based on subjective human judgments. For how are we to know beyond our perceptive faculty of judgment and perception what is valuable? Let alone the dimensions and nature of this value. So, when economist/art historian *Velthuis* and artist *Wilde* speak of *value of nature* and *real value*, we arrogantly claim that they have no idea what they are talking about. Do their indications of value refer to basic products like food, clothing and accommodation? Or to cars, televisions and computers? All of them are things we do value, certainly, but we have no idea how to attach a 'value of nature' to a computer for example. Useful things to modern man. But 'useful' is a subjective concept and the question is whether this is a 'value of nature' or a 'real value'.'

Philosophical speculations, I thought, but meanwhile having become familiar with the author's view, I wasn't surprised any longer.

'Nevertheless these statements by *Velthuis* and *Wilde* are of importance, because both indirectly refer to the abstract nature of art and money. Abstraction as an essential characteristic of both according to *Spoerri*: if we exchange art for money, we exchange one abstraction for another.

In this chapter we will meet a number of artists who are inspired by the phenomenon of money. The art they make, we will call money art and this money art has a few things in common with artificial money. Money art contains a series of art products which are based on our dealings and experiences with money or institutions that supply money, like banks. These products may take the shape of sculptures, paintings, installations and performances, but money also plays a part in other art forms like literature and acting. The best-known example is *The merchant of Venice* by William Shakespeare. In chapter 7 we have already mentioned this play in connection with the interest ban.'

And don't forget film, I added, just think of this famous film *Wall Street* from 1987 featuring Michael Douglas as Gordon Gekko. *"Every dream has a price"*, was his slogan, I think. Fits nicely into this book's theme, I thought, which deals with the money dream in our minds, a dream sometimes with a high price attached to it.

'But in this chapter on money art we restrict ourselves to the visual arts. The concepts of money art and artificial money aren't always easily distinguished. In general money art has not been made to be used as money, but is just art. Artificial money mostly is not meant as art, but as currency for special occasions like the Chinese ghost or spirit money (we will come to that later) or for games and festivities. Think of plastic coins or vouchers for consumptions during pop festivals for example.'

And games like monopoly particularly! I just thought of, as I used to play this game in the past. Buy streets, rule over houses and hotels, whether or not mortgaged, pretend to be a capitalist with fake monopoly money, or go bankrupt. But there are a lot more of these money games with fake money; you can find many in the internet, like the ones I had come across when searching them for my little nephew: like the old-fashioned 'Play Shops', 'Fish Money', 'The Money Game', 'Coinz!' and many others.

'And we think of more than just games and toy money', the author waved away my childlike enthusiasm, 'but also of more serious matters, like Chinese ghost and spirit money. This isn't real money, but artificial money used to be burnt for the deceased. It's a Taoist ritual, in which this artificial money is sent to deceased relatives in the hereafter, by being burnt. They need this money for their daily needs.'

Their daily needs? When they are dead?

'The Chinese believe life to go on beyond the grave in one way or another and that it isn't cheap either. That's why ghost money is supplied in high denominations of 10,000 up to 1 billion Yuan, but also in dollars or other currencies.'

A bit like this story of the Styx and Hades in Greek mythology, I thought, when the deceased are given a coin, an obol, to pay the ferryman Charon. And when thinking this, it reminded me of the famous BBC-television series of 1977: *Who Pays the Ferryman?*

'Because electronic payment to the hereafter doesn't exist, burning money is the quickest alternative to pay deceased loved ones - although nowadays cheques and paper credit cards are used as well.'

Well, this may not be electronic, it's quite virtual though, I thought. Money that ends up in smoke and materializes in the hereafter, it's as virtual as you can imagine, I guess, and it reminded me of the words *Scotty beam me up*, spoken by a crewmember in the *Star Trek* series if he wanted to be transported back from an alien planet to the spaceship *Enterprise*.

'This Chinese ghost money is a nice example of artificial money that isn't accepted as real money in real life. This is the most important characteristic of the concept 'artificial money', as from the moment it is accepted as real money, it will be real money! The shape of the money or the material it is made of, is of no importance at all, as we have said many times before, whether it is made of stone, wood, leather, salt, metal, paper, air or whatever.'

Money made of air?

'Money made of air is of course nothing but a metaphor for a verbal credit agreement, in the form of some money words hanging in the air like a radio signal between two parties.'

A financial agreement, without a written account, I nodded, a verbal IOU, merely a matter of trust, a promise that creates debt.

'Hence, artificial money isn't real money. It may be a form of money art, like the *AVL money* of 2001 designed by *Atelier Van Lieshout*, a series of banknotes in denominations of 1, 5, 25 and 100 AVL. But Van Lieshout wasn't the only artist who designed his own money. The American artist *JSG Boggs* (born 1955) did something similar. He drew his own banknotes in 1988 and tried to spend them in economic intercourse. He did quite well, as he bought for more than a million Euros, among other things a Harley Davidson motorbike, flight tickets, clothing, art, and rare banknotes.[1] Another example of an artist who produced his own money, is the American *Stephen Barnwell* (born 1960, Rutherford, NJ), who among other things made 'Antarctic' dollar notes of 4 and 7 dollars. He printed the homepage of his own company on the banknotes. 'Antarctica' was the name of that company at that time.[2] On his website he called the paper dollars, produced by himself, *dream-dollars*,[3] a characterization that goes well with the title of this book, and isn't only applicable to artificial dollars but also to all dollars, according to us.'

And to all other kinds of money, I added for the sake of completeness.

'The artificial money of Atelier Van Lieshout, Boggs and Barnwell is a form of money art at the same time, which even got a monetary function in the case of Boggs, because he used it literally as a currency. In his case his art got the status of money: Art = Money! A congruency that can be applied to a lot of art. We will go into that later.

Now we have almost arrived at our walk around money art. Almost, as first we should answer the question to which extend money itself is a kind of art. In deciding this the design and style may play a part, but in our view rather a supporting part than a principal part. For, isn't money, regardless of its form, a work of art by itself?'

I guess so, I thought, or he wouldn't have asked the question.

'Think of completely shapeless virtual money: can something invisible like that be art?'

I guess so, I thought again, as virtual money is pure abstraction! A form of money abstracted to a degree that not only the bearer but also the representation has disappeared, even more invisible than a white painting by *Malewitsch* for instance, as this virtual money can't be framed and hung on the wall! I remember that there was a kind of 'attack' by the Russian artist *Aleksander Davidovich Brener* (born 1957, Alma Ata) on this completely white painting on show in the Stedelijk Museum in Amsterdam in 1997: he sprayed a green dollar sign on the painting, and immediately turned himself in to a museum attendant and ended up in prison for half a year. But he didn't regret his action and didn't even consider it a crime. During his defence he said that it hadn't been directed against the painting, but that he had meant his action to be a dialogue with Malewitsch. From prison he told that his work had to be considered an avant-garde artwork. His dollar sign was a sign of trade and merchandise, pointing at how immoral the present-day elite had become and how devastating the money dealings in art. I read about it in the newspapers at the time and remembered it because I saw the fun of it. But why am I mentioning this? Ah yes, because of the association with virtual money, which couldn't even be hung on the wall like a white Malewitsch. If I were to compare this kind of money with a form of art, it would be a performance, a conceptual artwork, or a phantasmagoria maybe, a dance for figures and numbers on postmodern charivari. Virtual money isn't visible, doesn't have a body, and yet we pretend that it exists. And this is exactly what money is actually: a form of faith! But is faith a form of art as well? Nice speculations, I thought, if *George Simmel* could hear this, he might be chuckling in his grave. And he most certainly would have agreed with *Spoerri's* saying on the abstract nature of art and money. For hadn't he stressed that the step from concrete to abstract money had been a great leap forward in the reasoning of man?

'These questions must be answered affirmatively: money is a form of art, abstract art, and the medium used is of no importance. But in our walk around money art we will visit some works which have been put in some tangible form or other. Money art mostly isn't without a body, contrary to money as a product of art in itself. Let's not rack our brains over it and let's push off. In the scope of this book, this walk around money art will be a limited subjective selection, as in the course of time the number of productions in this field have been that large that even a substantial catalogue couldn't contain all of them. We believe that the money artworks we chose, represent the dualism between money spirit and money matter. They give a picture of how artists look at the phenomenon of money and in what way this money is in their minds.

With the artists inspired by money, often a conscious or unconscious perception of (the right) value plays a part too. By their works they implicitly or explicitly criticize money society and the chosen foundation of value. We can distinguish seven categories as foundations of value, sometimes melting in one another or combined by the artists:

Precious metal (gold and silver)
Dollar
Art
Trust
Earth (nature)
Labour (time)
Energy sources (like coal or oil)

We'll give some examples of money art which belong to a particular category.

Foundation of value precious metal: The Money Changer and His Wife

The most famous artwork in which money is the central point, may be *The Money Changer and His Wife* by the Flemish artist *Quinten Massijs* or *Quinten Metsys* (1464/5 - 1530) from 1514 which hangs in the Louvre in Paris. The painting has been chosen as an illustration on the cover of many books and stories on money, as on *Marc Shell's* book, which has been mentioned in the previous chapter. This artwork depicts a banker or money changer in his office, who is busy weighing coins. This weighing was necessary in those days to check the gold or silver content of the money, because, as we have told before, the coins suffered wear by daily use and besides these coins were prone to tampering.'

Oh yes, clipping, sweating, monarchs melting these old coins down for new ones with a lower precious metal content, things like that.

'Seated next to him is his wife, who looks up from her illustrated *Book of Hours*, a devout work with prayers and psalms. She has just turned a page with a picture of the Madonna and her child. But being distracted from her devout book by filthy lucre is a fateful sign. According to the Louvre's website[4] we are dealing with a painting with a moral message: it judges human vice and reminds the viewers of the fragility of life. The shining gold, together with the pearls (symbol of desire) and some jewels on the front of the table, have distracted the woman from her divine duties.'

Something like a divine spirit being distracted by an evil money spirit in the shape of a monetary Mephistopheles, I thought. Two spirits struggling for priority in the mind of the money changer's wife. For money is a kind of spirit too, the author's central proposition. There may be real coins lying on the money changer's table, but their attraction isn't caused by the discs themselves, but by what this coin material, this money body symbolizes to the money changer and his wife, and to us as well, as I had grasped meanwhile, so what they represented. And that's wealth, power, prosperity, independence, freedom from worry, status, happiness - yes, happiness too, although that representative side of money often turns out to be a fata morgana. Hence, when looking at it in this way, such a money changer behind his table is in cloud-cuckoo land, a kind of paradise. He is imagining all kinds of things. While weighing and counting, images and promises are circulating in his mind, promises of a land of milk and honey and his wife is in this promised land as well. That's why she has this faraway gaze. A gaze I came across in a number of similar paintings the writer drew my attention to:

'Compare this painting to two similar works by *Marinus van Reymerswaele*', he said, 'who lived in the same period of time (1490 - 1546). One is hanging in the *Alte Pinakothek* in München and the other in the *Koninklijk Museum voor Schone Kunsten* in Antwerp[5], but both represent the same as the money changer by Massijs, namely *The Banker and His Wife*. And also in these two paintings the bankers' wives are looking at the coins lying on the table with a similar faraway gaze. What do they see?'

Fantasies, I thought, ideals, options, undifferentiated purchasing power, well anything you can imagine. Those coins do lie on the table, but what they symbolize is in the minds of the money changers and their wives.

Foundation of value: Tower of Power

'Those bankers and their wives see the same things lying there as the contemporary artist *Chris Burden* (born 1946) wants to show with his *Tower of Power* from 1985.'

Ah, Tower of Power, I thought, the famous soul - funk - rhythm and blues band with many brass players. But it wasn't about this band at all, of course. Do pay attention to the lesson, I severely spoke to myself.

'This pyramid-like tower, with a bit of fantasy resembling a cathedral with a gold roof, consists of 100 kilo gold with a value of more than a million dollars, composed of 100 ingots of 1 kilogram each, constantly guarded by a security guard. According to the artist, the *Tower of Power* represents a connection between *aura* and *wealth* and also between *beauty* and *power*. In many works by *Burden* the meaning-making role of banks and museums is emphasized. And because a work of art is usually shown in a museological setting, the *Tower of Power* is also a metaphorical reference to the power of the museum as an institution. Burden shows that is not only a place where aesthetic and imaginary values are neutrally being exhibited, but also inevitably a place of evaluation and power and of inclusion and exclusion. In addition his installation refers to the link between aesthetic and social rules hidden in every work of art.

As far as we are concerned, the message of Burden's tower of power fits well into this book's theme, this book on money as a mind thing, as Burden is also depicting in his gold Tower a connection between *money spirit* and *money body*, between the *aura* of the gold and the *capital* it represents. For what do we actually see when looking at the Tower? Once more we see an illusion which appears to be surprisingly real. The same kind of illusion that put a spell on the money changer and his wife.

Foundation of value: dollar
More artists similarly depicted their fascination with the power and aura of money, but not with gold or silver as the foundation of value, but with the American dollar. As we have seen before in another connection, the dollar appears to have overthrown gold, because since 15 august 1971 the dollar price was no longer determined by the value of gold, but the gold price got more and more dependent on the value of the dollar.'

Yes indeed, Nixon, I remembered, his decision to disconnect the dollar from the monetary gold.

'From that time onwards almost any country increasingly considered the American dollar an equal substitute for gold. And when nowadays central banks all over the world calculate their supply of 'gold and currency', they mainly refer to dollars as 'currency'. The dollar has remained the most powerful currency, even though the Chinese Yuan and the Indian rupee are rapidly growing more and more important. But the power of the dollar apparently impresses many artists and their most famous representative may be *Andy Warhol*. He painted numerous dollar signs in all colours of the rainbow, like *192 One Dollar Bills* from 1962 and from the same year *200 One Dollar Bills*, sold at Sotheby's in 2009 for $43.8 million. This iconic money art is a form of pop art, comparable to his famous series *Campbell's* soup cans.

Foundation of value: One Billion Dollar (Most Expensive Artwork Ever)

Another artist who depicted his fascination or awe for the dollar was the Austrian *Michael Marcovici* (born 1969, Vienna) who built *One Billion Dollar (Most Expensive Artwork Ever)* in 2009. On twelve pallets he piled dollar bills of $100 each with a total value of one billion dollars. In an explanation he wrote that this artwork is not about what you see, but about the imagination what you might be able do with this money. Once more a clear reference to the dualism between money body and money spirit, in which it's all about this spirit, about the imagination of material and immaterial wealth these pallets loaded with money evoke.

Foundation of value dollar: 100,000 Dollar - Wall

Our last example of an artist who used dollars in his work, is conceptual artist *Hans - Peter Feldmann*, born 1941 in Düsseldorf, who displayed a *100,000 Dollar - Wall* in the Guggenheim Museum in New York in 2011. The installation literally consisted of 100,000 dollar bills he had pasted on the walls and pillars. We shouldn't try to read anything into this, he said, for it was just what it showed: *Money = Art*. He had received the money shortly before as winner of the *Hugo Boss Prize,* a biennial prize since 1996.'

Money = Art or Art = Money: a kind of economic cycle, I thought, but in this case a cycle of two countercyclical kinds of money, if I had understood the artist correctly. A kind of congruency. Because if he assumes that money is a form of art, and if I turn it around, we actually speak of two kinds of currency traded in a special kind of financial market, and this market is the currency market. In the currency market different currencies are being exchanged, like dollars for Euros, and according to *Hans - Peter Feldmann* art should be seen as a currency, if I'm right. And I was right, as:

'By which we have ended up with the artists who consider their art a form of money,' the author said.

Foundation of value money: Art = Money

'There have been many more artists who posed that Money and Art are identical, among whom *Joseph Beuys* (1921 - 1986) might have been the most famous, who wrote several versions of **Kunst = Kapital** (Art = Capital) on blackboards and notes among other things. He is supposed to have been the first artist who repeatedly posed this equalization, by which he made clear that to him art had a monetary foundation of value in itself.

But art as a foundation of value for money takes up a special position, because it has two identities, or rather: two masks, the one of the master and the other of the servant. With the first mask it presents itself as an independent manager of the designing spirit and pliable matter, with the second as the servant of the monetary society. Neither of both identities has a fixed form and sometimes they coincide chameleon-like when the artist presents his art as mere money. The question is whether the artist has become a money servant, or whether the money servant has freed himself from his subordinate status by means of his art and thus has become the master of the monetary form.'

Yes of course, my goodness, the master of the monetary form! Would that be a kind of monetary Zen master? A bit of a vague story about this artistic struggle with the inner master - servant relation. But aren't we all bothered once in a while by this struggle of who is in control, the money or we ourselves, but in most cases it won't be an artistic struggle.

'But a comparable view on art being the same as money can be found with *Damien Hirst* (born Bristol 1965), who once said that art is the most important currency in the world. It's held against *Hirst* that he is nothing but a charlatan and a money-grubber. It was the main criticism in 2007, when he exhibited his skull set with precious stones *For the Love of God*. The skull, a platinum cast of a skull of an 18th century European, had been encrusted with 8601 diamonds. In 2008 the skull was shown in the Rijksmuseum Amsterdam and attracted long queues of visitors. Hirst claimed that the production costs had been 14 million pounds and that it had been sold for 50 million pounds. But it's unclear whether this work deals with the dualism between money body and money spirit.'

Unclear? I thought. Well, it's quite obvious to me that it does.

'A foundation of value related to the dollar and art is faith. But these foundations of value 'dollar' and 'art' may be faith too. Couldn't we say as well that the value of both dollar and art are actually dependent on faith, as without it nobody would pay a penny for them.

Foundation of value art and faith: Danaë
The Russian pavilion in the Venice Biennale 2013 showed an installation of the Russian conceptual artist *Vadim Zakharov* (born 1959 Dushanbe, Tajikistan), who had been inspired by the story of *Danaë*, a myth from Greek mythology. This daughter of Akrisios, king of Argos, was seduced by a gold rain. Meant by it was the corrupting power of money. *Zakharov* made an installation in Venice in which it literally rained money, in the form of coins. From a pyramid shaped roof it was raining coins through a large shower head. The spectators were allowed to walk through the money rain with transparent umbrellas and pick up coins from the money pool on the floor. But after that they had to neatly put these coins into a bucket. When it had been filled, it was pulled up by a rope through a hole in the ceiling by the artist or his assistant and emptied into a conveyer belt (Jacob's ladder) which transported the coins upstairs again, after which the whole process was repeated.'

Again a kind of cycle model, I thought.

'The question is whether or not this is an example of an economic cycle,' the author took up my thought (was this man clairvoyant?). 'If this is the case, a flow of goods and/or services must run counterclockwise into a flow of money. Well, this money cycle is clearly visible here, but what kind of product flows in the opposite direction?'

Good question, I thought, art maybe?

'This product is an art product in this case: the installation of Zakharov, who renders a service to the public. They are presented an art performance. Comparable to a theatrical performance, when the audience pays for the theater product.'

Or a film, I added, a concert, a flower parade, or whatever. I guess that I understood the meaning of the *Danaë* installation meanwhile.

Foundation of value earth: Soil-erg
'A money artwork of quite another nature than the examples above, was shown at the art manifestation *Documenta 13* in Kassel in

2012. It playfully criticizes our gold stupidity. It was made by the American female artist *Claire Pentecost* (born 1956 Atlanta: professor at the 'School of Art Institute of Chicago') and exhibited in the Ottoneum in Kassel. The installation is called *Soil-erg* and consists among others of soup plate-sized coins and piles of ingots resembling gold ingots, but instead made of earth and compost. Large bank note-like drawings 'painted' in earth and compost too, were hanging on the wall. With this installation Pentecost meant to offer an alternative for the petrodollar.'[6]

Petrodollar, I thought, what was it again?

'This petrodollar came into existence after Nixon had stopped the free exchangeability of dollars for monetary gold in 1971.'

That year rang a bell: hadn't the author mentioned it before? The fact that the dollar was no longer determined by gold, but that the causality had been turned around? Yes, the value of gold was dependent on the value of the dollar from that moment onwards, as *Jean-Joseph Goux* had said, which he considered a kind of postmodern reversal of cause and effect.

'We came across this date of 14 august 1971 a few times before as the beginning of postmodernism, according to *Jean - Joseph Goux*', the author repeated. 'He argued that the dollar became the foundation of the price of gold, meaning that the gold price depended on the dollar's value. But this didn't happen without any resistance. For the immediate consequence of this stopping of the free exchangeability of dollars for monetary gold was an enormous devaluation of the dollar. In an attempt to end this, Nixon arranged with Saudi-Arabia that in exchange for support and weapons, from then onwards American dollars should be used as payment for oil supplies. After that the other OPEC countries also introduced the dollar as international currency for oil. It caused an increase of the international demand of dollars, which supported the dollar exchange rate. But these so-called petrodollars didn't circulate within America, and therefore weren't part of the domestic American money supply and so they couldn't cause inflation there. You might say that the Americans exported part of their inflation this way. The value of the dollar is supported by this privilege of the international use of the petrodollar and as a consequence of this the gold price is additionally determined by way of this oil-route. And this privileged position of the dollar is criticized by Claire Pentecost in het *Soil-erg* project.

That's why she shows ingots, coin sculptures and banknote drawings made from earth and natural compost. This soil is of vital importance and has all the necessary qualities a currency should have in future according to her. Sound soil and seeds are endangered from all sides nowadays in becoming privatized and poisoned by pesticides, fertilizer and other chemicals. Pentecost encourages people to face these facts and to start the production of sound soil themselves by learning how to compost. In view of this she added an 'auditory sculpture', in which a section of fertile soil is shown behind glass to the spectators, who can meanwhile listen to amplified sounds of worms productively turning up the soil.

By this artwork Claire Pentecost has returned the idea of money and value circulating in our minds to the place where in her view this entire value originates from, the earth. Our earth eventually delivers all our food and all our raw materials, and therefore we have to be careful with it.

Foundation of value work: Time/Bank

At the same *Documenta 13* was a pavilion of the artists *Julieta Aranda* (born 1975 Mexico city) and *Anton Vidokle* (born 1965 Moscow) titled *Time/Bank*. It showed an alternative currency with working hours as foundation of value. There were banknotes in many denominations, for instance half an hour, an hour, six hours or ten hours. The banknotes had been designed in different languages by various artists. The project Time/Bank started in 2010 and has got many departments all over the world meanwhile. The intention of the artists goes beyond merely showing an artwork, for they set up an online platform where people can exchange services and products based on working hours without the use of money. In their website you can find a survey of all the available skills.[7] Of which does this remind us?'

Adam Smth! I called out breathlessly - and our friend Simmel!, both with exclamation marks, but it made me almost choke. It made me think of *'toil and trouble'* by Adam Smith, which accompany work in his view, or the *'Mühe und Plage'* of work in the words of George Simmel. It has been dealt with in the first couple of chapters. And oh yes, this peculiar French philosopher Jean - Joseph Goux, who argued that only making sacrifices, suffering, could provide value. But this plague of labour, this suffering from work had been caused by the uncontrollable curiosity of two women: *Eva* and *Pandora*! You should have left that apple alone and never have opened that box, dear ladies! We might have liked going to our work instead - but then, work couldn't have provided any value, according to *Adam Smith*. And he hadn't been able to base his theory of values on it, either. For hadn't he been the one who had stated that labour was the only right criterion for exchange value or the price of a product? Had I remembered this correctly?

'It reminds us of the labour theory of values of classical economists like *Adam Smith* and *David Ricardo*', the author affirmed, 'but as we know also *Karl Marx* has based his theory of values on labour.'

Oh yes, with his famous idea that the surplus value of that labour was pruned away and stolen by capitalist employers, came to mind.

'Hence the artists of the Time/Bank actually return to this classical labour theory of values. Meanwhile similar timebanks have been founded all over the world, which use a comparable exchange system of time units. The question raised by this is whether it can be argued that this kind of exchange system operates essentially different from or is principally deviating from the regular monetary exchange.'

I guess not, when posed like this, I thought.

'In our view the answer is: no not in essence. It's just that the scale of these alternative monetary systems is smaller. But even a timebank like that is eventually based on faith, on the faith that someone else is prepared to do the job you want him to do in exchange for your time voucher. What counts in favour of a timebank, is that the price-fixing of the supplied services and products will be nearer to the 'fair price' we mentioned in chapter 2. Because the participants can't cheat with inexplicable profit margins not related to working hours. The quoted Christian thinkers *Thomas of Aquino* and *Albertus Magnus* might have been quite content with the justice and virtuousness of a timebank like that. *Aristotle* would have nodded approvingly and *Adam Smith* would have congratulated the participants for having managed to put his idea into practice, his idea of *"labour is the real measure of exchangeable value, and the first price paid for all things".*

Might be so, I thought, but the quality difference within labour won't be calculated in a timebank like that, for an hour is an hour, whatever kind of work it may be. So the value of all working hours are put on a par, whether it is an hour of garden work or brickwork, a teaching hour or a lawyer's hour. I guess it's a drawback for every time bank, for in accepting this total equalization of wages, you must be quite socially-minded or have a heart of gold. Hence, such an exchange system with time units presupposes a far-reaching kind of social equality, almost communism.

'In the past various similar economic projects based on time have gone on the rocks because of internal differences,' the author took up my objections. 'A well-known historical example was the *National Equitable Labour Exchange*, founded in 1832 by *Robert Owen*, which was closed within two years. And as mentioned before in the previous chapter, his little utopian town *New Harmony* in Indiana lasted less than four years as a cooperative village. We are curious therefore what will happen to the Time/Bank of the artist duo *Aranda* and *Vidokle*.'

That sounds rather skeptical, I thought, whereas the duo of the Time/Bank does have a chance of success, especially because they go about internationally with establishments in many cities as well as online activities - but I might be wrong though.

Foundation of value energy sources: coal

'In German crime films money is often called *Kohle*, dough in English. Female conceptual artist *Alicja Kwade*, born in Poland (1979) and working in Berlin, made a money artwork in 2008, consisting of a pile of 666 gilded coal briquettes of the Union firm, titled *Von Explosionen zu Ikonen*.'

666 - the holy figure, or the mark of the beast, I thought. Might Alicja have meant this? A reference to the *Book of Revelation*?

'It was a visualization of the "black gold", which had been the fuel for the economic engine for years. But this fuel was at the end of its heyday. Most mines had been closed down and present-day energy supply mainly comes from oil, gas, nuclear power and more and more sustainable energy sources like wind and sun. Hence, coal has become an old-fashioned energy source, as obsolete as the almost *"lächerlich altertümliche Goldbegehren"* as the artist calls it. This: "lächerlich altertümliche Goldbegehren" - the reader may understand that we wholeheartedly agree to these words (See chapter 9). Just like the similar view of *Claire Pentecost*, who spoke of 'gold stupidity' in her *Soil-erg* project.

With the additional printing of the word *Rekord* on her gilded briquettes *Alicja Kwade* shows our value structures to the point of absurdity. By treating coal, gold and money as equals, the artist dethrones gold of its holy value, which makes clear how randomly a foundation of value is chosen. Anything can be proclaimed a value-icon. The title of the artwork refers to this: *Von Explosionen zu Ikonen*. By gilding the briquettes and piling up 666 of them, the fuel, the 'explosion-product' gets the aura of an almost holy/diabolic icon.

Foundation of art: Art Reserve Bank (Kunst Reserve Bank)

At the time of writing this book (2014), a small square glass building could be seen in Amsterdam, containing an 'office' of the temporary *Art Reserve Bank* (Temporary, because the ARB will be ended after five years). The 'main office' has its seat in Eindhoven and annexes can be found all over the Netherlands.[8] The ARB has been set up as a cooperative society Without Reserve Liability, in which the members determine the financial and artistic course. The 'bank' in Amsterdam owns a coin press, a vault and an office window. The aim of the Art Reserve Bank is to investigate whether it is possible to introduce a new kind of currency: a *reserve coin with intrinsic art value*. Every month a prominent artist designs a series of four coins, every week a new one, and every coin is issued for one week only. Every time a limited edition of only 100 pieces, which can be changed for the current exchange-rate at the online exchange window or at one of the annexes. And the bank has a real **dealing room** on its website: *"The dealing room is an open market place where everybody can trade their coins (…) You can also try to obtain a coin on this public marketplace."*, it says.

The terms *reserve coin* and *intrinsic art value* raise several questions though. For what do the artists mean? The aim of the bank is to investigate whether a new kind of *currency* can be introduced, which can serve as a legal means of payment. Well, there are many kinds of currencies, but only a few reserve coins. Each country has its own currency - America the dollar, China the Yuan, Turkey the lira and Poland the zloty - but only the dollar (and sometimes also the euro, and in near future maybe the Yuan and the rupee) can be used as a reserve coin by many countries. A reserve coin is a national currency indeed, but the special privilege of being internationally accepted as money and being a reserve coin at the same time, has only been given to the dollar. We won't go into the background of this privilege, but those who studied economics at school may remember that countries and central banks regularly calculated their supply of *'gold and reserve currencies'*. The currencies in this supply of 'gold and reserve currencies' are the reserve coins and the question is whether the bankers of the Art Reserve Bank have this in mind, even though the word *Reserve* is prominently present in their name, as it is in the name of the American central bank, the *Federal Reserve Bank*. But aren't the artists of the ARB merely putting a new series of coins into circulation, which will be accepted as money?

Apart from this in our view rather ambiguous message, we also stumble over the concept of *intrinsic art value*. It looks like an absolute paradox to us. Just read the quotation of *Daniel Spoerri* at the top of this chapter and the lines by *Olav Velthuis*. Both art and money are abstractions, Spoerri says, and Velthuis speaks of art and money being symbol systems, which don't have any value by themselves. Our modern money doesn't have any intrinsic value, nor does art. The value we attach to both is based on subjective value judgment, we have elaborately discussed this before.

Nevertheless, the Art Reserve Bank is an interesting art project, because this is another example of how to put the view people have on value into perspective. The ARB chose art as a foundation of value and this choice is as valid as the choice of gold, labour, trust, compost, coal or whatever other value-icon.'

Like shelves, salt, cattle, corn, fish, Yap stones and the like, I added in thought.

'Coins of the ARB designed by artists having value, is evident because of their trade value, but this value isn't intrinsic, even though the ARB speaks of 'real value'! in this case the 'real value' is the market value of those coins, which like other art products is a subjective value, fluctuating daily, dependent on demand and supply.

Money design and symbolism
We've arrived at the end of our walk around money art. But there is a lot more on display for art lovers. We recommend a book like *Art & Money* of 1994 by Marc Shell, whom we have mentioned before. And Google is a good source for information on money art. It's astonishing, how many more artists than expected are engaged in this theme.

To end this chapter, we will briefly sketch the design of money itself. By means of this design the authorities traditionally tried to send a message into the world, a value message to inspire confidence that should nestle into the minds of the money users. How can the appearance of a coin or banknote contribute to the sense of trustworthiness of that money?'

With the help of a series of authenticity characteristics, came to mind, like our banknotes with a special kind of paper, watermark, raising printing, hologram, security thread, ultraviolet ink, glossy stripe - 'touch, look, turn', the ECB calls it, but surely the author wasn't heading for this side of the story, as he had done so before.

'By choosing pictures and symbols with the appearance of authority', he said, 'symbols of national pride, decisiveness, dignity and perseverance. The originally rather heroic symbolism gradually changed into power symbols with scenic, folkloric and abstract pictures. In the beginning those power symbols used to be mainly portraits of kings and emperors, whose face had been portrayed on the coins in profile or full face.'

Or going to battle on horseback or in a four, I thought, as I had seen some pictures like that.

'Well-known examples are various coins with the portraits of Greek an Roman kings and emperors like *Alexander the Great* on a silver Tetadrachme and *Julius Caesar* on a Roman denarius. This portrait gallery shows the glorification of persons, a monetary tradition living on in coins on which our kings and queens have been depicted.'

And they aren't the only ones, I thought, just look at the self-important presidents and dictators depicted on coins and banknotes. On all American banknotes are portraits of presidents, and various government buildings on the back.

'In the ancient Greek and Roman times they used to love gods as well. Among the gods depicted on coins, are for instance the god of light, music and poetry *Apollo*, the god of the forest *Pan* and the goddess of wisdom *Pallas Athena* who had been depicted on a Greek Tetadrachme together with the owl of Athens.

But these gods are of no importance to us any longer and …'

Of no importance? Well, yes this might be the case as regards to their portraits, but *"God zij met ons"* (God be with us) has always been the edge inscription on the Dutch guilder and even on the €2 coin.

'… and fortunately it hasn't remained limited to people worship, as quite early on in history also animals, plants and objects symbolic for a town or country were used. These early pictures sometimes referred to the goods money of the time before. This *"Neigung zur Symmetrie"* used to be *"allen unausgebildeten Kulturen eigen"*, according to *Georg Simmel*, whom we have quoted before in chapter 2. That's why we can find ears of corn, axes, fish or cattle on ancient coins. And in China in the period 475 - 221 before Christ money in the shape of bronze knives and spades, and a bronze imitation of a cowry shell were circulating.[9]

The animal parade on coins and banknotes is a long parade of lions, tigers, eagles, (winged) horses, hares, elephants, dolphins, frogs, owls, dragons, crabs and the like. There usually was a relation between the animals and the character, situation, culture, economy or politics of a town or country. *Pegasus*, the winged horse, is a figure from Greek mythology flying around on various coins. On a silver Tetadrachme of the town Messina town in the fifth century before Christ a hare jumps over a cicada (cricket) and a crab and other sea animals are crawling on a coin of the town Akragas (Agrigento nowadays) founded by the Greek in Sicily in the fifth century before Christ.

Of course once in a while heroic deeds had to be rewarded with a coin too, and that's why general *Julius Caesar* had a silver denarius minted depicting an elephant trampling on a snake (his opponents) in 49 or 48 before Christ. This coin was minted in the battle field as payment for his army.[10] Knights on horsebacks, lions and eagles have been repeatedly used as coin symbols to stress the courage of the monarch or the people.'

Ah well, I sighed, like the Dutch lion with the raised sword, a claw filled with arrows and a lolling tongue, symbolizing the national heraldry.

'It took a while before the money design became more abstract. Step by step the images on money became less realistic and more symbolic. This process didn't take place to the same extent and at the same speed all over the world, and even in modern times large differences in design still remain. The designs of the Dutch industrial designer *Bruno Ninaber van Eyben* meant a break with tradition. On the coins designed by him on the occasion of queen Beatrix's crowning in 1980, the queen was only visible in half and vague contours and on the back were some nominal figures of value in a screen of straight lines. Her silhouette had been drawn by him on Dutch euro coins as well. But he had nothing to do with the designs of the Dutch banknotes or euro notes in later years. In the past in designing the oldest Dutch banknotes, designers didn't play an important part. It had to do with the history of development of our paper money. Although paper money existed as early as the 7th century before Christ in China, where the design of the notes was taken great care of, the development of money design in the western world was quite different. Our paper money has developed from written IOUs like bills of exchange and promissory notes. That's why there are hardly any figurative elements in the beginning, but merely payment promises with a signature. A nice example is the Dutch *Robin*, the very first issued banknote by the DNB (Dutch Central Bank) in 1814. The first series of the banknote, which had been issued in a number of values, had been filled in and signed by hand.[11] Both short edges of the Robins had been decorated with scattered music notes, which were broken in some places as a secret security feature. In 1860 the Robin was succeeded by notes with an ornamental relief edge and a Dutch lion at the top, and various other designs followed.

It's hard to retrieve the names of the designers of the first Dutch banknotes, as they were often anonymous designers or employees of the printers. The self-proclaimed greatest printer of banknotes in the world is the English printer *De La Rue*, founded in 1821 by *Thomas de la Rue*, who printed the first banknote (for Mauritius) in 1860. His name is in small print on the famous Dutch *Lieftinck-tientje*, on which the Dutch had to manage a whole week during the currency reform after the war in 1945. Not only was *De La Rue* the printer of many kinds of paper money, but he also has a *banknote design facility* of his own. So for the greater part anonymous designers.

Similar to the arts, the design of banknotes has gradually developed from realistic towards abstract. But this hasn't been a straight line development. In fact not until the beginning of the eighties of the previous century did the realistic portrait tradition come to an end when *Oxenaar* issued his famous nature series of Dutch banknotes. Everybody paying with guilders in those days remembers the vivid yellow *Sunflower* of 1982, which is considered a top design in the history of Dutch banknotes. Just like the *Lighthouse* and the *Water snip* they all were typically Dutch symbols.

Since Oxenaar's banknotes designers of banknotes are spotlighted in the Netherlands. Their names might even be considered an extra quality mark for the money's value. Whereas the debtors' signatures and later on those of bank managers used to be enough to guarantee the value of a payment promise like paper money, nowadays banknotes can't do without the value suggesting name of a famous designer.

Apart from a few exceptions hardly any information on the designer of early guilder banknotes can be found. One of those exceptions was the 25 guilder banknote of 1949, with the designer's name in small print at the bottom: *J.B. Sleper*, in full *Johannes Bernardus Sleper* (1919-2000), sculptor, painter, graphic artist and draughtsman. The banknote shows king Salomon, and in the background the bishop town Tours, and Saint Martin cutting his cloak in two parts in order to share it with a beggar. *"Shortly after the issue there is a disturbance in the (Dutch) Lower House"*, mentioned DNB Magazine (Magazine of the Dutch Central Bank),[11] *" SGP (Dutch Reformed ± Presbyterian Party) vicar Zandt requests the withdrawal of the banknote because it should be roman catholic propaganda. This doesn't happen. The banknote remains in circulation until 1961".*

But comments and criticism on designs of banknotes can be found before that. In 1904 the first tenner (Dutch 10 guilders note) with *" a tough blacksmith representing Labour, and an elegantly dressed lady symbolizing Wealth, shaking hands"*. But: *"Others look upon it differently: They rather see a poor blacksmith's servant and a scandalized city miss. Hence the banknote led to cartoons and criticism."*[11] These examples show how sensitive people are towards money design, which isn't typically Dutch, but international. In each country national and religious sentiments crop up when cultural imagination of ideas is involved, in any form whatever: art, literature, plays, music, including money design. The examples of writers, painters, composers and other artists whom have been forbidden, exiled or imprisoned, because their ideas displeased the regime, are countless unfortunately.

Bearing this in mind careful attention was given to the design of the euro banknotes, when the euro was introduced. In spite of this a lot of criticism came up at the introduction of the euro banknotes in 2002. The design of these banknotes had been worked on for many years. As soon as 1992 a study group of the committee of the governors of the central banks started the preparations of the design of the euro banknotes. *"They all agreed on the condition that the banknotes' iconography should be more than national traditions and preference of a particular gender"*, mentions the *Museum of the National Bank of Belgium* on its website.'[12]

Oh yes, they still have their beautiful money museum, I thought. Our (Dutch) museum in the Mint of Utrecht has been closed because of economization in 2012 - stupid, quite stupid and short-sighted.

' *"Besides the banknotes should represent European values of openness and the cooperation among European countries and the rest of the world."* In November 1994 the 'Study Group Banknotes' was asked to develop a series of new design themes. *"Together with some experts in history (of art), psychology and design the Study Group suggested eighteen neutral themes, among which the European fauna and flora, common myths and legends, the founders of Europe, and so on. Out of the eighteen themes three were finally proposed to the Council of the EMI: 'Periods and styles of Europe', 'Abstract and modern' and 'European heritage'* ". Thereafter a competition was organized, but when this started in 1996, the candidates could only choose one of the first two themes. The Austrian graphic designer *Robert Kalina*, the definite winner, chose *'Periods and styles of Europe'*, and he neatly carried out the prescribed periods per denomination: classic for banknote €5, roman for €10, gothic for €20, renaissance for €50, baroque and rococo for €100, the period of iron & glass for €200, and the modern architecture of the 20th century for €500. Not everyone liked his designs, but most people thought that the idea of Europe had been most adequately represented by them, and thus they got into circulation from 1 January 2002. And what's on them?'

What's on them? Let me have a look … buildings on the front, arcades mostly, bridges on the back.

'Monumental buildings radiating a message, a message of …?'

Why doesn't he finish the sentence? But okay, I see what he means, for he mentioned this message before: the message is, sleep well, trust us, for the euro has a solidly constructed historic fundament and can't fall apart. And this rather traditional design should support and strengthen the idea of value in our minds.

'The reader may meanwhile be able to answer this question', sounded quizmaster- like. 'We suppose that by this the most important elements of money design have been mentioned briefly. And we hope that it has become clear that the money's design is of crucial importance in accepting the currency. The intrinsic value of money has stopped playing an important part centuries ago. It's exclusively the nominal or numerical value that counts now, and this sign value is a kind of faith. This faith is strengthened by the design's symbolism and settles in our minds as an idea of value.'

Notes:

1. Olav Velthuis, *Imaginary Economics: Contemporary Artists and the World of Big Money: Fascinations*, Rotterdam 2015

2. Sabine Krangler, Claudia Degold, **Geld*(kunst)stück***, article in Artenvielfalt, date unknown (2010?)
3. http://www.dream-dollars.com/press.htm
4. www.louvre.fr/en/oeuvre-notices/moneylender-and-his-wife
5. Basil S. Yamey, *Art & Accounting*, New Haven & London 1989
6. *Kunstforum International*, volume 217, August - September 2012
7. http://e-flux.com/timebank/about
8. http://artreservebank.com/
9. Catherine Eagleton and Jonathan Williams, *Money - A history*, New York 1997
10. Bert van Beek, Hans Jacobi and Marjan Scarloo, *Geld door de eeuwen heen - Geschiedenis van het geld in de Lage Landen*, Amsterdam 1984
11. DNB Magazine nr. 1, 2014
12. www.nbbmuseum.be/nl

BIBLIOGRAPHY

Achterhuis, H, *Het rijk van de schaarste - van Thomas Hobbes tot Michel Foucault*, Baarn 1988, Ambo (*The Realm of Scarcity. From Thomas Hobbes to Michel Foucault*)

Achterhuis, H., *De utopie van de vrije markt*, Rotterdam 2010, Lemniscaat

Barks, C., Walt Disney, *Oom Dagobert, avonturen van een steenrijke eend*, o.a. Haarlem, Amsterdam, Hoofddorp 1977-2006, Oberon BV, De Geïllustreerde Pers BV, Sanoma uitgevers (*Uncle Scrooge Adventures*)

Beek, Bert van; Jacobi, Hans; Scharloo, Marjan, *Geld door de eeuwen heen - Geschiedenis van het geld in de Lage Landen*, Amsterdam 1984, Pampus Associates U.A

Beutels, R, *Over de usura-doctrine of het kerkelijk renteverbod*, Maandschrift Economie / volume 54, 1990, p. 316-326 (*On the Ursula-doctrine or the ecclesiastical interest prohibition*)

Beutick, Frits; Kroeze, Cherelt *Kapitaal Nederland - 100 markante momenten uit de financiële geschiedenis van Nederland*, Arnhem 2011, Sonsbeek Publishers bv (*Capital Country - 100 memorable moments from the financial history of the Netherlands*)

Bevers, Ton, *Zuinigheid en verkwisting - Georg Simmel over geld en cultuur in onze tijd*

Lecture in het Geldcultuurcafé, Geldmuseum Utrecht, 14 June 2007 (The Dutch Money museum was closed in 2015)

Botton, Alain de, *Statusangst*, Amsterdam 2007, Olympus (*Status Anxiety*, London 2005)

Butler, C, *Postmodernisme - De kortste introductie*, Utrecht 2004, Het Spectrum B.V (*Postmodernism. A very short introduction*, New York 2002)

Critchley, Simon, *Geld is de ene ware God waar we allemaal in gelo-*

ven, article in Filosofie Magazine 2010

Defoort, J, *Het Grote Geld - keerpunten in de monetaire geschiedenis*, Leuven 2000, Van Halewyck

DNB Magazine, *DNB 200 jaar*, April 2014 (*Dutch Central Bank, Magazine*)

Eagleton, C; Williams, J, *Money - A History*, New York 1997, Firefly Books

Ferguson, N., *Het succes van geld - Een financiële geschiedenis van de wereld*, Amsterdam/Antwerp 2008, Contact (*The Ascent of Money. A Financial History In the World*, London 2008)

Ferguson, N., *De Geldmachine - Geld en macht in de moderne wereld, 1700-2000*, Amsterdam 2009, Contact (*The Cash Nexus, Money and Power in the Modern World 1700-2000*, New York 2001)

Foucault, M, *De woorden en de dingen, - Een archeologie van de menswetenschappen*, chapter 6, Baarn 1966, Ambo (*The order of things - An archeology of Human Science*, London 1966)

Freij, H.A.; Widemann, R, *Geld & Internationale economie - Schematische kern en oefenboek*, Groningen 1991, Wolters-Noordhoff

Ginneken, J. van, *Gek met geld - Over financiële psychologie*. Amsterdam/Antwerp 2010, Business Contact

Goff, J. Le, *De woekeraar en de hel. Economie en religie in de middeleeuwen*, Amsterdam 1987, Wereldbibliotheek (*Your money or your life: economy and religion in the Middle Ages*)

Gossen, Hermann Heinrich , *Entwicklung der Gesetze des menschlichen Verkehrs: und der daraus fliessenden Regeln für menschliches handels*, Braunschweig 1854, 1889, 1927

Goux, J.J., *Elektronisch geld, of de vingers van de onzichtbare hand*, article 1998

Goux, J.J., *Symbolic Economics. After Marx and Freud*, New York 1990, Cornell University Press, (originally Paris 1973)

Graeber, D, *Schuld - de eerste 5000 jaar*, Amsterdam, Antwerp 2012, Business Contact (*Debt: The First 5,000 Years*, New York 2011 Melville House)

Gude, R, *Stand-up filosoof - De antwoorden van René Gude*, Leusden 2013, ISVW

Guillet de Monthoux, P., *Monetarisierung und Organisation. Eine Geschichte des imaginären Geldes für Erwachsene*, essay in *Georg*

Simmels Philosophie des Geldes - Aufsätze und Materialien, Frankfurt am Main 2003, Suhrkamp

Hegel, G.W.F., *Das System der Bedürfnisse*, Werke, Band 7, Frankfurt a. M. 1979, S 346; (originally 1819)

Heijne, B., *Zo'n onttoverde rationele wereld roept verzet op*, NRC Handelsblad, 14/12/2013

Herodotus, *Het verslag van mijn onderzoek - Historiën*, Amsterdam 1995, Sun

Hobbes, Thomas, *Leviathan*, Amsterdam 2010, Boom (originally 1651)

Huizinga, J., *Vormverandering der geschiedenis*, 1941. Bron: *Geschiedwetenschap / hedendaagse cultuur*, Verzameld werk VII (Collected Works), Haarlem 1950, Tjeenk Willink & Zoon

Klever, W.N.A., *Archeologie van de Economie - de economische theorie in de Griekse oudheid*, Nijmegen 1986, Markant

Krangler, S.; Degold, C., *Geld(kunst)stück*, article in Artenvielfalt, date unknown (2010?)

Kunstforum International, Volume 217, August - September 2012

Laum, B., *Heiliges Geld. Eine historische Untersuchung über den Sakralen Ursprung des Geldes*, Tübingen, 1924

Leeuwen, Arend Th. van, *De nacht van het kapitaal*, Nijmegen 1985, Sun

Lietaer, B., *The Future of Money - Creating new wealth, work and a wiser world*, London 2001, Random House.

Locke, J., *Essay concerning human understanding*, London 1689

Lyotard, J.F., *Het postmoderne weten*, Kampen 1987, Kok Agora (*The Postmodern Condition: A Report on Knowledge*, Minneapolis, 1984)

Mandeville, B, *De fabel van de bijen*, Rotterdam 2008, Lemniscaat (*The Fable of the Bees or Private Vices, Public Benefits*, Oxford 1723)

Martin, F., *Geld - de ongeautoriseerde biografie*, Amsterdam/Antwerp 2013, Business Contact (*Money: The Unauthorized Biography*, New York 2015)

Marx, Karl, *Het Kapitaal*, Amsterdam 2010, Boom (originally *Das Kapital*, Hamburg 1867)

McMahon, Darrin M., *Geluk, een geschiedenis*, Amsterdam 2005,

De Bezige Bij (*Happiness: A History*, New York 2005, Atlantic Monthly Press)

Mujagić, E., *Geldmoord - Hoe de centrale banken ons geld vernietigen*, Amsterdam 2012, Balans (*Money Murder - How the Central Banks are Destroying Our Money*)

Mulder, E., *Freud en Orpheus*, p. 59-62, Utrecht 1987, HES Uitgevers

Pannwitz, R., *Die Krisis der Europäischen Kultur*, Nürnberg 1917

Papilloud, C., *Tausch. Autopsie eines soziologischen Topos*, in: *Georg Simmel's Philosophie des Geldes - Aufsätze und Materialen*, Frankfurt am Main 2003, Suhrkamp

Porter, E, *Alles heeft een prijs - De ontrafeling van de economische geheimen van ons dagelijks leven*, Houten - Antwerp 2011, Spectrum (*The price of everything*, London 2011, Portfolio - Penguin)

Poundstone, W., *Priceless - the hidden psychology of value*. Oxford 2011, Oneworld Publications

Rockoff, H., *The "Wizard of Oz" as a Monetary Allegory*, Journal of Political Economy, Vol. 98, 1990, pp. 739-760

Rotman, B., *Signifying Nothing: The semiotics of Zero*, Stanford, California 1993, Stanford University Press

Russell, B, *Geschiedenis der westerse filosofie*, Den Haag 2008, Servire (originally *History of Western Philosophy*, London 1946)

Sandel, M.J., *Niet alles is te koop - De morele grenzen van marktwerking*. Utrecht 2012, Ten Have (*What Money can't buy - The Moral Limits of the Markets*, New York 2012)

Schama, S., *Overvloed en onbehagen - De Nederlandse cultuur in de Gouden Eeuw*, Amsterdam 2006, Olympus (*The Embarrassment of Riches. An Interpretation of Dutch Culture in the Golden Age*, London 1997)

Schinkel, M., *De gillende geldpers van premier Abe*, NRC Handelsblad 20/21 May 2013

Schopenhauer, A., *De wereld als wil en voorstelling*, Amsterdam 2012, Wereldbibliotheek (Originally Frankfurt 1818 en 1844)

Scott, M., *Het wrede ontwaken van een nieuwe wereld - Ondergang en herrijzenis van het antieke Griekenland*, Amsterdam 2010, Uitgeverij Bert Bakker (*From Democrats to Kings. The Brutal Dawn of a New World from the Downfall of Athens to the Rise of Alexander the Great*, London 2010)

Shell, M., *Money, Language, and Thought*, Baltimore, London 1993, Softshell Books edition(originally, University of California Press 1982)

Simmel, G., *Philosophie des Geldes*, Frankfurt am Main 1989, Suhrkamp (originally Leipzig 1900; *The Philosophy of Money*, London, New York, 2004, 2011, Routledge)

Skidelsky, Robert & Edward, *Hoeveel is genoeg? - Geld en het verlangen naar een goed leven*, Antwerp 2012, De Bezige Bij (*How much is enough? - Money and the good life*, London 2012, Allen Lane)

Skynner, R. & Cleese, J., *Cleese over het leven*, Utrecht/Antwerp 1999, Kosmos (*Life, and How to Survive it*, London 1996)

Sloterdijk, P., *Sferen*, Amsterdam 2009, Boom (*Bubbles*, Cambridge 2011)

Smith, Adam, *The Wealth of Nations*, New York 2003, Bantam Classic (originally 1776)

Smith, D.K., *On Value and Values - Thinking Differently About We in an Age of Me*, Upper Saddle River, New Jersey 2004, Prentice Hall

Toonder, M., *De bovenbazen*, Amsterdam 1978, De Bezige Bij (*The Superbosses*)

Veblen, T., *The Theory of The Leisure Class*, New York 1899, Macmillan Company

Velthuis, O., *Imaginaire ecomomie - Hedendaagse kunstenaars en de wereld van het grote geld (Imaginary Economics - Contemporary Artists and the World of the Big money: Fascinations)* Rotterdam 2005, NAi Publishers

Wells, D.A., *Het Geld van Robinson Crusoe - populaire uiteenzetting omtrent den oorsprong en het gebruik van geld als ruilmiddel*, 's-Gravenhage 1919, W.P. van Stockum & Zoon (*Robinson Crusoe's Money; or, The remarkable fortunes of a remote island Community*, New York 1876)

Widdershoven-Heerding, C., c.s., *Wetenschapsleer*, Open University course, Heerlen 2003 (*Epistemology*)

Widemann, R., *Het Rentelabyrint - Conversaties over geld en intrest*, Dordrecht 2012,Convoy

Yamey, B.S., *Art & Accounting*, New Haven & London 1989, Yale University Press

Websites:
http://www.dream-dollars.com/press.htm
www.louvre.fr/en/oeuvre-notices/moneylender-and-his-wife
http://e-flux.com/timebank/about
http://artreservebank.com/
www.nbbmuseum.be/nl